CASEBOOK SERIES

T. S. Eliot: *The Waste Land*

Casebook Series

GENERAL EDITOR: A. E. Dyson

Jane Austen: *Emma* DAVID LODGE

T. S. Eliot: *The Waste Land* C. B. COX AND A. P. HINCHLIFFE

John Osborne: *Look Back in Anger* J. RUSSELL TAYLOR

Pope: *The Rape of the Lock* JOHN DIXON HUNT

Shakespeare: *Antony and Cleopatra* J. RUSSELL BROWN

Shakespeare: *Hamlet* JOHN JUMP

Shakespeare: *Macbeth* JOHN WAIN

Shakespeare: *The Tempest* D. J. PALMER

Shakespeare: *The Winter's Tale* KENNETH MUIR

Yeats: *Last Poems* JON STALLWORTHY

IN PREPARATION

William Blake: *'Songs of Innocence' and 'Songs of Experience'*
MARGARET BOTTRALL

Emily Brontë: *Wuthering Heights* MIRIAM ALLOTT

Joseph Conrad: *The Secret Agent* IAN WATT

Charles Dickens: *Bleak House* A. E. DYSON

T. S. Eliot: *Four Quartets* BERNARD BERGONZI

E. M. Forster: *A Passage to India* MALCOLM BRADBURY

D. H. Lawrence: *Sons and Lovers* GĀMINI SALGĀDO

D. H. Lawrence: *'The Rainbow' and 'Women in Love'*
COLIN CLARKE

Milton: *'Comus' and 'Samson Agonistes'* STANLEY FISH

Shakespeare: *Henry IV* Parts I and II G. K. HUNTER

Shakespeare: *Julius Caesar* PETER URE

Shakespeare: *Richard II* NICHOLAS BROOKE

Shakespeare: *The Merchant of Venice* JOHN WILDERS

Tennyson: *In Memoriam* JOHN DIXON HUNT

Wordsworth: *Lyrical Ballads* ALUN JONES

Wordsworth: *The Prelude* W. J. HARVEY

T. S. Eliot
The Waste Land

A CASEBOOK

EDITED BY

C. B. COX
and ARNOLD P. HINCHLIFFE

Aurora Publishers Incorporated
NASHVILLE/LONDON

FIRST PUBLISHED 1969 BY
MACMILLAN AND COMPANY LIMITED
LONDON, ENGLAND

COPYRIGHT © 1970 BY
AURORA PUBLISHERS INCORPORATED
NASHVILLE, TENNESSEE 37219
LIBRARY OF CONGRESS CATALOG CARD NUMBER: 70-127569
STANDARD BOOK NUMBER: 87695-040-3
MANUFACTURED IN THE UNITED STATES OF AMERICA

CONTENTS

ACKNOWLEDGEMENTS

EARLY reviews from the *Guardian*, the *Times Literary Supplement* and the *New Statesman*; George Watson, 'The Triumph of T. S. Eliot', from *Critical Quarterly*, 1965 (A. D. Peters & Co.); 'The Poetry of T. S. Eliot', from *Principles of Literary Criticism* (Harcourt, Brace & World Inc.; © I. A. Richards 1948); William Empson, *Seven Types of Ambiguity* (Chatto & Windus Ltd, New Directions Publishing Corporation); C. Day Lewis, *A Hope for Poetry* (A. D. Peters & Co.); Yvor Winters, *On Modern Poets* (The Swallow Press Inc., Chicago); *In Defense of Ignorance* (Random House Inc.; © Karl Shapiro 1960); Graham Hough, *Image and Experience* (Gerald Duckworth & Co. Ltd, The University of Nebraska); Stephen Spender, 'Remembering Eliot', from *The Sewanee Review*, LXXIV, No. 1 (Winter 1966) (© The University of the South); Daniel H. Woodward, 'Notes on the Publishing History and Text of *The Waste Land*', from *Papers of the Bibliographical Society of America* (July/September 1964) LVIII (The Bibliographical Society of America); Conrad Aiken, 'An Anatomy of Melancholy', from *T. S. Eliot: The Man and His Work*, ed. Allen Tate, pub. Chatto & Windus Ltd (A. M. Heath & Co.); Edmund Wilson, *Axel's Castle* (© Charles Scribner's Sons 1931; renewed © Edmund Wilson 1959); F. O. Matthiessen, *The Achievement of T. S. Eliot* (Oxford University Press Inc.); George L. K. Morris, 'Marie, Marie, Hold on Tight', from *Partisan Review*, XXI (March-April 1954) ii 231–3 (© *Partisan Review* 1954); *A Reader's Guide to T. S. Eliot* (Farrar, Straus & Giroux Inc.; © George Williamson 1953); Cleanth Brooks, *Modern Poetry and the Tradition* (The University of North Carolina Press); 'The Defeatism of *The Waste Land*', from

Critical Quarterly, 1960 (Mr David Craig and the Editor of *Critical Quarterly*); *The Invisible Poet: T. S. Eliot* (Mr Hugh Kenner and W. H. Allen & Co.); C. K. Stead, *The New Poetic* (Hutchinson & Co. (Publishers) Ltd); Frank Kermode, 'A Babylonish Dialect', from *T. S. Eliot: The Man and His Work*, ed. Allen Tate, pub. by Chatto & Windus Ltd.

GENERAL EDITOR'S PREFACE

EACH of this series of Casebooks concerns either one well-known and influential work of literature or two or three closely linked works. The main section consists of critical readings, mostly modern, brought together from journals and books. A selection of reviews and comments by the author's contemporaries is also included, and sometimes comments from the author himself. The Editor's Introduction charts the reputation of the work from its first appearance until the present time.

What is the purpose of such a collection? Chiefly, to assist reading. Our first response to literature may be, or seem to be, 'personal'. Certain qualities of vigour, profundity, beauty or 'truth to experience' strike us, and the work gains a foothold in our mind. Later, an isolated phrase or passage may return to haunt or illuminate. Where did we hear that? we wonder – it could scarcely be better put.

In these and similar ways appreciation begins, but major literature prompts to very much more. There are certain facts we need to know if we are to understand properly. Who were the author's original readers, and what assumptions did he share with them? What was his theory of literature? Was he committed to a particular historical situation, or to a set of beliefs? We need historians as well as critics to help us with this. But there are also more purely literary factors to take account of: the work's structure and rhetoric; its symbols and archetypes; its tone, genre and texture; its use of language; the words on the page. In all these matters critics can inform and enrich our individual responses by offering imaginative recreations of their own.

For the life of a book is not, after all, merely 'personal'; it is more like a tripartite dialogue, between a writer living 'then', a reader living 'now', and whatever forces of survival and honour link the two. Criticism is the public manifestation of this dialogue, a witness to the continuing power of literature to arouse and excite. It illuminates the possibilities and rewards of the dialogue, pushing 'interpretation' as far forward as it can go.

And here, indeed, is the rub: how far can it go? Where does 'interpretation' end and nonsense begin? Why is one interpretation superior to another, and why does each age need to interpret for itself? The critic knows that his insights have value only in so far as they serve the text, and that he must take account of views differing sharply from his own. He knows that his own writing will be judged as well as the work he writes about, so that he cannot simply assert inner illumination or a differing taste.

The critical forum is a place of vigorous conflict and disagreement, but there is nothing in this to cause dismay. What is attested is the complexity of human experience and the richness of literature, not any chaos or relativity of taste. A critic is better seen, no doubt, as an explorer than as an 'authority', but explorers ought to be, and usually are, well equipped. The effect of good criticism is to convince us of what C. S. Lewis called 'the enormous extension of our being which we owe to authors'. A Casebook will be justified only if it helps to promote the same end.

A single volume can represent no more than a small selection of critical opinions. Some critics have been excluded for reasons of space, and it is hoped that readers will follow up the further suggestions in the Select Bibliography. Other contributions have been severed from their original context, to which some readers may wish to return. Indeed, if they take a hint from the critics represented here, they certainly will.

A. E. DYSON

INTRODUCTION

'I THINK it is a piece of tripe.' [1] Amy Lowell's opinion sums up the response of many readers when *The Waste Land* first appeared. The contemporary reviews printed here from the *Times Literary Supplement*, the *Manchester Guardian* and the *New Statesman* reflect the bewilderment and scorn of many poetry-lovers. F. L. Lucas's comment in the *New Statesman*, that a 'poem that has to be explained in notes is not unlike a picture with "This is a dog" inscribed beneath',[2] had an obvious appeal to readers accustomed to simple poems about simple feelings and the thin melancholy of much popular Georgian poetry. Even Clive Bell, in a review in the *Nation and Athenaeum*, found the poem influenced by a lack of 'imagination'.[3] Quite a few early commentators suspected a hoax. Arnold Bennett asked the author whether the notes were 'a lark or serious', and in 1923 writers in the *Christian Science Monitor*, the *New York Herald-Tribune* and *Time* all suspected that their legs were being pulled.[4] In the same year N. P. Dawson, in the *Forum*, considered that it was natural for the poem to be enjoyed more in Prohibition America than in England: 'The Dirge is doubtless "Yo-ho-ho, and a bottle of rum," and the lament is "Oh how dry I am!" ' [5]

Ezra Pound, in 1940, felt that the poem had suffered because

[1] Quoted by E. K. Brown, in 'Mr Eliot and Some Enemies', in *University of Toronto Quarterly*, VIII (1938) 81.

[2] *New Statesman*, XXII (3 Nov. 1923) 116.

[3] *Nation and Athenaeum*, XXXIII (22 Sept. 1923) 772–3.

[4] For full details, see A. H. Nelson, 'The Critics and *The Waste Land*, 1922–1949', in *English Studies*, XXXVI (1955), a useful compilation of critical responses to the poem.

[5] N. P. Dawson, 'Enjoying Poor Literature', in *Forum*, LXIX (1923) 1373.

of the notes, the addition of which was, anyway, quite fortuitous:

The bearing of this poem was not over-estimated, nevertheless the immediate reception of it even by second-rate reviewers was due to the purely fortuitous publication of the notes, and not to the text itself. Liveright wanted a longer volume and the notes were the only available unpublished matter.[1]

Certainly when the poem was first published, in the first issue of the *Criterion* (October 1922) and reprinted in the *Dial* in November of the same year, it appeared without footnotes. In his excellent account of the publishing history of the poem, D. H. Woodward recounts how Gilbert Seldes, managing editor of the *Dial*, deliberately promoted the poem's American success, including in his efforts the commissioning of Edmund Wilson to write a review. This favourable review, 'The Poetry of Drouth', was later rewritten for *Axel's Castle* (1931) and the revised form is printed here. Wilson praises the poem as a mirror of post-war society, with a new music, even in its borrowings, although he recognizes in Eliot the peculiar conflicts of the Puritan turned artist. Seldes himself heaped eulogies on the poem in a review in the *Nation*, but it is interesting to note how little he understood the poem. He quotes Bertrand Russell, saying that since the Renaissance the clock of Europe has been running down, thus pointing to a reason for the poem's becoming so influential in the 1920s. It seemed to epitomize the intellectual's feeling that he was living in a broken, decaying civilization. Another influential review was Conrad Aiken's in the *New Republic*. In a postscript, reprinted here, he recalls his unique good fortune in having been Eliot's friend for fifteen years and having seen parts of the poem in draft. He also raises the crucial question that has absorbed critics down to the present day: what kind of unity and structure has the poem? For Aiken, *The Waste Land* is 'a brilliant and kaleidoscopic confusion', but this 'heap of broken images' is justified 'as a series of brilliant, brief, unrelated

[1] Written for the Gotham Book Mart's catalogue *We Moderns* (New York, 1940) p. 24, and quoted in D. Gallup's *T. S. Eliot: A Bibliography* (1952) p. 7.

or dimly related pictures by which a consciousness empties itself of its characteristic contents'. For him, then, its 'incoherence is a virtue because its *donnée* is incoherence'.

Such early commendations set an intellectual fashion for the 1920s, and by the time he came to write *Axel's Castle* Edmund Wilson could talk of how the poem 'enchanted and devastated a whole generation'. George Watson stresses the extraordinary quickness with which the poem was accepted as a masterpiece and its great effect on young readers. By 1930 E. M. Forster, Bonamy Dobrée, William Empson, Laura Riding and Robert Graves were among the many writers extolling its virtues. Perhaps the most influential was I. A. Richards, who in 1926 extended his *Principles of Literary Criticism* by an appendix on T. S. Eliot. He finds no logical scheme in *The Waste Land* but argues that readers react with a unified emotional response. The poetry achieves form by 'a music of ideas', a phrase repeatedly criticized and discussed by subsequent critics.

In the 1930s the academics took over. Both F. O. Matthiesssen and Cleanth Brooks, whom we reprint here, were highly influential, and their works have instructed thousands of students how to respond to T. S. Eliot. Equally important was the section on T. S. Eliot (chapter III) in F. R. Leavis's *New Bearings in English Poetry* (1932), which, unfortunately, we have not been allowed to reprint. Leavis's argument covers the two major objections to the poem, its 'rich disorganization' (and the qualifying adjective suggests the writer's attitude) and its 'erudition'. He refers to I. A. Richards's theory of the music of ideas, and himself talks of the poem's 'depth of orchestration': the poem does not lack organization, for it aims at the unity of an 'inclusive consciousness'.[1] The anthropological background plays 'an obvious part in evoking that particular sense of the unity of life which is essential to the poem' and is 'a peculiarly significant expression of the scientific spirit'.[2] He demonstrates in an analysis of 'The Burial of the Dead' how the organization of the poem is obvious without the aid of notes, but he admits

[1] *New Bearings in English Poetry* (1961) pp. 95, 100 and 103.
[2] Ibid. pp. 93, 94.

that the poem is available to only a limited audience, though this is itself a symptom of the culture that produced the poem. His book is really important in the way he uses the poem to illustrate his own views on history and minority culture. For Leavis *The Waste Land* accurately reflects the breakdown of tradition in contemporary civilization:

In considering our present plight we have also to take account of the incessant rapid change that characterizes the Machine Age. The result is breach of continuity and the uprooting of life. This last metaphor has a peculiar aptness, for what we are witnessing today is the final uprooting of the immemorial ways of life, of life rooted in the soil.[1]

Perhaps Leavis was the most powerful figure in the transformation of the poem into a myth, a representative symbol of the breakdown in modern consciousness. This leads him to declare that the poem can only exist for an extremely limited audience equipped with special knowledge, though his demonstration by analysis indicates that this is not as devastating as many critics have suggested. Nevertheless, in his view, works expressing the finest consciousness of the age inevitably appeal only to a minority of trained sensibilities who have cut themselves off from their hostile environment.

All these academic critics are convinced that the poem possesses its own kind of unity. Matthiessen talks, once more, of the 'musical organization' of the poem's dramatic structure and of its lyrical intensity, and Cleanth Brooks puts forward a subtle theory explaining how the irony works on different levels to create a sense of the oneness of experience and the unity of all periods. This kind of justification is continued in Hugh Kenner's more recent book *The Invisible Poet: T. S. Eliot* (1959), in which he describes the influence of F. H. Bradley's philosophy on Eliot and sees the loose sequence of poems in *The Waste Land* co-existing as a 'zone of consciousness'. All these critics balance their search for unity with enquiry into the erudition, showing considerable critical acumen in their analyses of ambiguities

[1] Ibid. p. 91.

found in particular passages. But the dangers of academic criticism can be seen in Grover Smith's *T. S. Eliot's Poetry and Plays* (1956) ominously sub-titled 'A Study in Sources and Meaning'. This is, undeniably, an invaluable source-book for the allusions in the poem. Asked by a student 'What does this mean?' a teacher too often feels obliged to answer, falling into the desire to provide a rational structure for each section and to hunt down every reference. In our opinion Grover Smith has carried this to extravagant lengths. We are told of 'the cock, crowing enigmatically in Portuguese', and that the young man carbuncular 'is the quester himself; the food laid out in tins is a kind of Grail repast which the Loathly Damsel has prepared'. A unified narrative is imposed on the poem by taking Tiresias as the central consciousness, every incident spoken by him or reflecting his memories: 'Blind and spiritually embittered, Tiresias wrestles with buried emotions unwittingly revived.' [1] Grover Smith himself seems to wrestle desperately to fit all the details into his pattern. The illogicalities and confusions he is drawn into are nicely demonstrated in the following passage:

At his meeting with the hyacinth girl in *The Waste Land*, Tiresias as the quester has omitted to ask the indispensable question of the Grail initiation. Evidently he has merely stood agape while she, bearing the sexual symbol – the spike-shaped blossoms representing the slain god Hyacinth of *The Golden Bough* – has awaited the word he cannot utter:

> – Yet when we came back, late, from the Hyacinth garden,
> Your arms full, and your hair wet, I could not
> Speak, and my eyes failed, I was neither
> Living nor dead, and I knew nothing,
> Looking into the heart of light, the silence.

Eliot diversified the pattern slightly, for the hyacinth is a male symbol, and then, too, the quester himself has given the flowers to the hyacinth girl. But the effect is the same as in the Grail narratives. [2]

[1] *T. S. Eliot's Poetry and Plays* (Chicago, 1960) pp. 95, 88 and 72.
[2] Ibid. pp. 74–5.

Ezra Pound rightly stressed that the poem's total effect demands no great knowledge of its sources. Invaluable as Grover Smith's work is, the attempt to impose a simple structure, for the student's benefit, betrays the true nature of the poem.

The early doubts about the poem's structure were not silenced by this mass of academic erudition which fell upon the poem in the post-1930 period and which, ironically, served only to emphasize the other objection to the poem, namely its 'erudition'. In 1943 the iconoclastic Yvor Winters declared that 'Eliot, in dealing with debased and stupid material, felt himself obliged to seek his form in this matter: the result is confusion and journalistic reproduction of detail'.[1] These criticisms were repeated by Karl Shapiro, while in *Image and Experience* (1960) Graham Hough argues, carefully and precisely, that the poem lacks unity of tone, and that those who justified the poem's structure came to very different conclusions about the relevance of specific passages; for example, about the significance of the hyacinth girl or Phlebas. In his view *The Waste Land* is in the imagist tradition, and this tradition is suited only to brilliant lyrics and short-term effects. Eliot and Pound were eccentrics, and their experiments, however dazzling they seemed at the time, resulted in no permanent revolution in poetics.

In the same year (1960) David Craig made a frontal attack on Leavis's position, insisting that the poem's attempt to create an impersonal portrait of society is a pretence and a sham. The poem is actually a romantic expression of personal depression, which some intellectuals have accepted because it reflects their own *malaise*, but which has no relevance to actual twentieth-century social conditions. For Craig, the poem is too genteel, too anti-life. Previously, in *Essays in Criticism* (1952), John Peter had emphasised the poet's revulsion from sexual relationships in a controversial article we have not been allowed to reprint.

We include at this point a section from C. K. Stead's interesting book *The New Poetic* (1964) now available in Penguin Books in which Mr Stead rejected critical procedures which look for a statement of beliefs rather than submitting to the

[1] *On Modern Poets* (New York, 1959) p. 70.

'direct experience' of the poem. As an example of this 'direct experience' we end the selection with Frank Kermode's brilliant study of modernism in *The Waste Land*. Early commentators, inevitably, had to take the poem section by section and make sense of it to bewildered readers. Now Kermode can step back and see the poem in the tradition of European and American experimental art. He can also write that the poem 'resists an imposed order; it is a part of its greatness, and the greatness of its epoch, that it can do so'.[1] This seems the proper starting-point today for any discussion of the poem; blindness is a central motif in *The Waste Land*, a sense of meaning hidden, ambiguous, uncertain, never fully and absolutely revealed.

But the arguments will continue: are the notes a waste of paper, a misuse of scholarship? Does the poem exhibit no progression, as Leavis says, or do we accept Helen Gardner's view that 'most people would agree today, in the light of Mr Eliot's later work, that the original critics of *The Waste Land* misread it, not recognizing it as an *Inferno* which looked towards a *Purgatorio*'?[2] Does the poem accurately record the society of post-1918, or, as Craig suggests, is it merely personal and defeatist? And has this last question any proper relevance to the poem's success as a work of art? Above all what *are* its structural principles? Is it a poem full of brilliant debris, as Hough would have us believe, or unified by theme like a piece of music (which, in the light of *Four Quartets*, remains a very tempting point of view)? Whatever future critics may decide, the poem will surely continue to fascinate and inspire its readers. Most of the best criticis *do agree* that the poem achieves greatness by its honesty. As Kathleen Raine has said, 'the statement of a terrible truth has a kind of healing power'.[3] In 1926 I. A. Richards wrote that 'only those unfortunate persons who are incapable of reading

[1] See pp. 231–2 of this collection.
[2] Helen L. Gardner, *'Four Quartets*: A Commentary', in *Focus Three: T. S. Eliot, A Study of His Writings by Several Hands*, ed. B. Rajan (1947) p. 60.
[3] 'The Poet of Our Time', in *T. S. Eliot: A Symposium*, compiled by R. March and Tambimuttu (1948) p. 79.

poetry can resist Mr Eliot's rhythms'.[1] For Frank Kermode, in 1967, 'to have Eliot's great poem in one's life involves an irrevocable but repeated act of love'.[2]

C. B. Cox and Arnold P. Hinchliffe

[1] See pp. 54–5.   [2] See p. 234.

PART ONE

The Author on the Poem

LETTERS CONCERNING
THE WASTE LAND 1921–2

ELIOT completed the original draft of *The Waste Land* towards the end of 1921. He visited Ezra Pound in Paris and gave the poem to him for his criticism. Pound suggested improvements that considerably reduced the poem from its original length. Unfortunately the original draft, with Pound's revisions, is now lost, and the only indication we have of the part played by Pound in determining the final form of the poem is contained in the following sequence of letters written after Eliot had returned to London. These letters, first published as an article by D. D. Paige in *Nine*, IV (Summer 1950) 176–9, and later incorporated in his edition of *The Letters of Ezra Pound* (1950) pp. 169–72, suggest Pound's function as *il miglior fabbro*. The dedication appears to mean precisely what it says.

References to parts of the original draft of the poem that were removed before the poem was published occur in the extract from an interview given by Eliot to the *Paris Review* in 1963. This extract also refers to a passage in 'Thoughts after Lambeth' which we reprint here. *Editors' note.*

1. ELIOT FROM POUND

Paris, 24 Saturnus, An. 1 (24 December 1921)

Caro mio: MUCH improved. I think your instinct had led you to put the remaining superfluities at the end. I think you had better leave 'em, abolish 'em altogether or for the present.

IF you MUST keep 'em, put 'em at the beginning before the

'April cruelest month.' The POEM ends with the 'Shantih, shantih, shantih.'

One test is whether anything would be lacking if the last three were omitted. I don't think it would.

The song has only two lines which you can use in the body of the poem. The other two, at least the first, does not advance on earlier stuff. And even the sovegna doesn't hold with the rest; which does hold.

(It also, to your horror probably, reads aloud very well. Mouthing out his OOOOOOze.)

I doubt if Conrad is weighty enough to stand the citation.

The thing now runs from 'April . . .' to 'shantih' without a break. That is 19 pages, and let us say the longest poem in the Englisch langwidge. Don't try to bust all records by prolonging it three pages further.

The bad nerves is O.K. as now led up to.

My squibs are now a bloody impertinence. I send 'em as requested; but don't use 'em with *Waste Land*.

You can tack 'em onto a collected edtn, or use 'em somewhere where they would be decently hidden and swamped by the bulk of accompanying matter. They'd merely be an extra and wrong note with the 19 page version.

Complimenti, you bitch. I am wracked by the seven jealousies, and cogitating an excuse for always exuding my deformative secretions in my own stuff, and never getting an outline. I go into nacre and objets d'art. Some day I shall lose my temper, blaspheme Flaubert, lie like a – – – – and say 'Art should embellish the umbelicus.'

SAGE HOMME

These are the poems of Eliot
By the Uranian Muse begot;
A Man their Mother was,
A Muse their Sire.

How did the printed Infancies result
From Nuptials thus doubly difficult?

> If you must needs enquire
> Know diligent Reader
> That on each Occasion
> Ezra performed the caesarean Operation.
>
> Cauls and grave clothes he brings
> Fortune's outrageous stings,
>   About which odour clings,
>   Of putrefaction,
> Bleichstein's dank rotting clothes
> Affect the dainty nose,
> He speaks of common woes
>   Deploring action.
>
> He writes of A.B.C.s
> And flaxseed poultices,
> Observing fate's hard decrees
>   Sans satisfaction;
> Breeding of animals,
> Humans and cannibals,
> But above all else of smells
>   Without attraction
>
> Vates cum fistula

— — — —

It is after all a grrrreat litttttterary period.
Thanks for the Aggymemnon.

2. To Pound from Eliot

[In early January Eliot wrote the following letter to Pound, who made his own notes in the margin (indicated here in bold type) and returned it to Eliot, apparently enclosed with letter 3.]

London (? *January 1922*)

Cher maître: Criticisms accepted so far as understood, with thanks.

Glowed on the marble where the glass
Sustained by standards wrought with fruited vines
Wherefrom . . . ? ?   **O.K.**
Footsteps shuffled on the stair . . .   **O.K.**
A closed car. I can't use taxi more than once.   **O.K.**
Departed, have *left no addresses . . . ???*   **O.K.**

What does THENCE mean (To luncheon at the Cannon St.
Hotel)???

Would D's difficulty be solved by inverting to
Drifting logs
The barges wash . . . ???

1. Do you advise printing 'Gerontion' as a prelude in book or
   pamphlet form?
2. Perhaps better omit Phlebas also???
3. Wish to use Caesarean Operation in italics in front.
4. Certainly omit miscellaneous pieces.   **Those at end.**
5. Do you mean not use the Conrad quote or simply not put
   Conrad's name to it? It is much the most appropriate I can
   find, and somewhat elucidative.

Complimenti appreciated, as have been excessively depressed.

— — — —

I would have sent Aeschule before but have been in bed with
flu, now out, but miserable.

Would you advise working sweats with tears etc. into nerves
monologue; only place where it can go?

Have writ to Thayer* asking what he can offer for this.

Trying to read Aristophane.

3. TO ELIOT FROM POUND

Paris (? January 1922)

Filio dilecto mihi: I merely queeried the dialect of 'thence'; dare
say it is O.K.

* Scofield Thayer, editor of the *Dial.*

D. was fussing about some natural phenomenon, but I thought I had crossed out her query. The wake of the barges washes etc., and the barges may perfectly well be said to wash. I should leave it as it is, and NOT invert.

I do *not* advise printing 'Gerontion' as preface. One don't miss it *at* all as the thing now stands. To be more lucid still, let me say that I advise you NOT to print 'Gerontion' as prelude.

I DO advise keeping Phlebas. In fact I more'n advise. Phlebas is an integral part of the poem; the card pack introduces him, the drowned phoen. sailor. And he is needed ABSOlootly where he is. Must stay in.

Do as you like about my obstetric effort.

Ditto re Conrad; who am I to grudge him his laurel crown? ...

PARIS REVIEW INTERVIEW (1959)

INTERVIEWER: Does the manuscript of the original, uncut *Waste Land* exist?

ELIOT: Don't ask me. That's one of the things I don't know. It's an unsolved mystery. I sold it to John Quinn. I also gave him a notebook of unpublished poems, because he had been kind to me in various affairs. That's the last I heard of them. Then he died and they didn't turn up at the sale.

INTERVIEWER: What sort of thing did Pound cut from *The Waste Land*? Did he cut whole sections?

ELIOT: Whole sections, yes. There was a long section about a shipwreck. I don't know what that had to do with anything else, but it was rather inspired by the Ulysses Canto in *The Inferno*, I think. Then there was another section which was an imitation *Rape of the Lock*. Pound said, 'It's no use trying to do something that somebody else has done as well as it can be done. Do something different.'

INTERVIEWER: Did the excisions change the intellectual structure of the poem?

ELIOT: No, I think it was just as structureless, only in a more futile way, in the longer version.

INTERVIEWER: I have a question about the poem which is related to its composition. In 'Thoughts after Lambeth' you denied the allegation of critics who said that you expressed 'the disillusionment of a generation' in *The Waste Land*, or you denied that it was your intention. Now F. R. Leavis, I believe, has said that the poem exhibits no progression; yet on the other hand, more recent critics, writing after your later poetry, found *The Waste Land* Christian. I wonder if this was part of your intention.

ELIOT: No, it wasn't part of my conscious intention. I think that in 'Thoughts after Lambeth' I was speaking of intentions more in a negative than in a positive sense, to say what was not my intention. I wonder what an 'intention' means! One wants to get something off one's chest. One doesn't know quite what it is that one wants to get off the chest until one's got it off. But I couldn't apply the word 'intention' positively to any of my poems. Or to any poem.

FROM 'THOUGHTS AFTER LAMBETH' (1931)

I DISLIKE the word 'generation'. When I wrote a poem called *The Waste Land* some of the more approving critics said I had expressed 'the disillusionment of a generation', which is nonsense. I may have expressed for them their own illusion of being disillusioned, but that did not form part of my intention.

PART TWO

Early Reviews

Manchester Guardian

THIS poem of 433 lines,* with a page of notes to every three pages of text, is not for the ordinary reader. He will make nothing of it. Its five sections, called successively 'The Burial of the Dead', 'A Game of Chess', and so on, for all they will signify to him, might as well be called 'Tom Thumb at the Giant's Causeway' or 'The Devil among the Bailiffs', and so on. The thing is a mad medley. It has a plan, because its author says so: and presumably it has some meaning, because he speaks of its symbolism; but meaning, plan, and intention alike are massed behind a smoke-screen of anthropological and literary erudition, and only the pundit, the pedant, or the clairvoyant will be in the least aware of them. Dr Frazer and Miss J. L. Weston are freely and admittedly his creditors, and the bulk of the poem is under an enormously composite and cosmopolitan mortgage: to Spenser, Shakespeare, Webster, Kyd, Middleton, Milton, Marvell, Goldsmith, Ezekiel, Buddha, Virgil, Ovid, Dante, St Augustine, Baudelaire, Verlaine, and others. Lines of German, French and Italian are thrown in at will or whim; so, too, are solos from nightingales, cocks, hermit-thrushes, and Ophelia. When Mr Eliot speaks in his own language and his own voice it is like this at one moment:

> April is the cruellest month, breeding
> Lilacs out of the dead land, mixing
> Memory and desire, stirring
> Dull roots with spring rain.
> Winter kept us warm, covering
> Earth in forgetful snow, feeding
> A little life with dried tubers;

and at another moment like this:

> Unreal City
> Under the brown fog of a winter noon

* *Editors' note*: Critics disagree on the number of lines in the poem. We have accepted 433 and have standardised references throughout this collection.

> Mr Eugenides, the Smyrna merchant
> Unshaven, with a pocket full of currants
> C.i.f. London: documents at sight,
> Asked me in demotic French
> To luncheon at the Cannon Street Hotel,
> Followed by a week-end at the Metropole.

For the rest one can only say that if Mr Eliot had been pleased to write in demotic English *The Waste Land* might not have been, as it just is to all but anthropologists and *literati*, so much waste paper.

(Charles Powell, 31 October 1923)

Times Literary Supplement

BETWEEN the emotion from which a poem rises and the reader there is always a cultural layer of more or less density from which the images or characters in which it is expressed may be drawn. In the ballad 'I wish I were where Helen lies' this middle ground is but faintly indicated. The ballad, we say, is *simpler* than the 'Ode to the Nightingale'; it evokes very directly an emotional response. In the ode the emotion gains resonance from the atmosphere of legendary association through which it passes before reaching us. It cannot be called better art, but it is certainly more sophisticated and to some minds less poignant. From time to time there appear poets and a poetic audience to whom this refractory haze of allusion must be very dense; without it the meanings of the words strike them so rapidly as to be inappreciable, just as, without the air, we could not detect the vibration of light. We may remember with what elaboration Addison, among others, was obliged to undertake the defence of the old ballads before it was recognized that their bare style might be admired by gentlemen familiar with the classics.

The poetic personality of Mr Eliot is extremely sophisticated. His emotions hardly ever reach us without traversing a zig-zag of allusion. In the course of his four hundred lines he quotes from a score of authors and in three foreign languages, though his artistry has reached that point at which it knows the wisdom of sometimes concealing itself. There is in general in his work a disinclination to awake in us a direct emotional response. It is only, the reader feels, out of regard for someone else that he has been induced to mount the platform at all. From there he conducts a magic-lantern show; but being too reserved to expose in public the impressions stamped on his own soul by the journey through the Waste Land, he employs the slides made by others, indicating with a touch the difference between his reaction and theirs. So the familiar stanza of Goldsmith becomes

> When lovely woman stoops to folly and
> Paces about her room again, alone,
> She smoothes her hair with automatic hand,
> And puts a record on the gramophone.

To help us to elucidate the poem Mr Eliot has provided some notes which will be of more interest to the pedantic than the poetic critic. Certainly they warn us to be prepared to recognize some references to vegetation ceremonies. This is the cultural or middle layer, which, whilst it helps us to perceive the underlying emotion, is of no poetic value in itself. We desire to touch the inspiration itself, and if the apparatus of reserve is too strongly constructed, it will defeat the poet's end. The theme is announced frankly enough in the title, *The Waste Land*; and in the concluding confession,

> These fragments I have shored against my ruins,

we receive a direct communication which throws light on much which had preceded it. From the opening part, 'The Burial of the Dead', to the final one we seem to see a world, or a mind, in disaster and mocking its despair. We are aware of the toppling of aspirations, the swift disintegration of accepted stability, the crash of an ideal. Set at a distance by a poetic method which is reticence itself, we can only judge of the strength of the emotion by the visible violence of the reaction. Here is Mr Eliot, a dandy of the choicest phrase, permitting himself blatancies like 'the young man carbuncular'. Here is a poet capable of a style more refined than that of any of his generation parodying without taste or skill – and of this the example from Goldsmith is not the most astonishing. Here is a writer to whom originality is almost an inspiration borrowing the greater number of his best lines, creating hardly any himself. It seems to us as if the *The Waste Land* exists in the greater part in the state of notes. This quotation is a particularly obvious instance:

> London Bridge is falling down falling down
> 　　　　　　　　　　　　　　falling down
> *Poi s' ascose nel foco che gli affina*
> *Quando fiam uti chelidon –* O swallow swallow
> *Le Prince d' Aquitaine à la tour abolie.*

The method has a number of theoretical justifications. Mr Eliot has himself employed it discreetly with delicious effect. It suits well the disillusioned smile which he had in common with Laforgue; but we do sometimes wish to hear the poet's full voice. Perhaps if the reader were sufficiently sophisticated he would find these echoes suggestive hints, as rich in significance as the sonorous amplifications of the romantic poets. None the less, we do not derive from this poem as a whole the satisfaction we ask from poetry. Numerous passages are finely written; there is an amusing monologue in the vernacular, and the fifth part is nearly wholly admirable. The section beginning

> What is that sound high in the air . . .

has a nervous strength which perfectly suits the theme; but he declines to a mere notation, the result of an indolence of the imagination.

Mr Eliot, always evasive of the grand manner, has reached a stage at which he can no longer refuse to recognize the limitations of his medium; he is sometimes walking very near the limits of coherency. But it is the finest horses which have the most tender mouths, and some unsympathetic tug has sent Mr Eliot's gift awry. When he recovers control we shall expect his poetry to have gained in variety and strength from this ambitious experiment.

(20 September 1923)

F. L. Lucas

Solitudinem faciunt, *poëma* appellant.

AMONG the maggots that breed in the corruption of poetry one of the commonest is the bookworm. When Athens had decayed and Alexandria sprawled, the new giant-city, across the Egyptian sands; when the Greek world was filling with libraries and emptying of poets, growing in erudition as its genius expired, then first appeared, as pompous as Herod and as worm-eaten, that *Professorenpoesie* which finds in literature the inspiration that life gives no more, which replaces depth by muddiness, beauty by echoes, passion by necrophily. The fashionable verse of Alexandria grew out of the polite leisure of its librarians, its Homeric scholars, its literary critics. Indeed, the learned of that age had solved the economic problem of living by taking in each other's dirty washing, and the *Alexandra* of Lycophron, which its learned author made so obscure that other learned authors could make their fortunes by explaining what it meant, still survives for the curious as the first case of this disease and the first really bad poem in Greek. The malady reappears at Rome in the work of Catullus' friend Cinna (the same whom with a justice doubly poetic the crowd in *Julius Caesar* 'tears for his bad verses'), and in the gloomy pedantry that mars so much of Propertius; it has recurred at intervals ever since. Disconnected and ill-knit, loaded with echo and allusion, fantastic and crude, obscure and obscurantist – such is the typical style of Alexandrianism.

Readers of *The Waste Land* are referred at the outset, if they wish to understand the poem or even its title, to a work on the ritual origins of the legends of the Holy Grail by Miss J. L. Weston, a disciple of Frazer, and to the *Golden Bough* itself. Those who conscientiously plunge into the two hundred pages of the former interesting, though credulous, work, will learn that the basis of the Grail story is the restoration of the virility of a Fisher King (who is an incarnation like so many others in Frazer, of the Life-spirit), and thereby of the fertility of a Waste Land, the Lance and the Grail itself being phallic symbols. While maintaining due caution and remembering how

> Diodorus Siculus
> Made himself ridiculous,
> By thinking thimbles
> Were phallic symbols,

one may admit that Miss Weston makes a very good case. With that, however, neither she nor Mr Eliot can rest content, and they must needs discover an esoteric meaning under the rags of superstitious Adam. Miss Weston is clearly a theosophist, and Mr Eliot's poem might be a theosophical tract. The sick king and the waste land symbolise, we gather, the sick soul and the desolation of this material life.

But even when thus instructed and with a feeling of virtuous research the reader returns to the attack, the difficulties are but begun. To attempt here an interpretation, even an intelligible summary of the poem, is to risk making oneself ridiculous; but those who lack the common modern gift of judging poetry without knowing what it means, must risk that. *The Waste Land* is headed by an allusion from Petronius to the Sibyl at Cumae, shrunk so small by her incredible age that she was hung up in a bottle and could only squeak, 'I want to die.' She typifies, I suppose, the timeworn soul's desire to escape from the 'Wheel' of things. The first of the five sections opens in spring with one of the snatches of poetry that occur scattered about the poem:

> April is the cruellest month, breeding
> Lilacs out of the dead land, mixing

> Memory and desire, stirring
> Dull roots with spring rain.

The next moment comes a spasm of futile, society conversation
from a Swiss resort, followed by a passionate outburst at the
sterile barrenness of life, though not without hope of its redemp-
tion. This is far the best passage in the book:

> What are the roots that clutch, what branches grow
> Out of this stony rubbish? Son of man,
> You cannot say, or guess, for you know only
> A heap of broken images where the sun beats,
> And the dead tree gives no shelter, the cricket no relief,
> And the dry stone no sound of water.

Then, suddenly, a verse of *Tristan und Isolde* and an echo of
Sappho (the vanity of human love?). Next instant there appears
a clairvoyante, and in the mystic 'Tarot' cards of her fortune-
telling are revealed those mysterious figures that flit through the
poem, melting into each other in a way that recalls Emerson's
'Brahma' – the Phœnician sailor, who 'is not wholly distinct
from Prince Ferdinand of Naples' and seems to be reincarnate
in the Smyrna currant-merchant; the Fisher King; and the
Frazerite Hanged Man or sacrificed priest, who merges later into
the Christ of the walk to Emmaus.

Then we are thrust into the squalid, 'unreal' Inferno of
London Bridge.

The second section contains a dialogue between two jaded
lovers in luxury, an interlude about the rape of Philomela the
nightingale (spiritual beauty violated by the world?), and a
pothouse story of a wrangle between two women about the
husband of one of them. In the third part the Fisher King appears
fishing in the first person behind the gashouse, and there recur
the *motifs* of the nightingale and of unreal London, also:

> Mr Eugenides, the Smyrna merchant
> Unshaven, with a pocket full of currants
> C.i.f. London.

But before the reader has time to breathe, 'I, Tiresias,' is watching the seduction of a tired typist after tea by a 'young man carbuncular' – a typical instance of that squalor which seems perpetually to obsess Mr Eliot with mixed fascination and repulsion. A note explains that Tiresias, being a person of double sex, unites in some way all the other persons in the poem. There is more suburban sordidness, and the section ends gasping half a sentence from St Augustine and another half from Buddha.

In 'IV – Death by Water' (one of the stock ways, in Frazer, of killing the vegetation king and ensuring rain by sympathetic magic) the Phœnician sailor is duly drowned. Section V, which brings the rain of deliverance to the Waste Land, is, by the author's account, a mixture of the Walk to Emmaus, of the approach to the Chapel Perilous in Arthurian Legend (taken by Miss Weston to signify initiation into the mysteries of physical and spiritual union), and of the state of Eastern Europe! Deliverance comes with the magic formula; 'Datta, dayadhvam, damyata – give, sympathise, control', and the poem ends:

> London Bridge is falling down falling down falling down
> *Poi s' ascose nel foco che gli affina*
> *Quando fiam uti chelidon* – O swallow, swallow
> *Le Prince d' Aquitaine à la tour abolie*
> These fragments I have shored against my ruins
> Why then Ile fit you. Hieronymo's mad againe.
> Datta. Dayadhvam. Damyata.
>   Shantih shantih shantih

(The punctuation largely disappears in the latter part of the poem – whether this be subtlety or accident, it is impossible to say. 'Shantih' is equivalent to the 'Peace that passeth understanding' – which in this case it certainly does.)

All this is very difficult; as Dr Johnson said under similar circumstances, 'I would it were impossible.' But the gist of the poem is apparently a wild revolt from the abomination of desolation which is human life, combined with a belief in salvation by the usual catchwords of renunciation – this salvation being also the esoteric significance of the savage fertility-rituals found in the *Golden Bough*, a watering, as it were, of the desert of the suffering soul.

About the philosophy of the poem, if such it be, it would be vain to argue; but it is hard not to regret the way in which modern writers of real creative power abandon themselves to the fond illusion that they have philosophic gifts and a weighty message to deliver to the world, as well. In all periods creative artists have been apt to think they could think, though in all periods they have beeen frequently harebrained and sometimes mad; just as great rulers and warriors have cared only to be flattered for the way they fiddled or their flatulent tragedies. But now, in particular, we have the spectacle of Mr Lawrence, Miss May Sinclair, and Mr Eliot, all sacrificing their artistic powers on the altar of some fantastic Mumbo-Jumbo, all trying to get children on mandrake roots instead of bearing their natural offspring.

Perhaps this unhappy composition should have been left to sink itself: but it is not easy to dismiss in three lines what is being written about as a new masterpiece. For at present it is particularly easy to win the applause of the *blasé* and the young, of the coteries and the eccentric. The Victorian 'Spasmodics' likewise had their day. But a poem that has to be explained in notes is not unlike a picture with 'This is a dog' inscribed beneath. Not, indeed, that Mr Eliot's notes succeed in explaining anything, being as muddled as incomplete. What is the use of explaining 'laquearia' by quoting two lines of Latin containing the word, which will convey nothing to those who do not know that language, and nothing new to those who do? What is the use of giving a quotation from Ovid which begins in the middle of a sentence, without either subject or verb, and fails to add even the reference? And when one person hails another on London Bridge as having been with him 'at Mylae', how is the non-classical reader to guess that this is the name of a Punic sea-fight in which as Phœnician sailor, presumably, the speaker had taken part? The main function of the notes is, indeed, to give the references to the innumerable authors whose lines the poet embodies, like a mediæval writer making a life of Christ out of lines of Virgil. But the borrowed jewels he has set in its head do not make Mr Eliot's toad the more prepossessing.

In brief, in *The Waste Land* Mr Eliot has shown that he can at moments write real blank verse; but that is all. For the rest he has quoted a great deal, he has parodied and imitated. But the parodies are cheap and the imitations inferior. Among so many other sources Mr Eliot may have thought, as he wrote, of Rossetti's 'Card-Dealer', of 'Childe Roland to the Dark Tower Came', of the 'Vision of Sin' with its same question:

> To which an answer peal'd from that high land,
> But in a tongue no man could understand.

But the trouble is that for the reader who thinks of them the comparison is crushing. *The Waste Land* adds nothing to a literature which contains things like these. And in our own day, though Professor Santayana be an inferior poet, no one has better reaffirmed the everlasting 'No' of criticism to this recurrent malady of tired ages, 'the fantastic and lacking in sanity':

> Never will they dig deep or build for time
> Who of unreason weave a maze of rhyme,
> Worship a weakness, nurse a whim, and bind
> Wreaths about temples tenantless of mind,
> Forsake the path the seeing Muses trod,
> And shatter Nature to discover God.
>
> (*New Statesman*, 3 November 1923)

Gilbert Seldes

In turning to Mr Eliot as poet I do not leave the critic behind since it is from his critical utterances that we derive the clue to his poetry. He says that the historical sense is indispensable to anyone who would continue to be a poet after the age of twenty-five, and follows this with a statement which cannot be too closely pondered by those who misunderstand tradition and by those who imagine that American letters stand outside of European letters and are to be judged by other standards:

The historical sense compels a man to write not merely with his own generation in his bones, but with a feeling that the whole of the literature of Europe from Homer and within it the whole of the literature of his own country has a simultaneous existence and composes a simultaneous order.

This is only the beginning of 'depersonalization'. It continues:

What happens is a continual surrender of himself [the poet] as he is at the moment to something which is more valuable. The progress of an artist is a continual self-sacrifice, a continual extinction of personality . . . the more perfect the artist, the more completely separate in him will be the man who suffers and the mind which creates; the more perfectly will the mind digest and transmute the passions which are its material. . . . The intensity of the poetry is something quite different from whatever intensity in the supposed experience it may give the impression of. . . . Impressions and experiences which are important for the man may take no place in the poetry, and those which become important in the poetry may play quite a negligible part in the man, the personality. . . .

And finally:

It is not in his personal emotions, the emotions provoked by particular events in his life, that the poet is in any way remarkable or interesting. His particular emotions may be simple, or crude, or flat. The emotion in his poetry will be a very complex thing, but not with the complexity of the emotions of people who have very complex or unusual emotions in life. . . . The business of the poet is not to find new emotions, but to use the ordinary ones and, in working them up into poetry, to express feelings which are not in actual emotions at all. . . . Poetry is not a turning loose of emotion, but an escape from emotion; it is not the expression of a personality, but an escape from personality. But, of course, only those who have personality and emotions know what it means to want to escape from these things.

The significant emotion has its life in the poem and not in the history of the poet; and recognition of this, Mr Eliot indicates, is the true appreciation of poetry. Fortunately for the critic he has written one poem, *The Waste Land*, to which one can apply his own standards. It develops, carries to conclusions, many things in his remarkable earlier work, in method and in thought. I have not that familiarity with the intricacies of French verse which could make it possible for me to affirm or deny the statement that technically he derives much from Jules Laforgue; if Remy de Gourmont's estimate of the latter be correct one can see definite points of similarity in the minds of the two poets:

His natural genius was made up of sensibility, irony, imagina-tion, and clairvoyance; he chose to nourish it with positive knowledge (*connaissances positives*), with all philosophies and all literatures, with all the images of nature and of art; even the latest views of science seem to have been known to him. . . . It is literature entirely made new and unforeseen, disconcerting and giving the curious and rare sensation that one has never read anything like it before. . . .

A series of sardonic portraits – of people, places, things – each the distillation of a refined emotion, make up Mr Eliot's 'Poems'. The deceptive simplicity of these poems in form and in style is exactly at the opposite extreme from false naïveté; they are unpretentiously sophisticated, wicked, malicious, humorous, and with the distillation of emotion has gone a condensation of expression. In *The Waste Land* the seriousness of the theme is matched with an intensity of expression in which all the earlier qualities are sublimated.

In essence *The Waste Land* says something which is not new: that life has become barren and sterile, that man is withering, impotent, and without assurance that the waters which made the land fruitful will ever rise again. (I need not say that 'thoughtful' as the poem is, it does not 'express an idea'; it deals with emotions, and ends precisely in that significant emotion, inherent in the poem, which Mr Eliot has described.) The title, the plan, and much of the symbolism of the poem, the author tells us in his 'Notes', were suggested by Miss Weston's remarkable book on the Grail legend, *From Ritual to Romance*; it is only indispensable to know that there exists the legend of a king rendered impotent, and his country sterile, both awaiting deliverance by a knight on his way to seek the Grail; it is interesting to know further that this is part of the Life or Fertility mysteries; but the poem is self-contained. It seems at first sight remarkably disconnected, confused, the emotion seems to disengage itself in spite of the objects and events chosen by the poet as their vehicle. The poem begins with a memory of summer showers, gaiety, joyful and perilous escapades; a moment later someone else is saying 'I will show you fear in a handful of dust', and this is followed by the first lines of *Tristan und Isolde*, and then again by a fleeting recollection of loveliness. The symbolism of the poem is introduced by means of the Tarot pack of cards; quotations, precise or dislocated, occur; gradually one discovers a rhythm of alternation between the visionary (so to name the memories of the past) and the actual, between the spoken and the unspoken thought. There are scraps, fragments; then sustained episodes; the poem culminates with the juxtaposition of the highest types of Eastern and Western asceticism, by means of allusions to St Augustine and Buddha; and ends with a sour commentary on the injunctions 'Give, sympathize, control' of the Upanishads, a commentary which reaches its conclusion in a pastiche recalling all that is despairing and disinherited in the memory of man.

A closer view of the poem does more than illuminate the difficulties; it reveals the hidden form of the work, indicates how each thing falls into place, and to the reader's surprise shows that the emotion which at first seemed to come in spite of the framework and the detail could not otherwise have been communicated. For the theme is not a distaste for life, nor is it a disillusion, a romantic pessimism of any kind. It is specifically concerned with the idea of the Waste Land – that the land *was* fruitful and now is not, that life had been rich, beautiful, assured, organized, lofty, and now is dragging itself out in a poverty-stricken and disrupted and ugly tedium, without health, and with no consolation in morality; there may remain for the poet the labor of poetry, but in the poem there remain only 'these fragments I have shored against my ruins' – the broken glimpses of what was. The poem is not an argument and I can only add, to

be fair, that it contains no romantic idealization of the past;
one feels simply that even in the cruelty and madness which
have left their record in history and in art, there was an intensity
of life, a germination and fruitfulness, which are now gone, and
that even the creative imagination, even hallucination and vision
have atrophied, so that water shall never again be struck from a
rock in the desert. Mr Bertrand Russell has recently said that
since the Renaissance the clock of Europe has been running
down; without the feeling that it was once wound up, without the contrasting emotions as one looks at the past and
at the present, *The Waste Land* would be a different poem,
and the problem of the poet would have been solved in another
way.

The present solution is in part by juxtaposition of opposites.
We have a passage seemingly spoken by a slut, ending

Goonight, Bill. Goonight, Lou. Goonight, May. Goonight. Ta
ta. Goonight, goonight.

and then the ineffable

Good night ladies, good night, sweet ladies, good night, good
    night.

Conversely the turn is accomplished from nobility or beauty
of utterance to

    The sounds of horns and motors, which shall bring
    Sweeney to Mrs Porter in the spring.

And in the long passage where Tiresias, the central character of
the poem, appears the method is at its height, for here is the
coldest and unhappiest revelation of the assault of lust made in
the terms of beauty:

    At the violet hour, when the eyes and back
    Turn upward from the desk, when the human engine waits
    Like a taxi throbbing waiting
    I Tiresias, though blind, throbbing between two lives,
    Old man with wrinkled female breasts, can see
    At the violet hour, the evening hour that strives

Homeward, and brings the sailor home from sea,
The typist home at tea-time, clears her breakfast, lights
Her stove, and lays out food in tins.
Out of the window perilously spread
Her drying combinations touched by the sun's last rays,
On the divan are piled (at night her bed)
Stockings, slippers, camisoles, and stays.
I Tiresias, old man with wrinkled dugs
Perceived the scene, and foretold the rest —
I, too, awaited the expected guest.
He, the young man carbuncular, arrives,
A small house-agent's clerk, with one bold stare,
One of the low on whom assurance sits
As a silk hat on a Bradford millionaire.
The time is now propitious, as he guesses,
The meal is ended, she is bored and tired,
Endeavors to engage her in caresses
Which still are unreproved, if undesired.
Flushed and decided, he assaults at once;
Exploring hands encounter no defence;
His vanity requires no response,
And makes a welcome of indifference.
(And I Tiresias have foresuffered all
Enacted on this same divan or bed;
I who have sat by Thebes below the wall
And walked among the lowest of the dead.)
Bestows one final patronizing kiss,
And gropes his way, finding the stairs unlit . . .

It will be interesting for those who have knowledge of
another great work of our time, Mr Joyce's *Ulysses*, to think of
the two together. That *The Waste Land* is, in a sense, the
inversion and the complement of *Ulysses* is at least tenable. We
have in *Ulysses* the poet defeated, turning outward, savoring the
ugliness which is no longer transmutable into beauty, and, in the
end, homeless. We have in *The Waste Land* some indication of
the inner life of such a poet. The contrast between the forms of
these two works is not expressed in the recognition that one is
among the longest and one among the shortest of works in its

genre; the important thing is that in each the theme, once it is comprehended, is seen to have dictated the form. More important still, I fancy, is that each has expressed something of supreme relevance to our present life in the everlasting terms of art.

(*Nation*, 6 December 1922)

PART THREE

Comments and Reactions

George Watson

WHEN a great poet dies, myths crowd in. In Eliot's case the myths began years before he died, which is natural enough when you remember that he lived the life of an established poet for over forty years. One of them concerns his early reputation. It now seems to be rather widely thought that Eliot had to fight hard and long to establish himself as the first living poet of the English-speaking world; and it is even believed by some that his followers suffered persecution and ignominy for upholding a cause called 'modernism'. This is a radical, and sometimes a wilful, misunderstanding of the facts. My own notion of what happened after 1922, the year of *The Waste Land* – the year after which it might reasonably be called foolish to deny Eliot's eminence as a poet – is based solely upon published evidence, since I cannot remember the Twenties. But the published evidence seems to me to contradict some of the assertions now confidently made by those who were there. In the circumstances, I don't apologise for the disqualification of not having proved these events on my own pulse. It is just because I have not lived through them, in fact, that I have taken the trouble to look the evidence up.

Eliot was a very successful poet. The acclaim for his early poems was, for all practical purposes, instantaneous. There seems to have been no period after 1922 when his significance as a poet was either doubted or radically misinterpreted in the literary journals. No doubt the word 'radically' needs special emphasis here; no doubt it would be easy to find isolated comments in the early reviews that would now look silly. But a judicial reading would support two conclusions: first, that they are overwhelmingly favourable; and second, that when they do make objections, the objections do not usually point either to a deep misunderstanding or a lack of sympathy. It would be quite wrong to suppose that Eliot had to create out of nothing, or even out of little, the taste by which he was appreciated. That appetite increased with the years, but it was always strongly there.

Admirers and detractors were equally agreed about the reality of his reputation. There is even an article of 1930 entitled 'On the Somewhat Premature Apotheosis of Thomas Stearns Eliot'. Richard Aldington, in an essay written even before the appearance of *The Waste Land*, called Eliot's verse the poetic equivalent of Joyce: 'The works of Mr James Joyce may be taken as typical of the best original prose of this [post-war] school; the poetry of Mr Eliot occupies a similar position' (*Literary Studies and Reviews*, 1924, p. 183). It seems to have been 'an international success', too, as John Crowe Ransom later called it in *The New Criticism* (1941), occurring simultaneously on both sides of the Atlantic. Mr E. M. Forster, in an article of 1928 later collected in *Abinger Harvest*, strikes the loudest of all echoing notes – that Eliot was the poet of a whole generation. As for the young, he wrote then, *The Waste Land* 'has made a profound impression on them, and given them precisely the food they needed'. For those under thirty he was 'the most important author of their day, his influence is enormous, they are inside his idiom as the young of 1900 were inside George Meredith's'. When Forster wrote that, Eliot had barely reached the age of forty; and there are still earlier testimonies.

In *Science and Poetry* (1926), Professor I. A. Richards, then a Cambridge lecturer in English in his early thirties, interrupted his discussion of the 'sense of desolation' felt by his generation to acknowledge his debt to a poem published only four years before. Eliot 'seems to me by this poem to have performed two considerable services for this generation': by accurately describing the contemporary state of mind, and by 'effecting a complete severance between his poetry and *all* beliefs' (pp. 64–5 n). Something of an irony now, this second point, but it serves as a reminder how little in the Twenties Eliot was thought of as a dogmatist, and how alien his progress towards belief would come to seem to the most ardent admirers of his first celebrity. *The Waste Land* could then seem a masterpiece of poetic impressionism by a rebel who refreshingly refused to have a cause; the causes were to come later. In the same year Richards extended his *Principles of Literary Criticism* (1924) with two appendices, in one of which, 'The Poetry of T. S. Eliot', he acknowledged the difficulty many found in reading the poems, but pleaded the case that 'very much of the best poetry is necessarily ambiguous in its immediate effect'. *The Waste Land*, in his view, had an emotional unity, and in any case every part of it succeeds in a more traditional sense. 'The poem as a whole may elude us, while every fragment, as a fragment, comes victoriously home.' Richards ends by making the point that Forster and many others were to echo through the Twenties and Thirties: some readers would find in Eliot's poems 'a clearer, fuller realisation of their plight, the plight of a whole generation'. Four years later Professor Empson, who had been Richards's pupil at Cambridge, was to use a passage from *The Waste Land* as an example in *Seven Types of Ambiguity* (1930).

Some views were balanced. In *The Calendar of Modern Letters* of May 1925 Edwin Muir had acclaimed Eliot's *Homage to Dryden* for its doctrine of a 17th-century 'dissociation of sensibility', an analysis of English poetry already 'accepted as a truism by intelligent people today'. But he disagreed with Eliot's abrupt dismissal of Milton and of the Romantics; and in his *Transition* (1928) he put his careful reservations about the poems, while still calling Eliot 'the most complete writer of our time'. Meanwhile, in a different context, Laura Riding and Robert Graves, in their *Survey of Modernist Poetry* (1927), had already compared *The Waste Land* favourably with Tennyson's *In Memoriam* and even with the *Aeneid*, on the grounds that Eliot does not confine himself to a single metre, but by metrical changes exploits 'delicate transitions from one atmosphere to another', so that the poem succeeds 'as a unified whole' (pp. 50–51). Other academics besides Richards were now crowding into the field. In a lecture written before *For Lancelot Andrewes* (1928) and collected soon after for the Clarendon Press in *The Lamp and the Lute* (1929), Professor Bonamy Dobrée unreservedly called Eliot's criticism 'the most important in English since Coleridge wrote his *Biographia Literaria*'; and as for the poetry, 'I would be prepared to lay odds that the year 1922, which saw *The Waste Land*, will prove to be as important a year in the history of the development of English poetry as the year 1798 . . .' (pp. 129–30). By 1932 at least six works had appeared entirely devoted to Eliot, published from points as scattered as London, Paris, Seattle, Finland and Peking. In one of them Mr Hugh Ross Williamson confirmed Dobrée's cataclysmic view of what had happened; in *The Poetry of T. S. Eliot* (1932) he calls Eliot 'the most important influence in English poetry at the present time', and *The Waste Land* comparable with *Lyrical Ballads* 'both as a turning-point and as a force' (p. 10). Among writers in their twenties, he goes on, Eliot by 1932 was 'an established and even slightly out-moded institution. . . . By them his importance has long been taken for granted', though he may still be suspected by older readers.

What is more, this immense celebrity was not confined to isolated admirers in literary cliques or in the little reviews, however much the more intense admirers were given, from the start, to striking embattled attitudes. The journals of the literary Establishment, if there is or was such a thing, acclaimed Eliot too. The *Times Literary Supplement*, it is true, disliked '*Prufrock*' (1917) as 'untouched by any genuine rush of feeling' and 'purely analytical' (21 June 1917); but it greeted *The Waste Land* with real warmth, recognized Eliot's debt to Laforgue, and called him 'a poet capable of a style more refined than that of any of his generation', though it found the parodies tasteless and the structure fragmentary (20 September 1923). It welcomed the early collections of essays, too – not surprisingly, since Eliot had been contributing to *TLS* since 1919, when he was thirty-one, and had first published some of the essays as reviews there. Years later he wrote a generous tribute to Bruce Richmond, the first editor, who had taught him 'to moderate my dislikes and crotchets, to write in a temperate and impartial way' (*TLS*, 13 January 1961), adding that he had tried to apply the same standards when in 1922 he began to edit the *Criterion*. By that date Eliot was a mere thirty-four. He seems to have been one who never had to wait.

('The Triumph of T. S. Eliot', from *Critical Quarterly*, 1965)

I. A. Richards

We too readily forget that, unless something is very wrong with our civilisation, we should be producing three equal poets at least for every poet of high rank in our great-great-grandfathers' day. Something must indeed be wrong; and since Mr Eliot is one of the very few poets that current conditions have not overcome, the difficulties which he has faced, and the cognate difficulties which his readers encounter, repay study.

Mr Eliot's poetry has occasioned an unusual amount of irritated or enthusiastic bewilderment. The bewilderment has several sources. The most formidable is the unobtrusiveness, in some cases the absence, of any coherent intellectual thread upon which the items of the poem are strung. A reader of 'Gerontion', or of 'Preludes', or of *The Waste Land*, may, if he will, after repeated readings, introduce such a thread. Another reader after much effort may fail to contrive one. But in either case energy will have been misapplied. For the items are united by the accord, contrast, and interaction of their emotional effects, not by an intellectual scheme that analysis must work out. The value lies in the unified response which this interaction creates in the right reader. The only intellectual activity required takes place in the realisation of the separate items. We can, of course, make a 'rationalisation' of the whole experience, as we can of any experience. If we do, we are adding something which does not belong to the poem. Such a logical scheme is, at best, a scaffolding that vanishes when the poem is constructed. But we have so built into our nervous systems a demand for intellectual coherence, even in poetry, that we find a difficulty in doing without it.

This point may be misunderstood, for the charge most usually brought against Mr Eliot's poetry is that it is over-intellectualised. One reason for this is his use of allusion. A reader who in one short poem picks up allusions to *The Aspern Papers*, *Othello*, 'A Toccata of Galuppi's', Marston, 'The Phœnix and the Turtle', *Antony and Cleopatra* (twice), 'The Extasie', *Macbeth*, *The Merchant of Venice*, and Ruskin, feels that his wits are being unusually well exercised. He may easily leap to the conclusion that the basis of the poem is in wit also. But this would be a mistake. These things come in, not that the reader may be ingenious or admire the writer's erudition (this last accusation has tempted several critics to disgrace themselves), but for the sake of the emotional aura which they bring and the attitudes they incite. Allusion in Mr Eliot's hands is a technical device for compression. *The Waste Land* is the equivalent in content to an epic. Without this device twelve books would have been neeeded. But these allusions and the notes in which some of them are elucidated have made many a petulant reader turn down his thumb at once. Such a reader has not begun to understand what it is all about.

This objection is connected with another, that of obscurity. To quote a recent pronouncement upon *The Waste Land* from Mr Middleton Murry: 'The reader is compelled, in the mere effort to understand, to adopt an attitude of intellectual suspicion, which makes impossible the communication of feeling. The work offends against the most elementary canon of good writing: that the immediate effect should be unambiguous.' Consider first this 'canon'. What would happen, if we pressed it, to Shakespeare's greatest sonnets or to *Hamlet?* The truth is that very much of the best poetry is necessarily ambiguous in its immediate effect. Even the most careful and responsive reader must reread and do hard work before the poem forms itself clearly and unambiguously in his mind. An original poem, as much as a new branch of mathematics, compels the mind which receives it to grow, and this takes time. Anyone who upon reflection asserts the contrary for his own case must be either a demigod or dishonest; probably Mr Murry was in haste. His remarks show that he has failed in his attempt to read the poem, and they reveal, in part, the reason for his failure – namely, his own overintellectual approach. To read it successfully he would have to discontinue his present self-mystifications.

The critical question in all cases is whether the poem is worth the trouble it entails. For *The Waste Land* this is considerable. There is Miss Weston's *From Ritual to Romance* to read, and its 'astral' trimmings to be discarded – they have nothing to do with Mr Eliot's poem. There is Canto xxvi of the *Purgatorio* to be studied – the relevance of the close of that canto to the whole of Mr Eliot's work must be insisted upon. It illuminates his persistent concern with sex, the problem of our generation, as religion was the problem of the last. There is the central position of Tiresias in the poem to be puzzled out – the cryptic form of the note which Mr Eliot writes on this point is just a little tiresome. It is a way of underlining the fact that the poem is concerned with many aspects of the one fact of sex, a hint that is perhaps neither indispensable nor entirely successful.

When all this has been done by the reader, when the materials with which the words are to clothe themselves have been collected, the poem still remains to be read. And it is easy to fail in this undertaking. An 'attitude of intellectual suspicion' must certainly be abandoned. But this is not difficult to those who still know how to give their feelings precedence to their thoughts, who can accept and unify an experience without trying to catch it in an intellectual net or to squeeze out a doctrine. One form of this attempt must be mentioned. Some, misled no doubt by its origin in a Mystery, have endeavoured to give the poem a symbolical reading. But its symbols are not mystical, but emotional. They stand, that is, not for ineffable objects, but for normal human experience. The poem, in fact, is radically naturalistic; only its compression makes it appear otherwise. And in this it probably comes nearer to the original Mystery which it perpetuates than transcendentalism does.

If it were desired to label in three words the most characteristic feature of Mr Eliot's technique, this might be done by calling his poetry a 'music of ideas'. The ideas are of all kinds: abstract and concrete, general and particular; and, like the musician's phrases, they are arranged, not that they may tell us something, but that their effects in us may combine into a coherent whole of feeling and attitude and produce a peculiar liberation of the will. They are there to be responded to, not to be pondered or worked out. This is, of course, a method used intermittently in very much poetry, and only an accentuation and isolation of one of its normal resources. The peculiarity of Mr Eliot's later, more puzzling, work is his deliberate and almost exclusive employment of it. In the earlier poems this logical freedom appears only occasionally. In 'The Love Song of J. Alfred Prufrock', for example, there is a patch at the beginning and another at the end, but the rest of the poem is quite straightforward. In 'Gerontion', the first long poem in this manner, the air of monologue, of a stream of associations, is a kind of disguise, and the last two lines,

> Tenants of the house,
> Thoughts of a dry brain in a dry season,

are almost an excuse. The close of 'A Cooking Egg' is perhaps the passage in which the technique shows itself most clearly. The reader who appreciates the emotional relevance of the title has the key to the later poems in his hand. I take Pipit to be the retired nurse of the hero of the poem, and *Views of the Oxford Colleges* to be the still treasured present which he sent her when he went up to the University. The middle section of the poem I read as a specimen of the rather withered pleasantry in which contemporary culture has culminated and beyond which it finds much difficulty in passing. The final section gives the contrast which is pressed home by the title. Even the most mature egg was new laid once. The only other title of equal significance that I can recall is Mrs Wharton's *The Age of Innocence*, which might well be studied in this connection. *The Waste Land* and 'The Hollow Men' (the most beautiful of Mr Eliot's poems, and in the last section a new development) are purely a 'music of ideas', and the pretence of a continuous thread of associations is dropped.

How this technique lends itself to misunderstandings we have seen. But many readers who have failed in the end to escape bewilderment have begun by finding on almost every line that Mr Eliot has written – if we except certain youthful poems on American topics – that personal stamp which is the hardest thing for the craftsman to imitate and perhaps the most certain sign that the experience, good or bad, rendered in the poem is authentic. Only those unfortunate persons who are incapable of reading poetry can resist Mr Eliot's rhythms. The poem as a whole may elude us while every fragment, as a fragment, comes victoriously home. It is difficult to believe that this is Mr Eliot's fault rather than his reader's, because a parallel case of a poet who so constantly achieves the hardest part of his task and yet fails in the easier is not to be found. It is much more likely that we have been trying to put the fragments together on a wrong principle.

Another doubt has been expressed. Mr Eliot repeats himself in two ways. The nightingale, Cleopatra's barge, the rats, and the smoky candle-end, recur and recur. Is this a sign of a poverty of inspiration? A more plausible explanation is that this repetition is in part a consequence of the technique above described, and in part something which many writers who are not accused of poverty also show. Shelley, with his rivers, towers, and stars, Conrad, Hardy, Walt Whitman, and Dostoevski spring to mind. When a writer has found a theme or image which fixes a point of relative stability in the drift of experience, it is not to be expected that he will avoid it. Such themes are a means of orientation. And it is quite true that the central process in all Mr Eliot's best poems is the same: the conjunction of feelings which, though superficially opposed – as squalor, for example, is opposed to grandeur – yet tend as they develop to change places and even to unite. If they do not develop far enough the intention of the poet is missed. Mr Eliot is neither sighing after vanished glories nor holding contemporary experience up to scorn.

Both bitterness and desolation are superficial aspects of his poetry. There are those who think that he merely takes his readers into the Waste Land and leaves them there, that in his last poem he confesses his impotence to release the healing waters. The reply is that some readers find in his poetry not only a clearer, fuller realisation of their plight, the plight of a whole generation, than they find elsewhere, but also through the very energies set free in that realisation a return of the saving passion.

(*Principles of Literary Criticism,* 1926)

William Empson

The Chair she sat in, like a burnished throne,
Glowed on the marble, where the glass
Held up by standards wrought with fruited vines
From which a golden Cupidon peeped out
(Another hid his eyes behind his wing)
Doubled the flames of seven-branched candelabra
Reflecting light upon the table as
The glitter of her jewels rose to meet it,
From satin cases poured in rich profusion;
In vials of ivory and coloured glass
Unstoppered, lurked her strange synthetic perfumes,
Unguent, powdered, or liquid – troubled, confused
And drowned the sense in odours; stirred by the air
That freshened from the window, these ascended
In fattening the prolonged candleflames,
Flung their smoke into the laquearia,
Stirring the pattern on the coffered ceiling.

What is *poured* may be *cases*, *jewels*, *glitter*, or *light*, and *profusion*, enriching its modern meaning with its derivation, is shared, with a dazzled luxury, between them; so that while some of the *jewels* are *pouring* out *light* from their *cases*, others are *poured* about, as are their *cases*, on the dressing-table. If referring to *glitter*, *poured* may, in any case, be a main verb as well as a participle. There is a more trivial point of the same kind in the next line, where *glass* may stand alone for a glass bottle or may be paired with *ivory* ('vials of glass'); and *unstoppered* may refer only to *glass*, or to *vials and glass*, or to *vials of glass and of ivory*; till *lurked*, which is for a moment taken as the same grammatical form, attracts it towards *perfumes*. It is because of this blurring of the grammar into luxury that the scientific word *synthetic* is able to stand out so sharply as a dramatic and lyrical high light.

The ambiguity of syntax in *poured* is repeated on a grander scale by

> Unguent, powdered, or liquid – troubled, confused,
> And drowned the sense in odours; stirred by the air ...

where, after *powdered* and the two similar words have acted as adjectives, it gives a sense of swooning or squinting, or the *stirring* of things seen through heat convection currents, to think of *troubled* and *confused* as verbs. They may, indeed, be kept as participles belonging to *perfumes*, to suggest the mingling of vapours against the disorder of the bedroom; for it is only with the culminating *drowned* that we are forced either to accept the *perfumes* as subject of a new sentence, or *the sense* as an isolated word, perhaps with 'was' understood, and qualified by three participles. For *stirred*, after all this, we are in a position to imagine three subjects as intended by *these*; *perfumes*, *sense*, and *odours* (from which it could follow on without a stop); there is a curious heightening of the sense of texture from all this dalliance; a suspension of all need for active decision; thus *ascended* is held back in the same way as either verb or participle in order that no climax, none of the relief of certainty, may be lacking to the last and indubitable verb *flung*.

It may be noted that the verse has no variation of sense throughout these ambiguities, and very little of rhythm; it loses nothing in definiteness from being the poetry of the English past participle.

(Seven Types of Ambiguity, 1930)

C. Day Lewis

ELIOT first came into prominence with the publication of *The Waste Land*. This poem called forth floods of abuse and storms of intellectual snobbery: it provided the reactionary with something they could really get their teeth into, and the fake-progressives with a new fashion. It does not to my mind contain his best poetry: for that, I would direct the reader to 'Prufrock', 'Gerontion', one or two of his later poems – in particular, 'Animula', and to such lines as –

> Eyes I dare not meet in dreams
> In death's dream kingdom
> These do not appear:
> There, the eyes are
> Sunlight on a broken column
> There, is a tree swinging
> And voices are
> In the wind's singing
> More distant and more solemn
> Than a fading star.

But the fact remains that, for good or ill, *The Waste Land* has had a greater influence on present-day verse than the rest of Eliot's work and probably a greater one than any other poetry of the century. This is due largely to its subject matter – more so, perhaps, than to the novelties of its technique. I. A. Richards, who gives a terribly inflated value to the poem, says that it effects 'a complete severance between poetry and all beliefs', an example of criticism at its most vicious. One can neither write nor exist completely severed from all beliefs, and the beliefs which a writer holds or against which he is reacting are bound to affect his writing. It is always dangerous and impertinent to commend a poem for anything but its poetry: however, I am compelled to say that *The Waste Land* seems to me chiefly important as a social document. It gives an authentic impression of the mentality of educated people in the psychological slump that took place immediately after the war. It makes us aware of the nervous exhaustion, the mental disintegration, the exaggerated self-consciousness, the boredom, the pathetic gropings after the fragments of a shattered faith – all those symptoms of the psychic disease which ravaged Europe as mercilessly as the Spanish influenza. But in doing so it enlarged our conception of the field of poetic activity: as Eliot himself has said; 'the essential advantage for a poet is not to have a beautiful world with which to deal; it is to be able to see beneath both beauty and ugliness; to see the boredom, and the horror, and the glory'.

(*A Hope for Poetry*, 1934)

Yvor Winters

THE subject matter of *The Waste Land* is in general similar to that of *Les Fleurs du Mal*. Yet if one will compare let us say 'Le Jeu' with 'A Game of Chess', one may perhaps note what Eliot overlooked. Eliot, in dealing with debased and stupid material, felt himself obliged to seek his form in this matter: the result is confusion and journalistic reproduction of detail. Baudelaire, in dealing with similar matters, sought to evaluate it in terms of eternal verity: he sought his form and his point of view in tradition, and from that point of view and in that form he judged his material, and the result is a profound evaluation of evil. The difference is the difference between triviality and greatness.

The difference is in part, however, merely the difference between a poet with a great native gift for poetic style and a poet with very little gift. Eliot has written in his essay on Massinger:

One of the surest of tests is the way in which a poet borrows. Immature poets imitate; mature poets steal; bad poets deface what they take, and good poets make it into something better, or at least something different. The good poet welds his theft into a whole of feeling which is unique, utterly different from that from which it was torn; the bad poet throws it into something which has no cohesion.

Such a statement might easily be used in defense of Pound who, except for Eliot, borrows more extensively than any other poet of our time: Pound's revery has a discernible consistency at its best, and the borrowed material is either selected or reworked so judiciously that it seems in place. And such a statement might be cited in defense of 'Gerontion' and even of some of Eliot's earlier work, frail as it is. But the meter of *The Waste Land* is not the suave meter of *The Cantos* or of 'Gerontion': it is a broken blank verse interspersed with bad free verse and rimed doggerel. And what is one to say of the last eight lines of *The Waste Land*, which are composed, as nearly as I can determine with the aid of the notes, of unaltered passages from seven sources? A sequence of such quotations cannot by any stretch of the imagination achieve unity, and its disunity can be justified on no grounds except the Adams–Eliot doctrine of modern art, of which the less said by this time the better. The method is that of a man who is unable to deal with his subject, and resorts to the rough approximation of quotation; it is the method of the New England farmer who meets every situation in life with a saw from *Poor Richard*; it betokens the death of the mind and of the sensibility alike. The last line, in fact, is a classic of its kind. It reads: 'Shantih shantih shantih', and in the note at the end of the poem Eliot tells us that ' "The Peace which passeth understanding" is a feeble translation of the content of this word'. Surely there was never another great sentiment expressed with such charming simplicity!

Eliot, in brief, has surrendered to the acedia which Baudelaire was able to judge; Eliot suffers from the delusion that he is judging it when he is merely exhibiting it. He has loosely thrown together a collection of disparate and fragmentary principles which fall roughly into two contradictory groups, the romantic on the one hand and on the other the classical and Christian; and being unaware of his own contradictions, he is able to make a virtue of what appears to be private spiritual laziness; he is able to enjoy at one and the same time the pleasures of indulgence and the dignity of disapproval.

(*On Modern Poets*, 1943)

Karl Shapiro

The Waste Land is the most important poem of the twentieth century, that is, the one that has caused the most discussion and is said by critics to be the culmination of the modern 'mythic' style. The poem, by Eliot's own admission, is a collaboration with Pound. Pound edited it and removed a third or two thirds of it. The 'continuity', we can assume, is therefore the work of Pound, who abhorred continuity in his own more ambitious poetry. As everyone knows how to read the poem or can find out by visiting the nearest library, I will say nothing about its meaning. I will speak rather of the success and the failure of the poem. That it is lacking in unity is obvious (assuming, as I do, that unity is a literary virtue). Any part of The Waste Land can be switched with any other part without changing the sense of the poem. Aside from the so-called 'mythic' form, which is worthless and not even true – for Eliot misread James Joyce's Ulysses when he saw it as a parallel to Homer – the underlying unity of the poem is tonal and dramatic, exactly as a Victorian narrative poem would be. Eliot tries to conceal this indispensable literary method by mixing languages, breaking off dramatic passages, and by dividing the poem into sections with titles. But what really keeps the poem moving is its rhetoric, its switches from description to exclamation to interrogation to expletive, sometimes very beautifully, as in the passages beginning 'Unreal City'. The straight descriptive passages are weak: 'A Game of Chess' is one of the dullest and most meretricious of Eliot's writings, indicating his own dissatisfaction with that kind of verse. The dialogue, on the other hand, is generally good. The best moments of all are the image passages, where the images are set in dramatic tonalities: 'What the Thunder Said' is the finest of these. The very worst passages are those which are merely quotes; even Eliot's most abject admirers can find no justification of the last lines of the poem, with its half-dozen languages and more than half a dozen quotations in a space of about ten lines.

The Waste Land, because of its great critical reputation, not because of any inherent worth it might have, is one of the curiosities of English literature. Its critical success was, I dare say, carefully planned and executed, and it was not beyond the realm of possibility that the poem was originally a hoax, as some of the first readers insisted. But hoax or not, it was very shortly made the sacred cow of modern poetry and the object of more pious literary nonsense than any modern work save the *Cantos* of Pound. The proof of the failure of the 'form' of this poem is that no one has ever been able to proceed from it, including Eliot himself. It is, in fact, not a form at all but a negative version of form. It is interesting to notice that in the conventional stanzas of the quatrain poems Eliot is more personally violent and ugly about his own beliefs; in his unconventional style the voice of the poet all but disappears and is replaced by characters from his reading.

(*The Death of Literary Judgement*, 1960)

Graham Hough

BUT the questions remain – above all the question of what really makes the poem a totality, if it is one at all. If we can imagine some ideal critic, acquainted with the poetical tradition of Europe, yet innocent of the spirit of our age, and if we can imagine ourselves persuading him to leave the question of total structure in abeyance, 'to allow the images to fall into his memory successively without questioning the reasonableness of each' – he would still be struck by the extraordinary rhetorical incongruities. He would find within its four hundred and thirty-three lines passages that are narrative, others that are dramatic, descriptive, lyric, hallucinatory and allusive. The theory of genres was never watertight or exhaustive, but never before was there a poem of this length, or perhaps of any other length, in which the modes were so mixed. Nor is the rhetorical level any more constant than the rhetorical mode. A modern and highly individual elegiac intensity, pastiche Renaissance grandeur, sharp antithetical social comment in the Augustan manner, the low mimetic of public-house conversation – all these and probably several other styles are found side by side. The relation of these is sometimes obvious; it is one of calculated contrast. But it is a question how hard such contrasts of texture can be worked in a relatively short poem without disastrous damage to the unity of surface. It is not so much in the obvious collisions of the high and the low styles that this is felt. That kind of calculated shock action is a limited effect, and the intention of producing the shock itself provides a medium between the two elements. It is the use of language in different and unrelated fashions in different parts of the poem that is disruptive. There is the lovely, romantically evocative manner of the hyacinth girl passage:

> Yet when we came back late from the Hyacinth garden
> Your arms full, and your hair wet, I could not
> Speak, and my eyes failed, I was neither
> Living nor dead, and I knew nothing,
> Looking into the heart of light, the silence.

These lines live unhappily in the same poem with:

> Endeavours to engage her in caresses
> Which still are unreproved, if undesired.
> Flushed and decided, he assaults at once;
> Exploring hands encounter no defence;
> His vanity requires no response,
> And makes a welcome of indifference.

The uneasiness does not arise from incompatibility of tone and feeling, but because the two passages are using language in utterly different ways; the first to evoke, by overtones and connotations, the trembling ghost of an intense emotion that is never located or defined; the second to define a situation by precise denotation and intelligent analysis. It is as though a painter were to employ a pointilliste technique in one part of a picture, and the glazes of the high renaissance in another.

When we come to the content of the separate passages the situation is disturbing in another way. It has become fashionable to refer to these contents as 'themes', suggesting a vaguely musical analogy; and suggesting, too, I suppose, that the 'themes' of a poem are related to each other only as the themes of a musical composition are. But themes in a poem are made of words, and words have meanings; our attention is never arrested at the verbal surface; it proceeds to what the words denote. They denote objects, persons and ideas; and it is very difficult altogether to dispel the notion that the objects, persons and ideas in a single poem should be in some intelligible relation to one another. A very little inspection of the commentaries, or questioning of readers of the poem, will show that this is not the case with *The Waste Land*; there is no certainty either about what is denoted, or how it is related to other denotations. It is sometimes suggested, for example, that the hyacinth girl is or might be the same as the lady who stayed with her cousin the archduke a few lines earlier. To me it has always been obvious that these fragmentary glimpses showed us, and were designed to show us, two different kinds of women and two different kinds of human relationship. Yet I suppose that those who think otherwise have taken at least as much trouble and are no greater fools than I. And I see no means by which the matter could be decided.

We have already remarked that Phlebas the Phoenician had a prior existence in another context and was included by chance or outside suggestion. True, a place is rather arbitrarily prepared for him; Madame Sosostris the clairvoyant, who is supposed to be using a Tarot pack, produces the card of the drowned Phoenician sailor – which is not a member of the Tarot pack – in order to suggest in advance that Phlebas has some part in the structure of the poem. But what his part is remains quite uncertain. Here the commentators for the most part insist on resolutely marking time, for fear of committing themselves to a false step; and we are even bidden to observe that the 'currents' which pick the drowned Phlebas's bones have a forerunner in the 'currants' in the pocket of Mr Eugenides the Smyrna merchant. Surely the last refuge of baffled imbecility.

It has been said that the poem adopts a 'stream of consciousness' technique;[1] and this sounds reassuring without committing us to anything very much. But it is precisely what the poem does not do. The advantage of the 'stream of consciousness' technique is that it allows a flood of images, more or less emancipated from narrative or logical continuity, while still preserving a psychological continuity – the continuity of inhering in a single consciousness. *The Waste Land* conspicuously forgoes this kind of unifying principle. One desperate expedient has been to fasten on Mr Eliot's note to line 218: 'Tiresias, although a mere spectator and not indeed a "character", is yet the most important personage in the poem, uniting all the rest. . . . What Tiresias *sees*, in fact, is the substance of the poem.' In the light of this it can be suggested that the whole poem is Tiresias's 'stream of consciousness'.[2] This is probably to give the note more weight than it can bear, and in any case, it does little to the purpose. Who was Tiresias? A man who had also been a woman, who lived for ever and could foretell the future. That is to say, not a single human consciousness, but a mythological catch-all, and as a unifying factor of no effect whatever.

I should like to commit myself to the view that for a poem to exist as a unity more than merely bibliographical, we need the sense of one voice speaking, as in lyric or elegiac verse: or of several voices intelligibly related to each other, as in narrative with dialogue or drama; that what these voices say needs a principle of connection no different from that which would be acceptable in any other kind of discourse; that the collocation of images is not a method at all, but the negation of method. In fact, to expose oneself completely, I want to say that a poem, internally considered, ought to make the same kind of sense as any other discourse.

(*Image and Experience*, 1960)

NOTES

1. Grover Smith, *T. S. Eliot's Poetry and Plays* (Chicago, 1956) p. 58.
2. Ibid. p. 58. See also George Williamson, *A Reader's Guide to T. S. Eliot* (New York, 1957) p. 123.

Stephen Spender

PART of the effect which a poem or a painting has is not what people think about it forty years later, but what they thought and felt about it when it was painted or written. In deciding, for example, whether *The Waste Land* adumbrates a Christian orthodoxy which became clarified in the *Four Quartets*, I. A. Richards's view (put forward in 1926) that it was a poetry 'severed from all beliefs' should be taken into account just as much as the view of someone today who using hindsight sees *The Waste Land* almost as a Christian poem. A different evolution of Eliot's ideas was possible, and if it had happened, would have made Richards right. Incidentally, if Eliot's own views are to be considered, I once heard him say to the Chilean poet Gabriela Mistral that at the time when he was writing *The Waste Land*, he seriously considered becoming a Buddhist. A Buddhist is as immanent as a Christian in *The Waste Land*.

('Remembering Eliot', from *T. S. Eliot: The Man and his Work*, ed. Allen Tate, 1967)

PART FOUR

Longer Studies

Daniel H. Woodward

NOTES ON THE PUBLISHING
HISTORY AND TEXT OF
THE WASTE LAND (1964)

IN 1952 William H. Marshall's comparison of the various texts of T. S. Eliot's 'Gerontion' demonstrated, rather surprisingly, 'that no printed edition up to the present has conformed in every detail with Eliot's full intentions'.[1] Then, in 1957, Robert L. Beare's important survey showed conclusively that Eliot has indeed been neglectful of the texts of many of his plays and poems.[2] But comparatively little attention has been given to the publishing history of *The Waste Land*. In a general way the publishing history of the poem points to the important assistances given to Eliot's literary career by a number of his friends and associates and, more specifically, a survey of the texts of the poem in various typescripts and printed editions is revealing about the development of Eliot's art and about the unfastidious attention which he has given to the publication of this poem. One major handicap to the historian of the poem is the absence of the original typescript of the poem as it stood before Ezra Pound's editing. Also unavailable is a manuscript notebook containing early drafts and some unpublished poems. Both of these items have been missing since the death in 1924 of their last owner, John Quinn, the New York lawyer, book collector, art patron; they are presumed to have been destroyed years ago.

The published versions of the letters which Eliot and Pound exchanged on *The Waste Land* in 1921–2 reveal much of what is known about the poem in its earliest form.[3] Aside from his letters to Eliot, what may be Pound's first reference to the poems occurs in an unpublished letter, dated 21 February 1922, to Mrs Jeanne Robert Foster, an American art critic and intimate friend of John Quinn, one of a series of letters the indefatigable Pound wrote for the as yet unnamed 'Bel Esprit' project: 'Eliot

produced a fine poem (19 pages) during his enforced vacation, but
has since relapsed. I wish something cd. be found for him, to get
him out of Lloyds bank.'⁴ Eliot had said in a recent letter to
Pound, 'Complimenti [about *The Waste Land*] appreciated, as
have been excessively depressed . . . I would have sent Aeschule
before but have been in bed with flu, now out, but miserable.'⁵
Pound also talked about the poem in an outline he drew up for
'Bel Esprit': 'Eliot, in bank, makes £500. Too tired to write,
broke down; during convalescence in Switzerland did *Waste
Land*, a masterpiece; one of the most important 19 pages in
English.' ⁶ Pound mentioned the poem for the first time publicly
on 30 March 1922, in an article drumming up support for 'Bel
Esprit': 'Rightly or wrongly some of us consider Eliot's employment in a bank the worst waste in contemporary literature.
During his recent three months' absence due to a complete
physical breakdown he produced a very important sequence of
poems: one of the few things in contemporary literature to
which one can ascribe permanent value. That seems a fairly clear
proof of restriction of output, due to enforced waste of his time
and energy in banking.'⁷

It is interesting that Pound refers to *The Waste Land* here as a
'sequence of poems', for Pound's letter to Eliot on 24 December
1921 suggests that he saw his editing job to consist of shaping
several poems into one: 'If you MUST keep 'em [i.e., lines eventually omitted by Eliot], put 'em at the beginning before the
"April cruelest month." The POEM ends with the "Shantih,
shantih, shantih." . . . The thing now runs from "April . . ." to
"shantih" without a break. That is 19 pages, and let us say the
longest poem in the Englisch langwidge. Don't try to bust all
records by prolonging it three pages further.'⁸ At least one of the
early critics felt that *The Waste Land* remained a series of poems
strung together, and not very satisfactorily. Even so, the critic,
Conrad Aiken, concluded generously, 'when our reservations
have all been made, we accept *The Waste Land* as one of the most
moving and original poems of our time. It captures us'.⁹ Eliot
himself insisted on the unity of the poem when he wrote to an
anthologist: '*The Waste Land* is intended to form a whole, and

I should not care to have anyone read *parts* of it; and further-more, I am opposed to anthologies in principle.' [10]

Despite the short life of 'Bel Esprit' and his failure to get Eliot out of Lloyds Bank until 1925, Pound showed both zeal in advancing his disciple's career and critical acumen that together must have been almost overpowering. Eliot has written: '[Pound] was ready to lay out the whole of life for anyone in whose life he was interested – a degree of direction which not all the beneficiaries deserved and which was sometimes embarras-sing. Yet, though the object of his beneficence might come to chafe against it, only a man of the meanest spirit could have come to resent it. He was so passionately concerned about the works of art which he expected his protégés to produce that he sometimes tended to regard them almost impersonally, as art or literature machines to be carefully tended and oiled, for the sake of their potential output. . . . It was in 1922 [actually, 1921] that I placed before him in Paris the manuscript of a sprawling, chaotic poem called *The Waste Land* which left his hands, reduced to about half its size, in the form in which it appears in print. I should like to think that the manuscript, with the suppressed passages, had disappeared irrecoverably: yet on the other hand, I should wish the blue penciling on it to be preserved as irrefutable evidence of Pound's critical genius.' [11]

Pound's poem, 'Sage Homme', which Eliot once considered putting at the head of *The Waste Land*, was never used. But the well-known dedication, 'For Ezra Pound *il miglior fabbro*', was added in the 1925 edition of Eliot's *Poems* and retained there-after, very likely as a token of Eliot's loyalty to his much-maligned friend and mentor. The exchange of letters between Pound and Eliot, and Hugh Kenner's report on Eliot's recollec-tions show that Eliot's debt to his 'cher maître' was indeed considerable. The published Pound–Eliot letters indicate that for the most part Eliot followed Pound's advice closely. Only once, after the poem had been published in the *Criterion*, did he have second thoughts, overruling Pound's approval of the un-common 'Wherefrom' (l. 80) and substituting 'From which' in all later editions. The other changes made as the various editions appeared seem not to have been influenced by Pound, one way or the other.[12]

Eliot attempted to find a publisher for the poem in January 1922, as he noted in a letter to Pound: 'Have writ to [Scofield] Thayer [editor of *The Dial*] asking what he can offer for this.' [13] Oddly enough, though, Eliot seems not to have sent a copy of the poem to the United States until the summer of 1922. Thayer and Eliot had been acquainted at Milton Academy, Harvard, and Oxford, and it was through the assistance of Thayer that Eliot met the first Lady Rothermere, whose patronage enabled him to found the *Criterion*.[14] Since 1920 Eliot had written London letters for the *Dial*. Eventually Eliot's correspondence with Thayer led to an agreement, for the first American publication of the poem occurred in the *Dial* for November 1922.[15] But when Thayer saw the poem in the summer of 1922 he was somewhat disappointed by it, and earlier in the year he and Eliot had disagreed about the rate of payment for it, so the negotiations were prolonged.[16] Meanwhile Pound looked for a publisher; on 6 May 1922 he wrote to Mrs Foster, who was associated with various periodicals in New York: 'What would *Vanity Fair* pay Eliot for *Waste Land*? cd. yr. friend there get in touch with T.S.E.?' Mrs Foster had published an article on Brancusi in *Vanity Fair*, but she turned Pound's letter over to John Quinn, who was a friend of Frank Crowninshield, the editor. When no offer for the poem was made, Mrs Foster wrote the news to Pound in Paris.[17]

In July 1922 Gilbert Seldes, managing editor of the *Dial*, took the initiative to get the poem into print. Seldes arranged a meeting in Quinn's office of Horace Liveright (the book publisher), Quinn (unofficially representing Eliot, who still had to approve any deal made), and Seldes himself. These persons agreed to the publication of the poem in the *Dial* and then in an edition by Boni & Liveright.[18] Quinn received a typescript copy of the poem, presumably from someone at the *Dial*, and almost immediately, on 31 July 1922, mailed it to Mrs Foster, who was temporarily in Schenectady, New York. This copy, made on American paper by someone other than Eliot, but not prepared in Quinn's office, was presented to the Houghton Library at

Harvard by Mrs Foster in 1961.[19] Dr James S. Watson, Jr, the publisher of the *Dial*, also had a typescript of the poem in the summer of 1922; he sent it from the Hotel Meurice, in Paris, to Thayer, in Vienna. This typescript, on Hotel Meurice stationery, is among the *Dial* papers in storage at the Worcester Art Museum in Massachusetts, but it is unavailable at present.[20] Dr Watson no longer recalls the source of it, and no one can identify the original from which it was made.

Seldes' expedition of Thayer's and Dr Watson's decision to publish the poem called for placing it in the *Dial*, paying Eliot at the regular rate ($20 for each page of poetry[21] – or $260), and then presenting him the *Dial* Award for 1922, worth $2000. Seldes also worked out the details of the Boni & Liveright edition, swelled to book length by the addition of Eliot's notes.[22] The poem appeared in the November issue, in which Pound trumpeted 'Bel Esprit' (pp. 549–52), to Eliot's acute embarrassment.[23] Then, after George Saintsbury declined the job,[24] Edmund Wilson wrote in the December issue a long, favorable review that included these comments: 'now the publication of his long poem, *The Waste Land*, confirms the opinion which we began gradually to cherish, that Mr Eliot, with all his limitations, is one of our only authentic poets. For this new poem – which presents itself as so far his most considerable claim to eminence – not only recapitulates all his earlier and already familiar motifs, but it sounds for the first time in all their intensity, untempered by irony or disguise, the hunger for beauty and the anguish at living which lie at the bottom of all his work. . . . I doubt whether there is a single other poem of equal length by a contemporary American which displays so high and so varied a mastery of English verse' (pp. 611, 615). Privately, Eliot was indignant about Wilson's review, which he felt used his achievement to disparage the work of his friend Pound.[25] Seldes himself reviewed the poem in the *Nation* for 6 December 1922: 'It will be interesting for those who have knowledge of another great work of our time, Mr Joyce's *Ulysses*, to think of the two together. That *The Waste Land* is, in a sense, the inversion and the complement of *Ulysses* is at least tenable. We have in *Ulysses* the poet defeated, turning outward, savoring the ugliness which is no longer transmutable into beauty, and, in the end, homeless. We have in *The Waste Land* some indication of the inner life of such a poet (p. 616). In effect, Eliot's American champions put on a grand show of publicity for the poem. There is, of course, absolutely no reason to doubt the sincerity of their admiration of the poem as well as the poet. But it is worth noting that the bombshell which literary historians often say was set off by the publication of the poem in 1922 was given a booster shot by the fireworks of the ingenious staff of the *Dial*. No one was more appreciative of this help than Eliot himself. He wrote to Seldes on 27 December 1922: 'I am deeply aware of the honour which the *Dial* has bestowed upon me as well as of the financial assistance which will be a very great help at a difficult time. May I be able to give the *Dial* still better work in the future!' And on 21 September 1922, he wrote to Quinn, approving the publishing scheme worked out by Quinn, Seldes, and Liveright:

I am quite overwhelmed by your letter, by all that you have done for me, by the results that have been effected, and by your endless kindness. . . . Of course, I am entirely satisfied with the arrangements that you have made. It is exactly what I should have liked; only I did not see how it could be done, if it was to be done at all, without calling upon you once more, which, after all you had already accomplished, I was absolutely determined not to do. I also felt that it would be in the nature of asking a favour from Liveright, and also I was loath to ask you to do this on my behalf. I gather that Liveright is quite satisfied that the arrangement will be ultimately to his advantage, and certainly the *Dial* have behaved very handsomely.

My only regret (which may seem in the circumstances either ungracious or hypocritical) is that this [*Dial*] award should come to me before it had been given to Pound. I feel that he deserves the recognition much more than I do, certainly 'for his services to Letters,' and I feel that I ought to have been made to wait until after he had received this public testimony.[26]

The Waste Land was first published in England, where it appeared in the October 1922, or initial number of the *Criterion*, edited anonymously by T. S. Eliot. Tentative arrangements for publishing the poem in England as well as in the United States seem to have been made early, for Pound could write on 9 July: 'Eliot's *Waste Land* is I think the justification of the "movement," of our modern experiment, since 1900. It shd. be published this year.'[27] Eliot was scrupulous about separating the English and American periodical versions of the poem, for his letters to Quinn on 21 September and Seldes on 12 November 1922 reveal that in order to prevent competition with the November *Dial* the first issue of the *Criterion* was not made readily available to American subscribers. A postscript in the letter to Seldes notes that by 12 November the first issue of the *Criterion* had been sold out. Oddly enough, in view of his ideas about the unity of the poem, Eliot once considered publishing the poem in two parts, divided between the first two issues of the *Criterion*. His reason for this was that in view of his anonymous editorship, his critical essays should not appear in the early issues, and thus the poem should be stretched to provide his only signed contributions.[28]

The first edition in book form (Boni & Liveright's) appeared on 15 December 1922, in New York.[29] According to Pound, the publication of the notes in this edition was 'purely fortuitous': 'Liveright wanted a longer volume and the notes were the only available unpublished matter.'[30] The requirements of the book may have altered Eliot's original plan: 'I had at first intended only to put down all the references for my quotations, with a view to spiking the guns of critics of my earlier poems who had accused me of plagiarism. Then, when it came to print *The Waste Land* as a little book ... it was discovered that the poem was inconveniently short, so I set to work to expand the notes, in order to provide a few more pages of printed matter, with the result that they became the remarkable exposition of bogus scholarship that is still on view to-day. I have sometimes thought of getting rid of these notes; but now they can never be unstuck. They have had almost greater popularity than the poem itself. ... I am penitent ... because my notes stimulated the wrong kind of interest among seekers of sources. It was just, no doubt, that I should pay tribute to the work of Miss Jessie Weston; but I regret having sent so many inquirers off on a wild goose chase after Tarot cards and the Holy Grail.'[31] It is certain, however, that the notes were in existence before the publication of the poem in the *Dial*. Seldes wrote to Dr Watson on 31 August 1922: 'We must assume that Eliot O.K.'s publication in the *Dial* without the notes . . . which are exceedingly interesting and add much to the poem, but don't become interested in them because we simply cannot have them.' [32] According to the plan of Seldes, Liveright, and Quinn, the notes were to be withheld from the *Dial* in order to make the book more attractive.

Roger Fry seems to have instigated Eliot's glosses, for according to Clive Bell he urged Eliot 'to elucidate the text of *The Waste Land* with explanatory notes'.[33] Mr Eliot has confirmed this: 'It may be as Mr Clive Bell says that it was Roger Fry who suggested that I should do notes to the poem. I remember reading the poem aloud to Leonard and Virginia Woolf before they ever read it and I know that the notes were added and were of such length as the poem by itself seemed hardly long enough for book form.'[34] In view of their mutual friendship and interest in each other's work, it is hardly necessary to speculate about the influence the Woolfs had on Eliot's poetry. Leonard Woolf has said that he 'had a hand in converting its author from an American to an English poet',[35] and this may be true in more than one way, since Eliot's *Poems*, 1919, and *The Waste Land*, 1923, were printed by hand at the Woolfs' Hogarth Press.

Both Mr Woolf and Mr Eliot have commented on the circumstances of the first English edition in book form. According to the latter: 'I think it would probably have been very difficult to find a commercial publisher for the poem in 1922 or 1923. I am certain that Miss Harriet Weaver [patroness of Joyce and backer of the Egoist Press] would have published the poem, but I am pretty sure she had gone out of business by that date. I had already . . . taken a set of seven or so short poems to Leonard Woolf which he published as a booklet bound in one or another of Roger Fry's papers.'[36] Mr Woolf has described the publishing ventures as the work of amateurs: 'No one in 1920 would have published *The Waste Land*. We started the Hogarth Press in 1917 as a hobby; really the hobby was printing. It was only casually that we published what we printed at first and we suggested to Eliot that we should print and publish poems of his. We first published the book called *Poems* [1919] and then *The Waste Land*. The above explains why we printed the book with our own hands.'[37] By publishing Eliot's poems the Woolfs made a gesture of faith in his work and also helped strengthen his position in England during a crucial period. Today, when the Hogarth Press edition of *The Waste Land* is a collector's item, every copy necessarily being an 'association copy', it is difficult to imagine that Eliot ever had trouble finding a publisher, or that when he found one, a small edition of about 460 copies, selling at 4s. 6d. each and published on 12 September 1923,[38] was still in print a year or so later. Pound did a great deal to publicize Eliot's work, especially among the critics and patrons of literature; as he wrote to Mrs Foster on 11 October 1922, about the American publications: 'I shall try to place a whoop for the pome THE *Waste Land* as soon as it is in print.' But the Woolfs' timely assistance in actually making Eliot's work available to the English reading public should never be overlooked.[39]

The Hogarth Press edition of *The Waste Land* is hardly a masterpiece of printing, and its text contains a number of errors. The fault must have been due to the skill rather than the will of the participants, however, for Leonard Woolf is quite positive: 'Mr Eliot certainly read the proofs.' [40] Eliot himself later corrected by hand three errors in presentation copies; in the Harvard copy, presented 'to Mother from Tom. 14.ix.23', *under* (l. 62) is corrected to *over*, the reading of all other editions; *coloured* (l. 96) to *carven* (*carven* was never printed, for *carvèd* appears in all other editions; in the Hogarth Press edition *coloured* obviously was transferred from the preceding line); and *Macmillan* (p. 29, heading to the notes) to *Cambridge Univ. Press*, the reading of the 1925 and all later editions.[41] But several other errors in this edition remained uncorrected, even in the hand-marked copies.

Eventually the Woolfs had to give up the hand printing they began in 1917, for the Hogarth Press became so successful that it was no longer a 'private press'. Even some of the earliest of their productions were reprinted by a commercial printer when the demand far exceeded the capacity of the Woolfs' hand press,[42] but such was not the case with Eliot's *Poems*, about two hundred copies printed,[43] or with *The Waste Land*. With these volumes the chief problem was merely completing the hand printing, the slowness of which delayed the publication of the Hogarth Press *Waste Land* until almost nine months after the Boni & Liveright edition came out in New York. On 24 June 1923 Virginia Woolf wrote from Hogarth House to a friend recovering from scarlet fever in a hospital: 'We've had a desperate afternoon printing, and I'm more in need of the love of my friends than you are. All the 14 pt. quads have been dissed into the 12 pt. boxes! Proof taking has been made impossible; and Eliot's poem delayed a whole week. I'm sure you'll see that this is much more worth crying over than the pox and the fever and the measles all in one. . . . Leonard is still trying to take proofs in the basement. I have cheered myself up by writing to you, so please don't say that I've plunged you into despair, as another invalid did the other day, when I cheered myself up by writing to her.'[44] The Woolfs bound the volume themselves, using three different labels on the front cover.[45] Their personal involvement in the routine of publishing was noticed by the poet and future publisher John Lehmann when he joined the Press in 1930; according to him, even at that time Virginia Woolf tied parcels and put labels on packages when rush orders came in,[46] and Leonard Woolf remained in some ways a private printer: 'In fact I learned the essentials of publishing in the most agreeable way possible: from a man who had created his own business, had never allowed it to grow so big that it fell into departments sealed off from one another, and who saw it all as much from the point of view of an author and amateur printer as of someone who had to make his living by it.'[47] The Woolfs must have been proud of their edition of *The Waste Land*, for it was listed with their 'books published' long after supplies of it were exhausted.[48]

Of the four editions of *The Waste Land* in 1922–3, that of Boni & Liveright has the most accurate text and is the closest to recent editions of the poem. It cannot be considered the standard text, however, for changes were made later in both the poem and the notes. Most of these changes were typographical, most of no significance, but a few were substantive. In evaluating the apparently insignificant changes in punctuation that occur in the various editions of the poem, one should keep in mind Eliot's remarks on punctuation in a letter to Quinn: 'I see reason in your objection to my punctuation; but I hold that the line itself punctuates, and the addition of a comma, in many places, seems to me to over-emphasize the arrest. That is because I always pause at the end of a line in reading verse, while perhaps you do not.'[49] A report on all the changes in punctuation as the poem was reprinted is an undertaking too large for this paper, but it can be said that Eliot's carelessness in seeing editions through the press is by no means proof that he was uninterested in fine pointing.

An unexpected development in regard to the text occurred in 1960, when Eliot prepared an autograph fair copy to be sold at auction for the benefit of the London Library, which Eliot served as President. After line 137 he added, '(The ivory men make company between us)', which Eliot said 'was in the original draft but for some reason or other was omitted from the published text. It came back to my mind when I was making the copy.'[50] This recollection certainly did not detract from the value of the manuscript, which sold at Christie's on 22 June 1960 for £2800.[51] The 1960 manuscript, now in the Humanities Research Center of the University of Texas, 'does not follow in exact detail the punctuation, spelling, or capitalization of any of the published versions of *The Waste Land*',[52] and its 'new' line is not canonized by inclusion in the signed, limited edition of the poem printed at the Officina Bodoni and published by Faber & Faber in 1961. About this edition Mr Eliot says: 'I think that it may be taken that the recent limited edition is the standard text. I have made one or two corrections in the notes in that edition and Mr Mardersteig, the publisher [i.e. printer] of that limited edition, suggested corrections in the quotations from Dante based on a more authentic text than the one I had used before.' [53] The 1961 edition is a tastefully produced volume containing only one obvious misprint, 'dampg round' for 'damp ground' (l. 193); it is generally close to the Boni & Liveright edition as later corrected; and it is, according to Mr Eliot, the standard text. The principal objections that one can make to it concern the small number of copies (300), the high price (10 guineas), and the omission of consecutive line numbers for reasons of typographical elegance, the notes being renumbered according to the lines on each page.

The 1963 Faber & Faber edition of *Collected Poems 1909–1962* reprints almost all of the changes in *1961*. It does not include the attribution of the epigraph, 'PETRONIUS. SATIRICON', and contains some minor misprints: *piante* for *pianto* (note on l. 64), *p. 306* for *p. 346, senti* for *senti*' (note on l. 411). It does not always follow *1961* in respect to punctuation, typographical conventions, and spacing, notably in the following places: *speak. Speak.* for *speak? Speak* (l. 112); *directors;* for *directors –* (l. 180); spaces before lines 187, 203, no space before line 206 (the reverse in *1961*); *Et* for *Et,* (l. 202); *spar.* for *spar* (l. 272); paragraph indentations in Section v (not found in *1961*). The text in the 1963 Harcourt, Brace & World edition of *Collected Poems 1909–1962*, which does not incorporate the changes made in *1961*, is interesting only for straightening out for the first time the misnumbering of lines 351–end in the text and the misnumbering of the notes on this part of the poem.[54]

The added line in the 1960 manuscript turns out to be an early reject, for, aside from this manuscript, it appears only in the twenty-page typescript copy presented to Harvard by Mrs Foster. The Harvard typescript copy clearly was never used by a printer for any edition. The line numbering and certain mechanical characteristics suggest that it and its original were prepared by a professional typist.[55] It antedates all the printed versions of the poem and possibly the only other extant typescripts, the one now among the *Dial* papers, and the one now in the library of John Hayward, editorial director of the *Book Collector*. About the latter Mr Hayward says: 'My typescript was not the printer's copy. It is authenticated in Eliot's hand "an early pre-publication typing by myself". Although his inscription goes on to say that "it may have been the printer's copy for *The Criterion*", it is clear that it was not in fact the printer's copy. I would infer that it was the penultimate copy from an earlier draft before the copy text was finally typed out. . . . None of the [major] variants in [the Harvard typescript copy] is present. Apart from a number of small and relatively trivial alterations of single words, the only curiosity is the omission (due to an obvious copying slip . . . [i.e. sight transference]) of lines 400–9.'[56] None of the extant typescripts contains the notes first printed in the Boni & Liveright edition. Even though the Harvard typescript is a copy-of-a-copy-of-a-copy, it would appear to be fairly close to the missing original typescript version (after Pound's editing) and possibly derives from the first copy Eliot sent to the United States in 1922. At any rate, when Quinn received it, for the second time an unpublished Eliot work passed through his hands: in 1917 Quinn had sent along to an American publisher the typescript of Eliot's *Ezra Pound: His Metric and Poetry*, Eliot's first book of criticism.[57]

Some of the readings peculiar to the Harvard typescript copy are of considerable interest.[58] Lines 105–6, which in the typescript read

                    staring forms
        Leaned, staring, hushing the room enclosed.

were changed to

                    staring forms
        Leaned out, leaning, hushing the room enclosed.

The image thus becomes more kinaesthetic. Line 115 was changed from

            I think we met first in rats' alley

to

            I think we are in rats' alley

learly less accusing and perhaps more desperate. Lines 124–5 were shortened from

> I remember
> The hyacinth garden. Those are pearls that were his eyes.

to

> I remember
> Those are pearls that were his eyes.

but the effect is to make more difficult the link between lines 35–42, 46–8, and Section IV, 'Death by Water', and this difficulty seems to have led some critics astray. Perhaps Eliot felt that the line after 137 was too obvious at this point

> The ivory men make company between us

(the 1960 parentheses are not present here) but the line did pick up the imagery of line 86 and perhaps led toward lines 263–5. The change in line 149 of 'theres many another will'. to 'there's others will, I said'. seems to tighten up the dialogue. Two other differences in this copy could be mere typing errors: line 143, 'done' typed as 'did', and line 150, 'Oh is' typed as 'Is'. In line 430 'de la' instead of 'à la' agrees only with the *Criterion* version. Aside from a few spelling errors, the other variants in the Harvard copy concern typographical conventions or punctuation.

The variants in the Harvard copy make the disappearance of the first autograph typescript especially tantalizing. After giving his copy to Mrs Foster in July, Quinn bought this autograph typescript from Eliot in the fall of 1922 for £100.[59] On 21 September 1922 Eliot wrote to Quinn from London:

In the manuscript of *The Waste Land* which I am sending you, you will see the evidences of his [Pound's] work, and I think that this manuscript is worth preserving in its present form solely for the reason that it is the only evidence of the difference which his criticism has made to this poem. I am glad that you, at least, will have the opportunity of judging this for yourself. Naturally, I hope that the portions which I have suppressed will never appear in print, and in sending them to you I am sending the only copies of these parts.

I have gathered together all of the manuscript in existence. The leather bound notebook is one which I started in 1909 and in which I entered all my work of that time as I wrote it, so that it is the only original manuscript (barring, of course, rough scraps and notes which were destroyed at the time) in existence. You will find a great many sets of verse which have never been printed and which I am sure you will agree never ought to be printed, and, in putting them in your hands, I beg you fervently to keep them to yourself and see that they never are printed.

I do not think that this manuscript is of any great value, especially as the large part is really typescript for which no manuscript, except scattered lines, ever existed.[60]

That the 'manuscript' of *The Waste Land* was a typescript is explained by the fact that when Eliot was in the Harvard Graduate School (1911–14), he strained one hand while rowing in a single shell and thereafter used a typewriter for composing.[61] These Eliot papers have been missing since Quinn's death. Mrs Foster, who arranged Quinn's literary papers and correspondence in 1924, never saw the first autograph typescript or the notebook.[62] Quinn may have taken Eliot's letter to heart and secretly destroyed them. But there is reason for supposing that they were stolen from Quinn's collection during his final illness or shortly after his death, and that they have been destroyed.[63]

Eliot seems not to have read the proofs of the *Dial* version of the poem, but was pleased by the printing. As editor he must have read the proofs of the first issue of the *Criterion*, and he is known to have done so for the Boni & Liveright[64] and Hogarth Press editions. Although he was still to make some changes in the text, in the fall of 1922 Eliot's attitude towards the poem that was becoming the most famous of the twentieth century was surprisingly offhand. On 12 November he wrote to Seldes: 'Nov. no. [of the *Dial*] just received. Poem admirably printed. I see some remarks by you which I find very flattering. But I find this poem as far behind me as Prufrock now: my present ideas are very different.' It is hardly unexpected, then, though still disconcerting, that Eliot did not bother to incorporate the changes of *1961* in the 1963 Harcourt, Brace & World edition of his *Collected Poems*.

NOTES

1. 'The Text of T. S. Eliot's "Gerontion" ' in *Studies in Bibliography*, IV (1951–2) 214.

2. 'Notes on the Text of T. S. Eliot: Variants from Russell Square', in *Studies in Bibliography*, IX (1957) 21–49.

3. See *The Letters of Ezra Pound*, ed. D. D. Paige (New York, 1950; London, 1951) pp. 169–72. Hugh Kenner, *The Invisible Poet: T. S. Eliot* (New York, 1959) pp. 145–52, has surveyed the *ur-Waste Land* as Eliot remembers it. As early as 9 May 1921 Eliot reported to Quinn that he had 'a long poem in mind and partly on paper . . .' (typescript of letter in the Quinn Collection, New York Public Library).

4. This letter and two others to Mrs Foster are quoted with the kind permission of Mrs Dorothy Pound and Mr William A. Jackson, Director, The Houghton Library, Harvard University. According to the 'Bel Esprit' plan, each of thirty contributors was to give ten pounds annually to a deserving writer, the first of which was to be Eliot. Eliot later refused any money from this source, and 'Bel Esprit' came to an end. (See further Donald Gallup, *A Bibliography of Ezra Pound* (1963) pp. 379–80.)

5. *Letters of Ezra Pound*, p. 171.

6. Ibid. p. 173 (from a typescript copy, dated 18 Mar 1922, sent to William Carlos Williams).

7. 'Credit and the Fine Arts', in *New Age*, 30 Mar 1922, pp. 284–5.

8. *Letters of Ezra Pound*, p. 169. Cf. Pound's phrase, 'a series of poems', quoted by Hugh Kenner, pp. 145–6.

9. Review in the *New Republic*, XXXIII (7 Feb 1923) 295. Aiken had been the intermediary who in 1914, after some unsuccessful peddling on his own, gave the typescript of Eliot's 'Prufrock' to Pound, who got it published in Harriet Monroe's *Poetry* (Conrad Aiken, letter to the editor, *Times Literary Supplement*, 3 June 1960, p. 353).

10. Quoted in *An Exhibition of Manuscripts and First Editions of T. S. Eliot* (Austin, 1961) p. 10.

11. T. S. Eliot, 'Ezra Pound', in *Ezra Pound: A Collection of Critical Essays*, ed. Walter Sutton (Englewood Cliffs, N. J., 1963) pp. 18–19.

12. Eliot let pass what may have been an oversight of Pound's. In the first of the published letters between Pound and Eliot on the poem, Pound said, 'I doubt if Conrad is weighty enough to stand the citation' (*Letters of Ezra Pound*, p. 169). Hugh Kenner (p. 145) learned from Eliot that Pound referred to Eliot's quotation of 'The horror! The horror!' from *Heart of Darkness*. As Pound suggested, Eliot removed the quotation. But Pound apparently was unaware that the

words in lines 268–70 of *The Waste Land* were derived from the first page of *Heart of Darkness* (pointed out by Kenner, p. 145, and rediscovered by John Frederick Nims, 'Greatness in Moderation', in *Saturday Review*, 19 Oct 1963, p. 26), and that the various passages in the poem concerning the Thames are strongly reminiscent of the first few pages of Conrad's novel.

13. *Letters of Ezra Pound*, p. 171.

14. Miss Pamela Barker, former secretary to Mr Eliot, letter to the author, dated 9 Sept 1963.

15. This phase in the history of the poem was first surveyed by William Wasserstrom, 'T. S. Eliot and *The Dial*', in *Southern Review*, LXX (Jan–Mar 1962) 81–92, and again in *The Time of the Dial* (Syracuse, 1963) pp. 102–5.

16. For information about these matters I am indebted to Professor Nicholas Joost, who has had access to the *Dial* papers and who has been generous in answering my questions.

17. Mrs Jeane Robert Foster, letter to the author, dated 9 Sept 1963.

18. Mr Gilbert Seldes, letters to the author, dated 25 Sept and 3 Nov 1963.

19. Mrs Foster is certain that the copy was not made in Quinn's office, and that Quinn received it only shortly before mailing it to her (letter to the author, dated 9 Sept 1963). The conclusions about the paper and the typist were reported to me by Mr John Hayward, in a letter dated 3 Sept 1963, and confirmed by Mr William A. Jackson (who once showed Eliot the typescript copy), in a letter dated 16 Sept 1963. See also *The Houghton Library Report of Accessions for the Year 1961–62* (Cambridge, Mass., 1962) pp. 45–6.

20. For information about this typescript I am indebted to Professor Joost.

21. William Wasserstrom, *A Dial Miscellany* (Syracuse, 1963) p. xiv.

22. The *Dial* did not pay for the edition but instead took 350 copies out of the 1000 numbered copies printed, and used them as an offer in a subscription campaign. See further Wasserstrom, *Time of the Dial*, pp. 103–4.

23. Public response to 'Bel Esprit', especially in the newspapers, often was unfavorable. In the Feb 1923, issue of the *Dial*, the editor had to defend Eliot's *Dial* Award against the charges of those opposed to 'Bel Esprit'. By May 1923 Pound had been fired as Paris correspondent of the *Dial*.

24. See further Wasserstrom, *Time of the Dial*, p. 104.

25. Eliot wrote to Seldes: 'While I wish to express my appreciation of Mr Wilson's praise, as well as of your own, there is one point in Mr Wilson's article to which I must strongly take exception. I do very

much object to be made use of by anyone for the purpose of disparaging the work of Ezra Pound. I am infinitely in his debt as a poet, as well as a personal friend, and I do resent being praised at his expense. Besides, what Mr Wilson said of him was most unfair. I sincerely consider Ezra Pound the most important living poet in the English language. And you will see that in view of my great debt to him in literature it is most painful to me to have such comments made. I should like Mr Wilson also to know this, if possible.' (Letter dated 27 Dec 1922; this letter and one other are quoted with the kind permission of Mr Eliot and Mr Seldes.) Evidently Edmund Wilson learned of Eliot's opinion, and when he wrote about Eliot's work in *Axel's Castle*, he greatly modified his remarks about the relative positions of Pound and Eliot, even though he continued to prefer Eliot's work.

26. Typescript of the letter in the Quinn Collection, New York Public Library. This letter and others to Quinn are quoted with the kind permission of Mr Eliot and the Library.

27. *Letters of Ezra Pound*, p. 180.

28. See further Eliot's letter to Quinn, 21 Sept 1922, a typescript of which is in the Quinn Collection, New York Public Library.

29. Donald Gallup, *T. S. Eliot: A Bibliography* (New York, 1953) p. 7.

30. *We Moderns* (New York, 1940), cited by Gallup, *T. S. Eliot*, p. 7.

31. T. S. Eliot, 'The Frontiers of Criticism', in *On Poetry and Poets* (1957) pp. 109–10.

32. Quoted by Wasserstrom, *Time of the Dial*, p. 104.

33. Clive Bell, *Old Friends* (New York, 1957) p. 119.

34. Letter to the author, 26 June 1963. Quoted with the kind permission of Mr Eliot.

35. *Sowing* (1960) p. 52.

36. Letter to the author, 26 June 1963.

37. Letter to the author, 5 Dec 1962. Quoted with the kind permission of Mr Woolf.

38. Gallup, *T. S. Eliot*, p. 8.

39. Among the consequences of the Hogarth Press edition were a review (not laudatory) in the *Times Literary Supplement*, 20 Sept 1923, p. 616, and a review (unfavorable) by Clive Bell in the *Nation and Athenæum*, 22 Sept 1923, pp. 772–3.

40. Letter to the author, 5 Dec 1962.

41. These manuscript corrections were first noticed by Robert L. Beare, p. 33.

42. See further B. J. Kirkpatrick, *A Bibliography of Virginia Woolf* (1957) pp. 7–8.

43. Gallup, *T. S. Eliot*, p. 4.

44. Quoted by Clive Bell, pp. 104, 107.

45. Leonard Woolf, letter to the author, 5 Dec 1962; and Gallup, *T. S. Eliot*, p. 8.

46. *The Open Night* (New York, 1952) p. 23.

47. *The Whispering Gallery* (New York, 1955) p. 168.

48. Ibid. p. 167.

49. From the typescript of a letter, 9 May 1921, in the Quinn Collection, New York Public Library.

50. *Exhibition of Manuscripts and First Editions*, p. 5.

51. 'Good Causes', in *Times Literary Supplement*, 1 July 1960, p. 424.

52. *Exhibition of Manuscripts and First Editions*, p. 5.

53. Letter to the author, 26 June 1963.

54. This error in numbering seems to have been noticed first by Hugh Kenner, p. 151.

55. John Quinn's possession of a copy of the poem in the summer of 1922, before publication anywhere, requires a slight revision of one of Aline B. Saarinen's anecdotes about Quinn: 'One morning in 1922 he received from T. S. Eliot a first copy of *The Waste Land*. He summoned a lovely lady [Mrs Foster] with a melodious voice to read the lengthy poem to him while he shaved. Thereafter, he could recite it without an error. . . . She [Mrs Foster] was an American, with burnished golden hair, black eyes and a lilting voice, who had written several volumes of verse, had been on the staffs of *Review of Reviews* and the *Transatlantic Review*, and was an intimate of the Yeats circle in New York and the "little magazine" group in Paris.' (*The Proud Possessors* (New York, 1958) pp. 208, 225. On Mrs Foster and Quinn, see also Ford Madox Ford, *It Was the Nightingale* (Philadelphia, 1933) p. 298.) The typescript copy did not come from Eliot, but Mrs Foster has confirmed that it is the copy of the poem mentioned in the anecdote.

56. Letter to the author, 16 Aug 1963. Quoted with the kind permission of Mr Hayward.

57. See further my short article, 'John Quinn and T. S. Eliot's First Book of Criticism', in *Papers of the Bibliographical Society of America*, LVI (second quarter, 1962) 259–65, and *Houghton Library Report of Accessions 1961–62*, pp. 45–6. Eliot wrote to Quinn on 9 July 1919: 'It is quite obvious that, without you, I should never get published in America at all.' (From the typescript in the Quinn Collection, New York Public Library.)

58. They are quoted here with the kind permission of Mr Eliot and Mr William A. Jackson.

59. John Hayward, letter to the author, 3 Sept 1963.

60. From the typescript of this letter in the Quinn Collection, New York Public Library. For telling me about this letter I am indebted to Professor Ben L. Reid, who is presently writing a biography of Quinn.

61. Miss Pamela Barker, letter to the author, 9 Sept 1963.

62. Mrs Foster, letters to the author and interview, Dec 1963.

63. Informed of this probable theft, Eliot has commented: 'I cannot feel altogether sorry that this [typescript] and the notebook have disappeared. The unpublished poems in the notebook were not worth publishing, and there was a great deal of superfluous matter in *The Waste Land* which Pound very rightly deleted. Indeed, the poem in the form in which it finally appeared owes more to Pound's surgery than anyone can realise' (letter to the author, dated 3 Apr 1964, quoted with the kind permission of Mr Eliot).

64. T. S. Eliot, letter to Gilbert Seldes, 12 Nov 1922.

Editors' note: In a letter to the editors, dated 16 Mar 1968, Mr Woodward writes 'that the story of the poem and its publication in *The Dial* is told in more detail by Nicholas Joost, *Scofield Thayer and The Dial* (Carbondale, Ill., 1964), pp. 159–65. This corrects a factual error about the payment for the poem: Eliot received $10 for each page, or $130, and not $20 per page, or $260, as I said, following Wasserstrom.'

Conrad Aiken

AN ANATOMY OF MELANCHOLY (1923)

PREFATORY NOTE

THE review of *The Waste Land*, with the above title, came out in the *New Republic* on 7 February 1923, in other words, four months after the poem's appearance in the *Criterion* of October 1922; and I suspect it was the first full-length favorable review the poem had then received – at any rate, I do not remember any predecessors. To be sure, I had the advantage of having known Eliot intimately for fifteen years – since my freshman year at Harvard – and had already, in 1917 and 1921, apropos of 'Prufrock' and *The Sacred Wood*, heralded him as the fugleman of many things to come. Of 'Prufrock' I said that in its wonderfully varied use of rhymed free verse there was a probable solution of the quarrel, at that time as violent as it is now, about the usefulness of rhyme or verse at all: the Imagists, and others, including of course Williams and his eternal Object, were already hard at it. I think 'Prufrock' still has its way.

As to *The Waste Land* and my review, it might be helpful for the general picture if I record here two episodes with Eliot, one before he had written the poem, and one after.

In the winter of 1921–2 I was in London, living in Bayswater, and Eliot and myself lunched together two or three times a week in the City, near his bank: thus resuming a habit we had formed many years before, in Cambridge. He always had with him his pocket edition of Dante. And of course we discussed the literary scene, with some acerbity and hilarity, and with the immense advantage of being outsiders (though both of us were already contributing to the English reviews); discussing also the then-just-beginning possibility of the *Criterion*, through the generosity of Lady Rothermere. And it was at one of these meetings, in midwinter, that he told me one day, and with visible concern, that although every evening he went home to his flat hoping that he could start writing again, and with every confidence that the material was *there* and waiting, night after night the hope proved illusory: the sharpened pencil lay unused by the untouched sheet of paper. What could be the matter? He didn't know. He asked me if *I* had ever experienced any such thing. And of course my reply that I hadn't wasn't calculated to make him feel any happier.

But it worried me, as it worried him. And so, not unnaturally, I mentioned it to a very good friend of mine, Dilston Radcliffe, who was at that time being analysed by the remarkable American lay analyst, Homer Lane. Radcliffe, himself something of a poet, was at once very much interested, and volunteered, at his next meeting with Lane, to ask him what he thought of it. And a few days later came the somewhat startling answer from Lane: 'Tell your friend Aiken to tell *his* friend Eliot that all that's stopping him is his fear of putting anything down that is short of perfection. He thinks he's God.'

The result was, I suppose, foreseeable, though I didn't foresee it. For when I told Eliot of Lane's opinion, he was literally speechless with rage, both at Lane and myself. The *intrusion*, quite simply, was one that was intolerable. But ever since I have been entirely convinced that it did the trick, it broke the log-jam. A month or two later he went to Switzerland, and there wrote *The Waste Land*.

Which in due course appeared in the first issue of the *Criterion*, by that time endowed by Lady Rothermere, and again in due course came to me from the *New Republic*, for review. And once more, it was as we proceeded from Lloyd's bank to our favorite pub, by the Cannon Street Station, for grilled rump steak and a pint of Bass, that another explosion occurred.

For I said, 'You know, I've called my long review of your poem "An Anatomy of Melancholy".'

He turned on me with that icy fury of which he alone was capable, and said fiercely: 'There is nothing melancholy about it!'

To which I in turn replied: 'The reference, Tom, was to BURTON's *Anatomy of Melancholy*, and the quite extraordinary amount of *quotation* it contains!'

The joke was acceptable, and we both roared with laughter.

To all of which I think I need add one small regret about that review. How could I mention that I had long been familiar with such passages as 'A woman drew her long black hair out tight', which I had seen as poems, or part-poems, in themselves? And now saw inserted into *The Waste Land* as into a mosaic. This would be to make use of private knowledge, a betrayal. Just the same, it should perhaps have been done, and the conclusion drawn: that they were not *organically* a part of the total meaning.   (*A Reviewer's ABC*, 1958)

Mr T. S. Eliot is one of the most individual of contemporary poets, and at the same time, anomalously, one of the most 'traditional'. By individual I mean that he can be, and often is (distressingly, to some), aware in his own way; as when he observes of a woman (in 'Rhapsody on a Windy Night') that the door 'opens on her like a grin' and that the corner of her eye 'Twists like a crooked pin'. Everywhere, in the very small body of his work, is similar evidence of a delicate sensibility, somewhat shrinking, somewhat injured, and always sharply itself. But also, with this capacity or necessity for being aware in his own way, Mr Eliot has a haunting, a tyrannous awareness that there have been many other awarenesses before; and that the extent of his own awareness, and perhaps even the nature of it, is a consequence of these. He is, more than most poets, conscious of his roots. If this consciousness had not become acute in 'Prufrock' or the 'Portrait of a Lady', it was nevertheless probably there: and the roots were quite conspicuously French, and dated, say, 1870–1900. A little later, as his sense of the past had become more pressing, it seemed that he was positively redirecting his roots – urging them to draw a morbid dramatic sharpness from Webster and Donne, a faded dry gilt of cynicism and formality from the Restoration. This search of the tomb produced 'Sweeney' and 'Whispers of Immortality'. And finally, in *The Waste Land*, Mr Eliot's sense of the literary past has become so overmastering as almost to constitute the motive of the work. It is as if, in conjunction with the Mr Pound of the *Cantos*, he wanted to make a 'literature of literature' – a poetry actuated not more by life itself than by poetry; as if he had concluded that the characteristic awareness of a poet of the twentieth century must inevitably, or ideally, be a very complex and very literary awareness, able to speak only, or best, in terms of the literary past, the terms which had molded its tongue. This involves a kind of idolatry of literature with which it is a little difficult to sympathize. In positing, as it seems to, that there is nothing left for literature to do but become a kind of parasitic growth on literature, a sort of mistletoe, it involves, I think, a definite astigmatism – a distortion. But the theory is interesting if only because it has colored an important and brilliant piece of work.

The Waste Land is unquestionably important, unquestionably brilliant. It is important partly because its 433 lines summarize Mr Eliot, for the moment, and demonstrate that he is an even better poet than most had thought; and partly because it embodies the theory just touched upon, the theory of the 'allusive' method in poetry. *The Waste Land* is, indeed, a poem of allusion all compact. It purports to be symbolical; most of its symbols are drawn from literature or legend; and Mr Eliot has thought it necessary to supply, in notes, a list of the many quotations, references, and translations with which it bristles. He observes candidly that the poem presents 'difficulties', and requires 'elucidation'. This serves to raise, at once, the question whether these difficulties, in which perhaps Mr Eliot takes a little pride, are so much the result of complexity, a fine elaborateness, as of confusion. The poem has been compared, by one reviewer, to a 'full-rigged ship built in a bottle', the suggestion being that it is a perfect piece of construction. But is it a perfect piece of construction? Is the complex material mastered, and made coherent? Or, if the poem is not successful in that way, in what way *is* it successful? Has it the formal and intellectual complex unity of a microscopic *Divine Comedy*; or is its unity – supposing it to have one – of another sort?

If we leave aside for the moment all other consideration, and read the poem solely with the intention of understanding, with the aid of notes, the symbolism; of making out what it is that is symbolized, and how these symbolized feelings are brought into relation with each other and with other matters in the poem; I think we must, with reservations, and with no invidiousness, conclude that the poem is not, in any formal sense, coherent. We cannot feel that all the symbolisms belong quite inevitably where they have been put; that the order of the parts is an inevitable order; that there is anything more than a rudimentary progress from one theme to another; nor that the relation between the more symbolic parts and the less is always as definite as it should be. What we feel is that Mr Eliot has not wholly annealed the allusive matter, has left it unabsorbed, lodged in gleaming fragments amid material alien to it. Again, there is a distinct weakness consequent on the use of allusions which may have both intellectual and emotional value for Mr Eliot, but (even with the notes) none for us. The 'Waste Land' of the Grail Legend might be a good symbol, if it were something with which we were sufficiently familiar. But it can never, even when explained, be a good symbol, simply because it has no immediate associations for us. It might, of course, be a good *theme*. In that case it would be given us. But Mr Eliot uses it for purposes of overtone; he refers to it; and as overtone it quite clearly fails. He gives us, superbly, *a* waste land – not *the* waste land. Why, then, refer to the latter at all – if he is not, in the poem, really going to use it? Hyacinth fails in the same way. So does the Fisher King. So does the Hanged Man, which Mr Eliot tells us he associates with Frazer's Hanged God – we take his word for it. But if the precise association is worth anything, it is worth putting into the poem; otherwise there can be no purpose in mentioning it. Why, again, Datta, Dayadhvam, Damyata? Or Shantih? Do they not say a good deal less for us than 'Give: sympathize: control' or 'Peace'? Of course; but Mr Eliot replies that he wants them not merely to mean those particular things, but also to mean them in a particular way – that is, to be remembered in connection with a Upanishad. Unfortunately, we have none of us this memory, nor can he give it to us; and in the upshot he gives us only a series of agreeable sounds which might as well have been nonsense. What we get at, and I think it is important, is that in none of these particular cases does the reference, the allusion, justify itself intrinsically, make itself felt. When we are aware of these references at all (sometimes they are unidentifiable) we are aware of them simply as something unintelligible but suggestive. When they have been explained, we are aware of the material referred to, the fact (for instance, a vegetation ceremony), as something useless for our enjoyment or understanding of the poem, something distinctly 'dragged in', and only, perhaps, of interest as having suggested a pleasantly ambiguous line. For unless an allusion is made to live identifiably, to flower where transplanted, it is otiose. We admit the beauty of the implicational or allusive method; but the key to an implication should be in the implication itself, not outside of it. We admit the value of the esoteric pattern; but the pattern should disclose its secret, should not be dependent on a cypher. Mr Eliot assumes for his allusions, and for the fact that they actually allude to something, an importance which the allusions themselves do not, as expressed, aesthetically command, nor, as explained, logically command; which is pretentious. He is a little pretentious, too, in his 'plan' – *qui pourtant n'existe pas*. If it is a plan, then its principle is oddly akin to planlessness. Here and there, in the wilderness, a broken finger-post.

I enumerate these objections not, I must emphasize, in derogation of the poem, but to dispel, if possible, an allusion as to its nature. It is perhaps important to note that Mr Eliot, with his comment on the 'plan', and several critics, with their admiration of the poem's woven complexity, minister to the idea that *The Waste Land* is, precisely, a kind of epic in a walnut shell: elaborate, ordered, unfolded with a logic at every joint discernible; but it is also important to note that this idea is false. With or without the notes the poem belongs rather to that symbolical order in which one may justly say that the 'meaning' is not explicitly, or exactly, worked out. Mr Eliot's net is wide, its meshes are small; and he catches a good deal more – thank heaven – than he pretends to. If space permitted one could pick out many lines and passages and parodies and quotations which do not demonstrably, in any 'logical' sense, carry forward the theme, passages which unjustifiably, but happily, 'expand' beyond its purpose. Thus the poem has an emotional value far clearer and richer than its arbitrary and rather unworkable logical value. One might assume that it originally consisted of a number of separate poems which have been telescoped – given a kind of forced unity. The Waste Land conception offered itself as a generous net which would, if not unify, at any rate contain these varied elements. We are aware of this superficial 'binding' – we observe the anticipation and repetition of themes, motifs; 'Fear death by water' anticipates the episode of Phlebas, the cry of the nightingale is repeated; but these are pretty flimsy links, and do not genuinely bind because they do not reappear naturally, but arbitrarily. This suggests, indeed, that Mr Eliot is perhaps attempting a kind of program music in words, endeavoring to rule out 'emotional accidents' by supplying his readers, in notes, with only those associations which are correct. He himself hints at the musical analogy when he observes that 'In the first part of Part V three themes are employed'.

I think, therefore, that the poem must be taken – most invitingly offers itself – as a brilliant and kaleidoscopic confusion; as a series of sharp, discrete, slightly related perceptions and feelings, dramatically and lyrically presented, and violently juxtaposed (for effect of dissonance), so as to give us an impression of an intensely modern, intensely literary consciousness which perceives itself to be not a unit but a chance correlation or conglomerate of mutually discolorative fragments. We are invited into a mind, a world, which is a 'broken bundle of mirrors', a 'heap of broken images'. Isn't it that Mr Eliot, finding it 'impossible to say just what he means' – to recapitulate, to enumerate all the events and discoveries and memories that make a consciousness – has emulated the 'magic lantern' that throws 'the nerves in pattern on a screen'? If we perceive the poem in this light, as a series of brilliant, brief, unrelated or dimly related pictures by which a consciousness empties itself of its characteristic contents, then we also perceive that, anomalously, though the dropping out of any one picture would not in the least affect

D   C.H.W.

the logic or 'meaning' of the whole, it would seriously detract from the value of the portrait. The 'plan' of the poem would not greatly suffer, one makes bold to assert, by the elimination of 'April is the cruellest month' or Phlebas, or the Thames daughters, or Sosostris or 'You gave me hyacinths' or 'A woman drew her long black hair out tight'; nor would it matter if it did. These things are not important parts of an important or careful intellectual pattern; but they are important parts of an important emotional ensemble. The relations between Tiresias (who is said to unify the poem, in a sense, as spectator) and the Waste Land, or Mr Eugenides, or Hyacinth, or any other fragment, is a dim and tonal one, not exact. It will not bear analysis, it is not always operating, nor can one say with assurance, at any given point, how much it is operating. In this sense *The Waste Land* is a series of separate poems or passages, not perhaps all written at one time or with one aim, to which a spurious but happy sequence has been given. This spurious sequence has a value – it creates the necessary superficial formal unity; but it need not be stressed, as the Notes stress it. Could one not wholly rely for one's unity – as Mr Eliot *has* largely relied – simply on the dim unity of 'personality' which would underlie the retailed contents of a single consciousness? Unless one is going to carry unification very far, weave and interweave very closely, it would perhaps be as well not to unify it at all; to dispense, for example, with arbitrary repetitions.

We reach thus the conclusion that the poem succeeds – as it brilliantly does – by virtue of its incoherence, not of its plan; by virtue of its ambiguities, not of its explanations. Its incoherence is a virtue because its *donnée* is incoherence. Its rich, vivid, crowded use of implication is a virtue, as implication is always a virtue – it shimmers, it suggests, it gives the desired strangeness. But when, as often, Mr Eliot uses an implication beautifully – conveys by means of a picture-symbol or action-symbol a feeling – we do not require to be told that he had in mind a passage in the *Encyclopedia*, or the color of his nursery wall; the information is disquieting, has a sour air of pedantry. We 'accept' the poem as we would accept a powerful, melancholy tone-poem. We do not want to be told what occurs; nor is it more than mildly amusing to know what passages are, in the Straussian manner, echoes or parodies. We cannot believe that every syllable has an algebraic inevitability, nor would we wish it so. We could dispense with the French, Italian, Latin, and Hindu phrases – they are irritating. But when our reservations have all been made, we accept *The Waste Land* as one of the most moving and original poems of our time. It captures us. And we sigh, with a dubious eye on the 'notes' and 'plan', our bewilderment that after so fine a performance Mr Eliot should have thought it an occasion for calling 'Tullia's ape a marmosyte'. Tullia's ape is good enough.

Edmund Wilson

THE PURITAN TURNED ARTIST (1931)*

ELIOT's most complete expression of the theme of emotional starvation is to be found in the later and longer poem called *The Waste Land* (1922). The Waste Land of the poem is a symbol borrowed from the myth of the Holy Grail: it is a desolate and sterile country ruled by an impotent king, in which not only have the crops ceased to grow and the animals to reproduce, but the very human inhabitants have become incapable of having children. But this sterility we soon identify as the sterility of the Puritan temperament. On the first pages we find again the theme of the girl with the hyacinths (themselves a symbol for the re-arisen god of the fertility rites who will save the rainless country from drought) which has already figured in 'La Figlia Che Piange' and 'Dans le Restaurant' – a memory which apparently represents for the poet some fulfilment foregone in youth and now agonisingly desired; and in the last page it is repeated. We recognise throughout *The Waste Land* the peculiar conflicts of the Puritan turned arist: the horror of vulgarity and the shy sympathy with the common life, the ascetic shrinking from sexual experience and the distress at the drying up of the springs of sexual emotion, with the straining after a religious emotion which may be made to take its place.

Yet though Eliot's spiritual and intellectual roots are still more firmly fixed in New England than is, I believe, ordinarily understood, there is in *The Waste Land* a good deal more than the mere gloomy moods of a New Englander regretting an emotionally undernourished youth. The colonisation by the

* *Editors' note*: Edmund Wilson's essay, 'The Poetry of Drouth', appeared in the Dec 1922 issue of the *Dial*. It was later revised for *Axel's Castle*, and we print this revised version here.

Puritans of New England was merely an incident in that rise of the middle-class which has brought a commercial-industrial civilisation to the European cities as well as to the American ones. T. S. Eliot now lives in London and has become an English citizen; but the desolation, the aesthetic and spiritual drought, of Anglo-Saxon middle-class society oppresses London as well as Boston. The terrible dreariness of the great modern cities is the atmosphere in which *The Waste Land* takes place – amidst this dreariness, brief, vivid images emerge, brief pure moments of feeling are distilled; but all about us we are aware of nameless millions performing barren office routines, wearing down their souls in interminable labours of which the products never bring them profit – people whose pleasures are so sordid and so feeble that they seem almost sadder than their pains. And this Waste Land has another aspect: it is a place not merely of desolation, but of anarchy and doubt. In our post-War world of shattered institutions, strained nerves and bankrupt ideals, life no longer seems serious or coherent – we have no belief in the things we do and consequently we have no heart for them.

The poet of *The Waste Land* is living half the time in the real world of contemporary London and half the time in the haunted wilderness of the medieval legend. The water for which he longs in the twilight desert of his dream is to quench the spiritual thirst which torments him in the London dusk; and as Gerontion, 'an old man in a dry month', thought of the young men who had fought in the rain, as Prufrock fancied riding the waves with mermaids and lingering in the chambers of the sea, as Mr Apollinax has been imagined drawing strength from the deep sea-caves of coral islands – so the poet of *The Waste Land*, making water the symbol of all freedom, all fecundity and flowering of the soul, invokes in desperate need the memory of an April shower of his youth, the song of the hermit thrush with its sound of water dripping and the vision of a drowned Phœnician sailor, sunk beyond 'the cry of gulls and the deep sea swell', who has at least died by water, not thirst. The poet, who seems now to be travelling in a country cracked by drought, can only feverishly dream of these things. One's head may be well stored

with literature, but the heroic prelude of the Elizabethans has
ironic echoes in modern London streets and modern London
drawing-rooms: lines remembered from Shakespeare turn to
jazz or refer themselves to the sound of phonographs. And now
it is one's personal regrets again – the girl in the hyacinth-
garden – 'the awful daring of a moment's surrender which an age
of prudence can never retract' – the key which turned once, and
once only, in the prison of inhibition and isolation. Now he
stands on the arid plain again, and the dry-rotted world of
London seems to be crumbling about him – the poem ends in a
medley of quotations from a medley of literatures – like Gérard
de Nerval's 'Desdichado', the poet is disinherited; like the author
of the 'Pervigilium Veneris', he laments that his song is mute
and asks when the spring will come which will set it free like
the swallow's; like Arnaut Daniel, in Dante, as he disappears
in the refining fire, he begs the world to raise a prayer
for his torment. 'These fragments I have shored against my
ruins.'

The Waste Land, in method as well as in mood, has left
Laforgue far behind. Eliot has developed a new technique, at
once laconic, quick, and precise, for representing the transmuta-
tions of thought, the interplay of perception and reflection.
Dealing with subjects complex in the same way as those of
Yeats's poem 'Among School Children' and Valéry's 'Cimetière
Marin', Eliot has found for them a different language. As May
Sinclair has said of Eliot, his 'trick of cutting his corners and his
curves makes him seem obscure when he is clear as daylight. His
thoughts move very rapidly and by astounding cuts. They move
not by logical stages and majestic roundings of the full literary
curve, but as live thoughts move in live brains.' Let us examine,
as an illustration, the lovely nightingale passage from *The Waste
Land*. Eliot is describing a room in London:

> Above the antique mantel was displayed
> As though a window gave upon the sylvan scene
> The change of Philomel, by the barbarous king
> So rudely forced; yet there the nightingale
> Filled all the desert with inviolable voice

> And still she cried, and still the world pursues,
> 'Jug Jug' to dirty ears.

That is, the poet sees, above the mantel, a picture of Philomela changed to a nightingale, and it gives his mind a moment's swift release. The picture is like a window opening upon Milton's earthly paradise – the 'sylvan scene', as Eliot explains in a note, is a phrase from *Paradise Lost* – and the poet associates his own plight in the modern city, in which some 'infinitely gentle, infinitely suffering thing', to quote one of Eliot's earlier poems, is somehow being done to death, with Philomela, raped and mutilated by Tereus. But in the earthly paradise, there had been a nightingale singing: Philomela had wept her woes in song, though the barbarous king had cut out her tongue – her sweet voice had remained inviolable. And with a sudden change of tense, the poet flashes back from the myth to his present situation:

> And still she *cried*, and still the world *pursues*,
> 'Jug Jug' to dirty ears.

The song of birds was represented in old English popular poetry by such outlandish syllables as 'Jug Jug' – so Philomela's cry sounds to the vulgar. Eliot has here, in seven lines of extraordinary liquidity and beauty, fused the picture, the passage from Milton and the legend from Ovid, into a single moment of vague poignant longing.

The Waste Land is dedicated to Ezra Pound, to whom Eliot elsewhere acknowledges a debt; and he has here evidently been influenced by Pound's *Cantos*. *The Waste Land*, like the *Cantos*, is fragmentary in form and packed with literary quotation and allusion. In fact, the passage just discussed above has a resemblance to a passage on the same subject – the Philomela–Procne myth – at the beginning of Pound's Fourth Canto. Eliot and Pound have, in fact, founded a school of poetry which depends on literary quotation and reference to an unprecedented degree. Jules Laforgue had sometimes parodied, in his poems, the great lines of other poets:

O Nature, donne-moi la force et le courage
De me croire en âge . . .

And Eliot had, in his early poetry, introduced phrases from
Shakespeare and Blake for purposes of ironic effect. He has
always, furthermore, been addicted to prefacing his poems with
quotations and echoing passages from other poets. But now, in
The Waste Land, he carries this tendency to what one must
suppose its extreme possible limit: here, in a poem of only four
hundred and thirty-three lines (to which are added, however,
seven pages of notes), he manages to include quotations from,
allusions to, or imitations of, at least thirty-five different writers
(some of them, such as Shakespeare and Dante, laid under
contribution several times) – as well as several popular songs;
and to introduce passages in six foreign languages, including
Sanskrit. And we must also take into consideration that the
idea of the literary medley itself seems to have been borrowed
from still another writer, Pound. We are always being dismayed,
in our general reading, to discover that lines among those which
we had believed to represent Eliot's residuum of original invention had been taken over or adapted from other writers (sometimes very unexpected ones: thus, it appears now, from Eliot's
essay on Bishop Andrewes, that the first five lines of 'The
Journey of the Magi', as well as the 'word within a word, unable
to speak a word' of 'Gerontion', had been salvaged from
Andrewes's sermons; and the 'stiff dishonoured shroud' of
'Sweeney Among the Nightingales' seems to be an echo of the
'dim dishonoured brow' of Whittier's poem about Daniel
Webster). One would be inclined *a priori* to assume that all this
load of erudition and literature would be enough to sink any
writer, and that such a production as *The Waste Land* must be a
work of second-hand inspiration. And it is true that, in reading
Eliot and Pound, we are sometimes visited by uneasy recollec-
tions of Ausonius, in the fourth century, composing Greek-and-
Latin macaronics and piecing together poetic mosaics out of
verses from Virgil. Yet Eliot manages to be most effective precisely – in *The Waste Land* – where he might be expected to be

least original – he succeeds in conveying his meaning, in communicating his emotion, in spite of all his learned or mysterious allusions, and whether we understand them or not.

In this respect, there is a curious contrast between Eliot and Ezra Pound. Pound's work *has* been partially sunk by its cargo of erudition, whereas Eliot, in ten years' time, has left upon English poetry a mark more unmistakable than that of any other poet writing in English. It is, in fact, probably true at the present time that Eliot is being praised too extravagantly and Pound, though he has deeply influenced a few, on the whole unfairly neglected. I should explain Eliot's greater popularity by the fact that, for all his fragmentary method, he possesses a complete literary personality in a way that Pound, for all his integrity, does not. Ezra Pound, fine poet though he is, does not dominate us like a master imagination – he rather delights us like a miscellaneous collection of admirably chosen works of art. It is true that Pound, in spite of his inveterate translating, is a man of genuine originality – but his heterogeneous shorter poems, and the heterogeneous passages which go to make his longer ones, never seem to come together in a whole – as his general prose writing gives scrappy expression to a variety of ideas, a variety of enthusiasms and prejudices, some ridiculous and some valid, some learned and some half-baked, which, though valuable to his generation as polemic, as propaganda and as illuminating casual criticism, do not establish and develop a distinct reasoned point of view as Eliot's prose-writings do. T. S. Eliot has thought persistently and coherently about the relations between the different phases of human experience, and his passion for proportion and order is reflected in his poems. He is, in his way, a complete man, and if it is true, as I believe, that he has accomplished what he has credited Ezra Pound with accomplishing – if he has brought a new personal rhythm into the language – so that he has been able to lend even to the borrowed rhythms, the quoted words, of his great predecessors a new music and a new meaning – it is the intellectual completeness and soundness which has given his rhythm its special prestige.

Another factor which has probably contributed to Eliot's

extraordinary success is the essentially dramatic character of his imagination. We may be puzzled by his continual preoccupation with the possibilities of a modern poetic drama – that is to say, of modern drama in verse. Why, we wonder, should he worry about drama in verse – why, after Ibsen, Hauptmann, Shaw and Chekov, should he be dissatisfied with plays in prose? We may put it down to an academic assumption that English drama ended when the blank verse of the Elizabethans ran into the sands, until it occurs to us that Eliot himself is really a dramatic poet. Mr Prufrock and Sweeney are characters as none of the personages of Pound, Valéry or Yeats is – they have become a part of our modern mythology. And most of the best of Eliot's poems are based on unexpected dramatic contrasts: *The Waste Land* especially, I am sure, owes a large part of its power to its dramatic quality, which makes it peculiarly effective read aloud. Eliot has even tried his hand at writing a play, and the two episodes from 'Wanna Go Home, Baby' which he has published in the *Criterion* seem rather promising. They are written in a sort of jazz dramatic metre which suggests certain scenes of John Howard Lawson's 'Processional'; and there can be no question that the future of drama in verse, if it has any future, lies in some such direction. 'We cannot reinstate', Eliot has written, 'either blank verse or the heroic couplet. The next form of drama will have to be a verse drama, but in new verse forms. Perhaps the conditions of modern life (think how large a part is now played in our sensory life by the internal combustion engine!) have altered our perception of rhythms. At any rate, the recognised forms of speech-verse are not as efficient as they should be; probably a new form will be devised out of colloquial speech.'

In any case, that first handful of Eliot's poems, brought out in the middle of the War (1917) and generally read, if at all, at the time, as some sort of modern *vers de société*, was soon found, as Wyndham Lewis has said, to have had the effect of a little musk that scents up a whole room. And as for *The Waste Land*, it enchanted and devastated a whole generation. Attempts have been made to reproduce it – by Aldington, Nancy Cunard, etc. – at least a dozen times. And as Eliot, lately out of Harvard, assumed the rôle of the middle-aged Prufrock and to-day, at forty, in one of his latest poems, 'The Song of Simeon', speaks in the character of an old man 'with eighty years and no to-morrow' – so 'Gerontion' and *The Waste Land* have made the young poets old before their time. In London, as in New York, and in the universities both here and in England, they for a time took to inhabiting exclusively barren beaches, cactus-grown deserts, and dusty attics overrun with rats – the only properties they allowed themselves to work with were a few fragments of old shattered glass or a sparse sprinkling of broken bones. They had purged themselves of Masefield as of Shelley for dry tongues and rheumatic joints. The dry breath of the Waste Land now blighted the most amiable country landscapes; and the sound of jazz, which had formerly seemed jolly, now inspired only horror and despair. But in this case, we may forgive the young for growing prematurely decrepit: where some of even the finest intelligences of the elder generation read *The Waste Land* with blankness or laughter, the young had recognised a poet.

F. O. Matthiessen

THE ACHIEVEMENT OF T. S. ELIOT (1935)*

After such knowledge, what forgiveness?

IN such a passage as the conclusion of 'The Burial of the Dead' Eliot reveals the way in which he himself possesses 'a sense of his own age', that 'peculiar honesty, which, in a world too frightened to be honest, is peculiarly terrifying. It is an honesty against which the whole world conspires because it is unpleasant'. Eliot used those words in describing Blake, and a further extension of the passage is likewise relevant to his own aims in *The Waste Land* (which he was to publish two years after this essay): 'Nothing that can be called morbid or abnormal or perverse, none of the things which exemplify the sickness of an epoch or a fashion, have this quality; only those things which, by some extraordinary labour of simplification, exhibit the essential sickness or strength of the human soul.'

In Eliot's earlier work, in such a poem as 'Sweeney among the Nightingales', or, more particularly, 'A Cooking Egg', it at first looked as though he was so absorbed in the splendours of the past that he was capable of expressing only the violent contrast between its remembered beauty and the actual dreary ugliness of contemporary existence, that he was merely prolonging one mood inherited from Flaubert in viewing human life crushed into something mean and sordid by bourgeois 'civilization'. But on closer examination it appears that his contrasts are not so clear-cut, that he is not confining himself to voicing anything so essentially limited and shallow as the inferiority of the present to the past. He is keenly aware of our contemporary historical

* *The Achievement of T. S. Eliot* was first published in 1935, with subsequent editions in 1947 and 1958.

consciousness, and of the problems which it creates. The modern educated man possesses a knowledge of the past to a degree hardly glimpsed a century ago, not only of one segment of the past, but, increasingly, of all pasts. If he is sensitive to what he knows, he can feel, in Eliot's words, 'that the whole of the literature of Europe from Homer ... has a simultaneous existence'. But also, owing to the self-consciousness which results from so much knowledge (scientific and psychological as well as historical and literary), he will have a sense in any given moment, as Eliot has remarked of Joyce, 'of everything happening at once'.

Such a realization can lead either to chaos or to a sense of the potential unity of life. The difficulty with our knowledge to-day consists in the fact that instead of giving the individual's mind release and freedom, the piling up of so many disparate and seemingly unrelated details can merely oppress him with their bewildering variety, with 'being too conscious and conscious of too much',[1] with the futility of any certainty, or, as Eliot has reflected, with the feeling that 'everybody is conscious of every question, and no one knows any answers'. The problem for the artist is to discover some unified pattern in this variety; and yet, if he believes as Eliot does that poetry should embody a man's reaction to his whole experience, also to present the full sense of its complexity. He can accomplish this double task of accurately recording what he has felt and perceived, and at the same time interpreting it, only if he grasps the similarity that often lies beneath contrasting appearances, and can thus emphasize the essential equivalence of seemingly different experiences. Such understanding and resultant emphasis constitute Eliot's chief reason for introducing so many reminiscences of other poets into the texture of his own verse. In this way he can at once suggest the extensive consciousness of the past that is inevitably possessed by any cultivated reader of to-day, and, more importantly, can greatly increase the implications of his lines by this tacit revelation of the sameness (as well as the contrasts) between the life of the present and that of other ages.[2]

This emphasis is a leading element in the method of *The*

Waste Land, whose city, as we have seen, is many cities, or rather certain qualities resulting from the pervasive state of mind bred by mass civilization. But the structure of the poem embraces more than that. In his desire to make available for poetry the multiplicity of the modern world in the only way that the artist can, by giving it order and form, Eliot had discovered a clue in anthropology, in its exploration of ancient myths. It was not accidental or owing to any idiosyncrasy that he was affected profoundly by his reading of such a work as *The Golden Bough*, since the investigations of anthropology along with those of psychology have produced the most fundamental revolutions in contemporary thought and belief. It is noteworthy that Jessie Weston's *From Ritual to Romance* appeared in 1920, at the very time when Eliot was seeking a coherent shape for the mass of intricate material that enters into his poem. For reading that book gave to his mind the very fillip which it needed in order to crystallize.[3] What he learned especially from it was the recurring pattern in various myths, the basic resemblance, for example, between the vegetation myths of the rebirth of the year, the fertility myths of the rebirth of the potency of man, the Christian story of the Resurrection, and the Grail legend of purification. The common source of all these myths lay in the fundamental rhythm of nature – that of the death and rebirth of the year; and their varying symbolism was an effort to explain the origin of life. Such knowledge, along with the researches of psychology, pointed to the close union in all these myths of the physical and spiritual, to the fact that their symbolism was basically sexual – in the Cup and Lance of the Grail legend as well as in the Orpheus cults; pointed, in brief, to the fundamental relation between the well-springs of sex and religion.

The consequence of so much knowledge presents a condensed example of the general problem of the modern consciousness outlined above. When the investigations of anthropology reveal that surface differences between the customs and beliefs of mankind tend to mask profound resemblances, the result is both a freeing and a destruction. Taboos are removed, but sanctions wither. The purity of the Grail legend seems lost in symbols of generative significance; and yet at the same time it takes on a rich depth of primitive force that was wholly lost by Tennyson's denatured picture-book version. In such a perception of the nature of myths, of 'a common principle underlying all manifestations of life',[4] Eliot found a scaffold for his poem, a background of reference that made possible something in the nature of a musical organization. He found the specific clue to the dramatic shaping of his material when he read in Miss Weston of the frequent representation of the mystery of death and rebirth by the story of a kingdom where, the forces of the ruler having been weakened or destroyed by sickness, old age, or the ravages of war, 'the land becomes Waste, and the task of the hero is that of restoration',[5] not by pursuing advantages for himself, but by giving himself to the quest of seeking the health and salvation of the land.

The poem thus embodies simultaneously several different planes of experience, for it suggests the likenesses between various waste lands. Its quest for salvation in contemporary London is given greater volume and urgency by the additional presence of the haunted realm of medieval legend. The name of the battle where Stetson fought is that of one in which the Carthaginians were defeated, pointing the essential sameness of all wars. The opening of the final section in particular furnishes an example of the way Eliot is portraying the equivalence of different experiences by linking together various myths:

> After the torchlight red on sweaty faces
> After the frosty silence in the gardens
> After the agony in stony places
> The shouting and the crying
> Prison and palace and reverberation
> Of thunder of spring over distant mountains
> He who was living is now dead
> We who were living are now dying
> With a little patience.

Reminiscence here is not only of the final scenes in the life of

Christ and of the gnawing bafflement of his disciples before his appearance at Emmaus. The vigil of silence and the agony of spiritual struggle are not limited to one garden; they belong to the perilous quest of Parsival or Galahad as well. The 'shouting and the crying' re-echo not only from the mob that thronged Jerusalem at the time of the Crucifixion, but also, as is made clearer in ensuing lines, from the 'hordes swarming over endless plains' in revolt in contemporary Russia. In the 'thunder of spring over distant mountains' there is likewise a hint of the vegetation myths, of the approaching rebirth of the parched dead land through the life-giving rain. Thus he who 'is now dead' is not Christ alone, but the slain Vegetation God; he is Adonis and Osiris and Orpheus.[6] And with the line, 'We who were living are now dying', the link is made back to the realm of death in life of the opening section, the realm which focuses all the elements of the poem and resounds through all its lines, the waste land of contemporary existence, likewise waiting for salvation, salvation that can come only through sacrifice, as is revealed in the final apocalyptic command reverberating through 'What the Thunder Said': 'Give, Sympathize, Control.'

As a result of this method of compressing into a single moment both the memory and the sameness of other moments, it becomes apparent that in 'The Fire Sermon', the section of the poem which deals in particular with the present and the past of London, no sharply separating contrast is made between them. Squalor pollutes the modern river as it did not in Spenser's 'Prothalamion'; but there are also glimpses of beauty where

> The river sweats
> Oil and tar
> The barges drift
> With the turning tide
> Red sails
> Wide
> To leeward, swing on the heavy spar.

And, conversely, although mention of Elizabeth and Leicester brings an illusion of glamour, closer thought reveals that the stale pretence of their relationship left it essentially as empty as that between the typist and the clerk.

Use of such widely divergent details in a single poem indicates the special problem of the contemporary artist. Faced with so great a range of knowledge as a part of the modern consciousness, he can bring it to satisfactory expression in one of two ways: either by expansion or compression. It can hardly be a coincidence that each of these ways was carried to its full development at almost the same time, in the years directly following the War. Joyce chose the first alternative for *Ulysses* and devoted more than a quarter of a million words to revealing the complexity involved in the passage of a single ordinary day. In the following year Eliot concentrated an interpretation of a whole condition of society into slightly over four hundred lines. That Eliot was aware of similarities in their aims is indicated in a brief essay which he published during the year after the appearance of *The Waste Land* on 'Ulysses, Order, and Myth'.[7] He recognized how important it had been for Joyce to find a scaffold for his work in the structure of the *Odyssey* when he remarked that:

In using the myth, in manipulating a continuous parallel between contemporaneity and antiquity, Mr Joyce is pursuing a method which others must pursue after him. They will not be imitators, any more than the scientist who uses the discoveries of an Einstein in pursuing his own, independent, further investigations. It is simply a way of controlling, of ordering, of giving a shape and a significance to the immense panorama of futility and anarchy which is contemporary history. It is a method already adumbrated by Mr Yeats, and of the need for which I believe Mr Yeats to have been the first contemporary to be conscious. It is, I seriously believe, a step toward making the modern world possible in art.

The utilization of such a discovery would clearly differ for the novelist and the poet. With the example of the nineteenth century behind him, Eliot naturally felt that, if the long poem was to continue to exist, there must be more to distinguish it than length, that its energy must be increased by the elimination of everything superfluous. To convey in poetry the feeling of the

actual passage of life, to bring to expression the varied range and
volume of awareness which exists in a moment of consciousness,
demanded, in Eliot's view, the strictest condensation. Above all,
the impression of a fully packed content should not be weakened
through the relaxed connectives of the usual narrative structure.
Whatever may have been right at the time of the composition
of *The Ring and the Book*, it was apparent to Eliot that to-day
'anything that can be said as well in prose can be said better in
prose'. Poetry alone, through its resources of rhythm and sound,
can articulate the concentrated essence of experience, and thus
come closest to the universal and permanent; but it can do so only
through the mastery of a concentrated form. Though he
approaches the question with a much broader understanding of
all the factors involved than was possessed by the author of 'The
Poetic Principle', Eliot is at one with Poe in his insistence on the
necessary economy of a work of art, in his belief that a poem
should be constructed deliberately with the aim of producing a
unified effect. Consequently, after composing the first draft of
The Waste Land, his revisions shortened it to less than two-
thirds of its original length, in order that he might best create a
dramatic structure that would possess at the same time a lyrical
intensity.

That Eliot does not hold up such a method of construction as
an ideal necessarily to be followed is indicated by an extended
comment at the very close of *The Use of Poetry*:

To return to the question of obscurity: when all exceptions
have been made, and after admitting the possible existence of
minor 'difficult' poets whose public must always be small, I
believe that the poet naturally prefers to write for as large and
miscellaneous an audience as possible, and that it is the half-
educated and ill-educated, rather than the uneducated, who stand
in his way: I myself should like an audience which could neither
read nor write. The most useful poetry, socially, would be one
which could cut across all the present stratifications of public
taste – stratifications which are perhaps a sign of social disintegration. The ideal medium for poetry, to my mind, and the most
direct means of social 'usefulness' for poetry is the theatre. In a

play of Shakespeare you get several levels of significance. For the simplest auditors there is the plot, for the more thoughtful the character and conflict of character, for the more literary the words and phrasing, for the more musically sensitive the rhythm, and for auditors of greater sensitiveness and understanding a meaning which reveals itself gradually. And I do not believe that the classification of audience is so clear-cut as this; but rather that the sensitiveness of every auditor is acted upon by all these elements at once, though in different degress of consciousness.

This is the kind of passage which tantalizes and infuriates pragmatic critics of the sort who believe that a good author should simply decide what he wants to do and should then go ahead and do it. They would declare such reflections either to be disingenuous or to damn out of hand the validity of Eliot's own work. But one of the fundamental secrets of art as of life is that the mature artist finds his strength partly by coming to recognize and reckon with his limitations. Just as an individual starts by accepting certain technical conventions of a given art as a means of facilitating his search for a form that will enable him to embody what he wants to express, so, as he grows in the practice of that art and as he comes to closer grips with his own character, he will know that there are only certain things that he is best fitted to do, and that he can do those adequately only through selection and long perseverance.

Eliot's extreme awareness of the boundaries of his own work is very similar to Hawthorne's detached perception of the contrast between the bustling everyday Salem which surrounded him, and the realm of dim lights and dark shadows which he was meanwhile creating in *The Scarlet Letter*. Eliot's preference for a very different kind of poetry from that which he is capable of writing likewise recalls Hawthorne's repeated statement that the novels he really liked were not his own tenuous explorations of the soul, but the solid beef-and-ale stories of Trollope. This unusual degree of detachment which reverberates with loneliness, but which brings with it in compensation a special development of spiritual understanding, has grown organically out of the conditions of American life, out of the isolation of the individual from the centre of European culture. Kindred isolation enabled Thoreau and Emily Dickinson to study themselves with such rare mastery. It has also enabled Poe and Henry James and Eliot, all of them possessing the excessive provincial consciousness of elements in literary tradition which Europeans would have taken for granted – and ignored – by that very consciousness to lead their European contemporaries into a more penetrating comprehension of the nature of art.

When he wrote that passage on the different levels of appeal, Eliot had experimented with drama only in his unfinished *Sweeney Agonistes*. He knew that poems like *The Waste Land* and *Ash Wednesday*, richly significant as they may be on all the higher levels, virtually ignore the level of the pit. But the fact remains that the sincere artist writes not the way he would, but the way he must. And the most important value of the artist to society, and the one element that lends his work enduring significance, is to give expression to the most pervading qualities of life *as he has actually known it*. That Landor and Donne have appealed to restricted audiences defines but does not destroy their excellence. And no one would think of quarrelling with Lucretius for not reaching a 'popular' level.

If, in severest analysis, the kind of poetry Eliot writes gives evidence of social disintegration, he has expressed that fact as the poet should, not by rhetorical proclamation, but by the very feeling of contemporary life which he has presented to the sensitive reader of his lines. And he has presented this not merely as something which the reader is to know through his mind, but is to know primarily as an actual physical experience, as a part of his whole being, through the humming pulsating evidence of his senses.

But when a poet is as conscious of his aims and effects as Eliot has revealed himself to be in his remarks on *Ulysses* as well as in *The Use of Poetry*, there is always the suspicion lingering in the minds of some readers that his way of giving order to the content of his work is too intellectually controlled and manipulated, that what he says cannot be wholly sincere because it is not sufficiently spontaneous. It may be that the large task which Eliot set himself in *The Waste Land* 'of giving a shape and a significance to the immense panorama of futility and anarchy' of contemporary history, caused some of the experiments which he made to gain that end to appear too deliberate. Certainly some of his analogies with musical structure, in particular the summation of the themes in the broken ending of the final part, have always seemed to me somewhat forced and over-theoretical. But this is very different from saying that he is a too conscious artist. Indeed, such a charge would overlook the fact that some of the poetry of the past which across the remove of time seems most 'spontaneous', that of Chaucer, for example, was actually a product of long experimentation in poetic theory fully as calculated as Eliot's. The greatest narrative poem in the language, *Troilus and Criseyde*, beats with equally geniune emotion in the passages where Chaucer is translating Boccaccio directly and in those where he is manipulating the structure of the Italian's poem to suit his own ends.

Despite some of the protests of the nineetenth century on behalf of the untutored genius, it still appears that the more conscious the artist the better, if that consciousness implies the degree to which he has mastered the unending subtleties of his craft. But I have mentioned Chaucer also to point a difference in modern art. As my paragraphs on our highly developed historical sense tried to indicate, Eliot as a poet is not only inevitably acquainted with a great range of possible techniques, as all expert poets since the Renaissance have increasingly been; he is, in addition, highly aware of the processes of the mind itself. This particular kind of consciousness is in part what led him to feel the necessity of grounding the structure of his longest poem in something outside himself, in an objective pattern of myths.

Ulysses, to be sure, furnishes an even fuller example of how a contemporary artist has mastered the problem of consciousness in a similar way. When one contemplates the overwhelming elaborateness of Joyce's construction, the almost unbelievable degree to which he worked out the parallel of even the smallest details in his narrative with those in the *Odyssey* (to say nothing of his intricate scheme of correspondences between the sections

of his work and various colours, arts, bodily organs, and so on),
one begins by wondering why his huge creative power was not
stultified by this fantastic heaping up of seemingly pointless
erudition, of practically none of which is it necessary for the
reader to be aware in order to follow with full understanding the
progress of Bloom's and Stephen's day. But finally one realizes
that the very *completeness* of this arbitrary external structure
may have been the one thing that gave to Joyce's scholastic
mind, deprived of faith but still possessing the ingrained habits
of logical formal thought, the greatest creative release possible
to him, by providing him with an entire scaffold – and one which
has the advantage of being one of the best stories in Western
civilization – on which to build his work.

And in case there should be some feeling that either Joyce
or Eliot has revealed a kind of bookish weakness in turning for
his structure to literature rather than to life, it should be recol-
lected that Shakespeare himself created hardly any of his plots,
and that by the very fact of taking ready-made the pattern of his
characters' actions, he could devote his undivided attention to
endowing them with life. It is only an uninformed prejudice
which holds that literature must start from actual personal
experience. It certainly must end with giving a sense of life; but
it is not at all necessary that the poet should have undergone in
his own person what he describes. Indeed, the more catholic the
range of the artist, the more obviously impossible that would be.
The poet's imagination can work as well on his reading as on the
raw material of his senses. It is a mark of human maturity, as Eliot
noted in his discussion of the metaphysical poets, that there
should not be a separation in an individual's sensibility between
reading and experience any more than between emotion and
thought.[8]

NOTES

1. F. R. Leavis, *New Bearings in English Poetry* (1932), uses a
similar phrase on p. 94. Mr Leavis's interpretation of Eliot, though

acutely perceptive of certain details ... suffers from a certain over-intensity. He seems to be writing continually on the defensive as though he were the apostle of modern art to an unappreciative world. As a result his criticism, though eager, is somewhat wanting in balance and perspective.

2. This matter of Eliot's use of his reading (a hint of which he picked up from the symbolists, but which he has carried to far greater lengths) has been a stumbling-block to so many readers of his poetry that it requires further comment. On the one hand are those who believe that it is impossible to understand him without possessing the ability to recognize all his varied allusions, and who, therefore, indifferent to the seemingly hopeless and unrewarding task of tracing down both the wide and specialized range of his particular equipment of knowledge, have given him up as 'a poet for the learned'. On the other hand are the smaller body of readers who have done the greatest disservice to his reputation – I mean those who regard his poetry as a kind of hidden mystery for the *cognoscenti*. They cast the snob-vote for him. 'What?' they ask, 'you haven't read *The Golden Bough*? You don't own a Tarot pack? You haven't studied the Upanishads? You didn't even recognize that allusion to Verlaine? Why, my dear, how can you expect to understand Mr Eliot?'

The shortest answer (which, I hope, is given full confirmation during the course of my essay) is that you begin to understand Eliot precisely as you begin to understand any other poet: by listening to the lines, by regarding their pattern as a self-enclosed whole, by listening to what is being communicated instead of looking for something that isn't. On the particular matter of what is accomplished by Eliot's literary allusions, and what equipment is necessary to comprehend them, consider the opening passage of 'The Fire Sermon':

> The river's tent is broken: the last fingers of leaf
> Clutch and sink into the wet bank. The wind
> Crosses the brown land, unheard. The nymphs are departed.
> Sweet Thames, run softly, till I end my song.
> The river bears no empty bottles, sandwich papers,
> Silk handkerchiefs, cardboard boxes, cigarette ends
> Or other testimony of summer nights. The nymphs are departed.
> And their friends, the loitering heirs of city directors;
> Departed, have left no addresses.
> By the waters of Leman I sat down and wept ...
> Sweet Thames, run softly till I end my song,
> Sweet Thames, run softly, for I speak not loud or long.
> But at my back in a cold blast I hear
> The rattle of the bones, and chuckle spread from ear to ear.

If one reads these lines with an attentive ear and is sensitive to their

sudden shifts in movement, the contrast between the actual Thames
and the idealized vision of it during an age before it flowed through a
megalopolis is conveyed by that movement itself, whether or not one
recognizes the refrain to be from Spenser. If one does have the lovely
pictures of his 'Prothalamion' in mind, there is then added to the
contrast a greater volume and poignancy. In like manner with the
startling quickening of pace in the final two lines and the terrifying
shudder they induce: it is not necessary to refer this effect to Marvell's
'Coy Mistress', although if the effect of the sudden shift in cadence in
that poem is also in the reader's ear, there is again a heightening.

In neither of these cases is anything demanded of the reader different
in kind from what is demanded by Milton's 'Lycidas'. A single careful
reading of that poem can fascinate the reader with its extraordinary
melodic richness and make him want to press on to a full comprehension of its intricate form, of the way its structure builds up through a
series of climaxes. But this can be understood only through some
knowledge of the whole elaborate convention that Milton inherited
from the classical and Renaissance pastoral. In particular, there are
many passages, the fullest relish of which depends upon the reader's
bringing with him the memory of the way a similar situation has been
handled by Virgil and Theocritus. In addition, certain well-known
lines require for the grasp of their sense at least as much literary
annotation as any passage in Eliot. For instance,

> Next Camus, reverend sire, went footing slow,
> His mantle hairy, and his bonnet sedge,
> Inwrought with figures dim, and on the edge
> Like to that sanguine flower inscribed with woe.

The wealth of mythology compressed into those lines would require
a long paragraph if it were to be elucidated in prose.

The point with any poem is that if the reader starts by being
enchanted by the movement of the lines, then gradually his mind can
furnish itself with the information necessary to understand what they
are telling him. In the case of the modern reader of a poem in a
Renaissance tradition, this means reminding himself of certain
mythological details once common property among educated readers,
but now increasingly forgotten. In the case of reading a contemporary
poet, it is more a question of accustoming yourself to an unfamiliar
procedure that breaks through your preconceptions of what poetry
should be (as Wordsworth broke through preconceptions inherited
from the eighteenth century). As Eliot remarked in the Conclusion to
The Use of Poetry:

The uses of poetry certainly vary as society alters, as the public to be addressed changes. . . . The difficulty of poetry (and modern poetry is supposed to be difficult) . . . may be due just to novelty: we know the ridicule accorded in turn to Wordsworth, Shelley and Keats, Tennyson and Browning – but must remark that Browning was the first to be *called* difficult; hostile critics of the earlier poets found them difficult, but called them silly. Or difficulty may be caused by the reader's having been told, or having suggested to himself, that the poem is going to prove difficult. The ordinary reader, when warned against the obscurity of a poem, is apt to be thrown into a state of consternation very unfavourable to poetic receptivity. Instead of beginning, as he should, in a state of sensitivity, he obfuscates his senses by the desire to be clever and to look very hard for something, he doesn't know what – or else by the desire not to be taken in. There is such a thing as stage fright, but what such readers have is pit or gallery fright. The more seasoned reader, he who has reached, in these matters, a state of greater *purity*, does not bother about understanding; not, at least, at first. I know that some of the poetry to which I am most devoted is poetry which I did not understand at first reading; some is poetry which I am not sure I understand yet: for instance, Shakespeare's.

And finally, there is the difficulty caused by the author's having left out something which the reader is used to finding; so that the reader, bewildered, gropes about for what is absent, and puzzles his head for a kind of 'meaning' which is not there, and is not meant to be there.

It is also relevant to note how the passage from 'The Fire Sermon' is an example of Eliot's way of suggesting sameness at the heart of contrast. 'The nymphs are departed': the first use of that statement, followed as it is by the line from Spenser, serves to build up the pastoral atmosphere: 'The river nymphs are departed with the oncoming of winter.' But as the ensuing lines present the picture of the present Thames in summer, the statement takes on another meaning: 'The age of romantic loveliness is gone.'

Then, when the statement is repeated a few lines later, the nymphs themselves have altered; they have now become decidedly flesh and blood. But the feeling expressed is not that the past was wholly noble and the present base. Instead, it is being suggested, if only in a minor undertone, that this glimpse of present life along the river, depressingly sordid as it is, being human cannot be wholly different from human life in the past. And, concurrently, the idealized Elizabethan young men and women who appear as attendants in Spenser's marriage songs begin to be seen with new eyes. They cannot be wholly unlike the present idle young men about town and their nymphs; and this touch of humanity removes them from the realm of the abstract and endows them with actuality. In such a manner the undertones of this 'resembling contrast' have grown directly from the depth of Eliot's psychological perception into the nature of life, of the way, for example, in which nobility and baseness are inextricably mingled in even the finest individual.

3. A point necessary to mention is that an appreciation of Eliot's poem is not dependent upon reading Miss Weston's study. I had been enjoying *The Waste Land* for several years before an interest in exploring the effect of Eliot's reading upon his development brought me to *From Ritual to Romance*. As a result of having read that book I can now follow more distinctly the logical steps by which Eliot was led to compose his structure, and can also perceive in detail the kind of stimulus and release that the book gave to his mind. I am also enabled to understand more fully how some of the widely disparate details fall into the completed pattern. For example, I had previously taken the presence of the 'wicked pack of cards' in the opening section to be simply a sharp dramatic device by which Eliot introduced his characters and at the same time stressed the point of their shifting identity: that, observed under varying and contrasting appearances, human beings remain essentially the same throughout different ages. I have never seen a Tarot pack (and, if I had to bet, my money would say that neither had Eliot himself). But Miss Weston mentions that its four suits are Cup, Lance, Sword, and Dish, which thus correspond to the sexual symbolism of the Grail; and that the original use of these cards was 'not to foretell the Future in general, but to predict the rise and fall of the waters which brought fertility to the land' (p. 76). Through such knowledge the emotional relevance to the poem of this 'wicked pack' is obviously increased.

But with the exception of a few such illuminating details, I question whether Miss Weston's valuable study has enabled me to feel the poem more intensely. For nearly everything of importance from her book that is apposite to an appreciation of *The Waste Land*, particularly her central emphasis on the analogous ways by which various myths express the mysteries of sex and religion, has been incorporated into the structure of the poem itself, or into Eliot's Notes. Unlike many sections of Pound's *Cantos*, *The Waste Land* does not require recourse to the poet's reading in order to become comprehensible. Its structure is pre-eminently self-contained.

The very presence of the Notes may seem to give a denial to that assertion. They are certainly an extremely artificial device, though not without precedent in English poetry, as *The Shepherds' Calendar* could illustrate. But Spenser's desire to have his poems rival the works of classical antiquity even to their appearance in a volume with annotations by the anonymous E.K. (who was most probably Spenser himself or at least a close collaborator), does not play any part in Eliot's intention. His Notes are simply a consequence of his desire to strip the form of his poem to its barest essentials in order to secure his concentrated effect. Such elimination, particularly when added to his method of using his reading as an integral part of his experience, demanded certain signposts of elucidation if the reader was to follow the exact course. And, as I have already indicated in my discussion of the closing lines of 'The Burial of the Dead', it is obviously necessary, for *full* understanding of some of his passages, to be aware of the special context of his allusions to other poets. In all cases when Eliot thinks that context essential to the reader of *The Waste Land* he has given the reference, as in this instance to the *Inferno, The White Devil,* and *Les Fleurs du Mal.* In the case of some of his less familiar allusions where the actual phrasing of the original constitutes part of his effect, he has also quoted the relevant passage. For example:

> But at my back from time to time I hear
> The sound of horns and motors, which shall bring
> Sweeney to Mrs Porter in the spring.

These lines, by themselves, without the need of any reference, etch a sharp description of the surroundings of 'the dull canal . . . round behind the gashouse'. Most present-day readers of poetry would be able to supply the surprising contrast:

> But at my back I always hear
> Time's wingèd chariot hurrying near,

so that Eliot simply mentions 'To His Coy Mistress' in a note. But to enable the reader also to hear this 'sound of horns' in a double way, it is necessary for Eliot to add the lines from the little-known Elizabethan poet, John Day:

> When of the sudden, listening, you shall hear
> A noise of horns and hunting, which shall bring
> Actaeon to Diana in the spring,
> Where all shall see her naked skin . . .

And no matter how much one may object to the existence of the Notes in general, it would be hard to deny the flash of tightly packed wit that is struck by the incongruous contrast between the 'naked skin' of Diana and that of Mrs Porter.

Some of the more general references in the Notes help to sharpen the outlines of Eliot's structure. The self-consuming burning of sterile passion which is the theme of 'The Fire Sermon' receives added emphasis from the pertinent reminder of the expression of that theme by Buddha and St Augustine, though no reading of their work is required for understanding the poem. I have not yet read the Upanishad from which Eliot borrowed the onomatopoeic representation of 'what the thunder said'; but it is perfectly clear from his own lines what an excellent 'objective correlative' he found in that legend.

My own chief objection to the Notes is the occasional tone of what Eliot himself, in relation to passages in *The Sacred Wood*, described as 'pontifical solemnity'. But that impression should be qualified by the admission that some of the notes which struck me at first as useless pedantry or deliberate mystification of the reader, particularly the one on Tiresias, I now recognize as very useful to the interpretation of the poem. The objection to stiffness in phrasing still remains, but this quality was perhaps due in part to Eliot's desire to state the necessary details as briefly as he could; and owing to the largeness of his undertaking in this poem and the inevitable limitations of his own temperament, this was possibly the price he had to pay in order to avoid what he would have considered muffling the energy of his poem by extended connecting links in the text itself.

The stiffness may also be due to Eliot's shyness at speaking in his own person, a quality which has likewise taken itself out in the occasional ponderous over- and under-statements in his Prefaces, and in his *Criterion* Commentaries. In these Notes it crops up in a curious double-edged irony, where he appears to be mocking himself for writing the note at the same time that he wants to convey something by it. Certainly the note on the hermit-thrush which tells us that it is *turdus aonalaschkae pallasii* and quotes a description from Chapman's *Handbook of Birds of Eastern North America*, would seem as though it were the desperate effort of J. Alfred Prufrock himself to say something important, but ending only in irrelevance. But actually the note ends with a telling sentence: 'Its "water-dripping song" is justly celebrated.' By that sentence Eliot has given a suggestion of the very sound from which his lines took rise (as remarked at the close of my chapter on the auditory imagination); and for ornithologists even the passage from Chapman would have the advantage of exact description.

Comparable to Eliot's use of Notes in *The Waste Land* is the frequent presence, throughout his work, of epigraphs for individual poems – though this device is not at all open to the objection of not being sufficiently structural. Again the intention is to enable the poet to secure a condensed expression in the poem itself, as well as to induce the reader to realize, even from the moment before the poem begins, that in reading poetry every word should be paid full attention. In each case the epigraph is designed to form an integral part of the effect of the poem; and in the most successful instances a subtle aura of association is added. 'Mistah Kurtz – he dead' – the harrowing climax of Conrad's *Heart of Darkness*, his expression of utter horror, epitomizes in a sentence the very tone of blasphemous hopelessness which issues from 'The Hollow Men'. And certainly the closed circle of Prufrock's frightened isolation is sharply underlined by inscribing this speech from the *Inferno*: 'If I thought my answer were to one who ever could return to the world, this flame should shake no more; but since, if what I hear be true, none ever did return alive from this depth, without fear of infamy I answer thee.' Prufrock can give utterance in soliloquy to his debate with himself only because he knows that no one will overhear him. The point of calling this poem a 'Love Song' lies in the irony that it will never be sung; that Prufrock will never dare to voice what he feels.

And as a final detail to this note on Notes, it is worth observing that Eliot uses his titles as well as his epigraphs as integral elements in his effect, to reiterate his belief that in writing poetry every word on the page should be designed to count. Often, in the earlier poems, the aim of the title was to surprise the reader out of all complacency. Thus 'Sweeney among the Nightingales', which is in itself a condensed metaphysical conceit; thus also the double meaning of 'Sweeney Erect'. 'Burbank with a Baedeker: Bleistein with a Cigar' dramatically sets a stage; but in this case the ensuing epigraph which is largely composed of phrases from other writers referring to events in Venice – for example, from *Othello, The Aspern Papers*, and Browning's 'A Toccata of Galuppi's', though calculated to call up the reader's usual wide range of associations with that city, is too much of a pastiche to be very effective. And lastly, the startling 'A Cooking Egg' requires for its comprehension the occult knowledge that an egg which is no longer fresh enough to be eaten by itself, but must be used in cooking, is so described with the accent on the participle. Thus the title relates to the epigraph from Villon, which also tells the age and condition of the hero of the poem:

> En l'an trentiesme de mon aage
> Que toutes mes hontes j'ay beues ...

4. Weston, *From Ritual to Romance*, p. 36.

5. Ibid. p. 21.

6. This point was noted by Hugh Ross Williamson, *The Poetry of T. S. Eliot* (1933) p. 135. Mr Williamson's book, though not wholly decisive in its critical observations, is a useful manual of relevant explanation, to which I have been frequently indebted.

7. *Dial*, Nov 1923, pp. 480–3.

8. Since writing this paragraph I have re-read the passage in

Henry James's essay 'The Art of Fiction' which expresses so exactly
the relation between literature and experience which I have attempted
to elucidate that I reproduce it here. In addition, it indicates once again
a fundamental sameness in point of view between James and Eliot.
James's rejoinder to the statement that 'the novelist must write from
experience' runs as follows:

It is equally excellent and inconclusive to say that one must write
from experience. . . . What kind of experience is intended, and
where does it begin and end? Experience is never limited, and it is
never complete; it is an immense sensibility, a kind of huge spider-
web, of the finest silken threads, suspended in the chamber of
consciousness and catching every air-borne particle in its tissue. It is
the very atmosphere of the mind; and when the mind is imaginative
– much more when it happens to be that of a man of genius – it
takes to itself the faintest hints of life, it converts the very pulses of
the air into revelations. The young lady living in a village has only
to be a damsel upon whom nothing is lost to make it quite unfair
(as it seems to me) to declare to her that she shall have nothing to
say about the military. Greater miracles have been seen than that,
imagination assisting, she should speak the truth about some of these
gentlemen. I remember an English novelist, a woman of genius,
telling me that she was much commended for the impression she
had managed to give in one of her tales of the nature and way of
life of the French Protestant youth. She had been asked where she
learned so much about this recondite being, she had been con-
gratulated on her peculiar opportunities. These opportunities consisted in her having once, in Paris, as she ascended a staircase, passed
an open door where, in the household of a *pasteur*, some of the young
Protestants were seated at table round a finished meal. The glimpse
made a picture; it lasted only a moment, but that moment was
experience. She had got her impression, and she evolved her type.
She knew what youth was, and what Protestantism; she also had
the advantage of having seen what it was to be French; so that she
converted these ideas into a concrete image and produced a reality.
Above all, however, she was blessed with the faculty which when
you give it an inch takes an ell, and which for the artist is a much
greater source of strength than any accident of residence or of place
in the social scale. The power to guess the unseen from the seen, to
trace the implication of things, to judge the whole piece by the
pattern, the condition of feeling life, in general, so completely that
you are well on your way to knowing any particular corner of it –
this cluster of gifts may almost be said to constitute experience, and
they occur in country and in town, and in the most differing stages

of education. If experience consists of impressions, it may be said that impressions *are* experience, just as (have we not seen it?) they are the very air we breathe. Therefore, if I should certainly say to a novice, 'Write from experience, and experience only', I should feel that this was rather a tantalizing monition if I were not careful immediately to add, 'Try to be one of the people on whom nothing is lost!'

Cleanth Brooks

THE WASTE LAND:
CRITIQUE OF THE MYTH (1939)

THOUGH much has been written on *The Waste Land*, it will not be difficult to show that most of its critics misconceive entirely the theme and the structure of the poem. There has been little or no attempt to deal with it as a unified whole. F. R. Leavis and F. O. Matthiessen have treated large sections of the poem in detail, and I am obviously indebted to both of them. I believe, however, that Leavis makes some positive errors of interpretation. I find myself in almost complete agreement with Matthiessen in his commentary on the section which he deals with in his *Achievement of T. S. Eliot*, but the plan of his book does not allow for a complete consecutive examination of the poem.

In view of the state of criticism with regard to the poem, it is best for us to approach it frankly on the basis of its theme. I prefer, however, not to raise just here the question of how important it is for the reader to have an explicit intellectual account of the various symbols and a logical account of their relationships. It may well be that such rationalization is no more than a scaffolding to be got out of the way before we contemplate the poem itself as poem. But many readers (including myself) find the erection of such a scaffolding valuable – if not absolutely necessary – and if some readers will be tempted to lay more stress upon the scaffolding than they should, there are perhaps still more readers who, without the help of such a scaffolding, will be prevented from getting at the poem at all.

The basic symbol used, that of the waste land, is taken of course, from Miss Jessie Weston's *From Ritual to Romance*. In the legends which she treats there, the land has been blighted by a curse. The crops do not grow and the animals cannot reproduce. The plight of the land is summed up by, and connected with, the plight of the lord of the land, the Fisher King, who has been rendered impotent by maiming or sickness. The curse can be removed only by the appearance of a knight who will ask the meanings of the various symbols which are displayed to him in the castle. The shift in meaning from physical to spiritual sterility is easily made, and was, as a matter of fact, made in certain of the legends. As Eliot has pointed out, a knowledge of this symbolism is essential for an understanding of the poem.

Of hardly less importance to the reader, however, is a knowledge of Eliot's basic method. *The Waste Land* is built on a major contrast – a device which is a favorite of Eliot's and is to be found in many of his poems, particularly his later poems. The contrast is between two kinds of life and two kinds of death. Life devoid of meaning is death; sacrifice, even the sacrificial death, may be life-giving, an awakening to life. The poem occupies itself to a great extent with this paradox, and with a number of variations upon it.

Eliot has stated the matter quite explicitly himself in one of his essays. In his 'Baudelaire' he says: 'One aphorism which has been especially noticed is the following: *la volupté unique et suprême de l'amour gît dans la certitude de faire le mal*. This means, I think, that Baudelaire has perceived that what distinguishes the relations of man and woman from the copulation of beasts is the knowledge of Good and Evil (of *moral* Good and Evil which are not natural Good and Bad or puritan Right and Wrong). Having an imperfect, vague romantic conception of Good, he was at least able to understand that the sexual act as evil is more dignified, less boring, than as the natural, "life-giving", cheery automatism of the modern world. . . . So far as we are human, what we do must be either evil or good; so far as we do evil or good, we are human; and it is better, in a paradoxical way, to do evil than to do nothing: at least, *we exist* [italics mine].' The last statement is highly important for an understanding of *The Waste Land*. The fact that men have lost the knowledge of good and evil, keeps them from being alive, and is the justification for viewing the modern waste land as a realm in which the inhabitants do not even exist.

E   C.H.W.

This theme is stated in the quotation which prefaces the poem. The Sybil says: 'I wish to die.' Her statement has several possible interpretations. For one thing, she is saying what the people who inhabit the waste land are saying. But she may also be saying what the speaker of 'The Journey of the Magi' says: '... this Birth was/Hard and bitter agony for us, like Death, our death/ ... I should be glad of another death.'

I

The first section of 'The Burial of the Dead' develops the theme of the attractiveness of death, or of the difficulty in rousing oneself from the death in life in which the people of the waste land live. Men are afraid to live in reality. April, the month of rebirth, is not the most joyful season but the cruelest. Winter at least kept us warm in forgetful snow. The idea is one which Eliot has stressed elsewhere. Earlier in 'Gerontion' he had written

> In the juvescence of the year
> Came Christ the tiger

. . .

> The tiger springs in the new year. Us he devours.

More lately, in *Murder in the Cathedral*, he has the chorus say

> We do not wish anything to happen.
> Seven years we have lived quietly,
> Succeeded in avoiding notice,
> Living and partly living.

And in another passage: 'Now I fear disturbance of the quiet seasons.' Men dislike to be roused from their death-in-life.

The first part of 'The Burial of the Dead' introduces this theme through a sort of reverie on the part of the protagonist— a reverie in which speculation on life glides off into memory of an actual conversation in the Hofgarten and back into speculation again. The function of the conversation is to establish the class and character of the protagonist. The reverie is resumed with line 19.

> What are the roots that clutch, what branches grow
> Out of this stony rubbish?

The protagonist answers for himself:

> Son of man,
> You cannot say, or guess, for you know only
> A heap of broken images, where the sun beats,
> And the dead tree gives no shelter, the cricket
>   no relief,
> And the dry stone no sound of water.

In this passage there are references to Ezekiel and to Ecclesiastes, and these references indicate what it is that men no longer know: The passage referred to in Ezekiel 2, pictures a world thoroughly secularized:

1. And he said unto me, Son of man, stand upon thy feet, and I will speak unto thee.

2. And the spirit entered into me when he spake unto me, and set me upon my feet, that I heard him that spake unto me.

3. And he said unto me, Son of man, I send thee to the children of Israel, to a rebellious nation that hath rebelled against me: they and their father have transgressed against me, even unto this very day.

Other passages from Ezekiel are relevant to the poem, Chapter 37 in particular, which describes Ezekiel's waste land, where the prophet, in his vision of the valley of dry bones, contemplates the 'burial of the dead' and is asked: 'Son of man, can these bones live? And I answered, O Lord God, thou knowest. 4. Again he said unto me, Prophesy over these bones, and say unto them, O ye dry bones, hear the word of the Lord.'

One of Ezekiel's prophecies was that Jerusalem would be conquered and the people led away into the Babylonian captivity. That captivity is alluded to in Section III of *The Waste Land*, line 182, where the Thames becomes the 'waters of Leman'.

The passage from Ecclesiastes 12, alluded to in Eliot's notes, describes the same sort of waste land:

1. Remember now thy Creator in the days of thy youth, while the evil days come not, nor the years draw nigh, when thou shalt say, I have no pleasure in them;

2. While the sun, or the light, or the moon, or the stars, be not darkened, nor the clouds return after the rain;

3. In the day when the keepers of the house shall tremble, and the strong men shall bow themselves, and the grinders cease because they are few, and those that look out of the windows be darkened,

4. And the doors shall be shut in the streets, when the sound of the grinding is low, and he shall rise up at the voice of the bird, and all the daughters of musick shall be brought low;

5. Also when they shall be afraid of that which is high, and fears shall be in the way, and the almond tree shall flourish, and the grasshopper shall be a burden, *and desire shall fail* [italics mine]: because man goeth to his long home, and the mourners go about the streets;

6. Or ever the silver cord be loosed, or the golden bowl be broken, or the pitcher be broken at the fountain, or the wheel broken at the cistern.

7. Then shall the dust return to the earth as it was: and the spirit shall return unto God who gave it.

8. Vanity of vanities, saith the preacher; all is vanity.

A reference to this passage is also evidently made in the nightmare vision of Section V of the poem.

The next section of 'The Burial of the Dead' which begins with the scrap of song quoted from Wagner (perhaps another item in the reverie of the protagonist), states the opposite half of the paradox which underlies the poem: namely, that life at its highest moments of meaning and intensity resembles death. The song from Act I of Wagner's *Tristan und Isolde*, 'Frisch weht der Wind', is sung in the opera by a young sailor aboard the ship which is bringing Isolde to Cornwall. The 'Irisch kind' of the song does not properly apply to Isolde at all. The song is merely one of happy and naïve love. It brings to the mind of the protagonist an experience of love – the vision of the hyacinth girl as she came back from the hyacinth garden. The poet says

> . . . my eyes failed, I was neither
> Living nor dead, and I knew nothing,
> Looking into the heart of light, the silence.

The line which immediately follows this passage, 'Oed' und leer das Meer', seems at first to be simply an extension of the last figure: that is, 'Empty and wide the sea [of silence]'. But the line, as a matter of fact, makes an ironic contrast; for the line, as it occurs in Act III of the opera, is the reply of the watcher who reports to the wounded Tristan that Isolde's ship is nowhere in sight; the sea is empty. And, though the 'Irisch kind' of the first quotation is not Isolde, the reader familiar with the opera will apply it to Isolde when he comes to the line 'Oed' und leer das Meer'. For the question in the song is in essence Tristan's question in Act III: 'My Irish child, where dwellest thou?' The two quotations from the opera which frame the ecstasy-of-love passage thus take on a new meaning in the altered context. In the first, love is happy; the boat rushes on with a fair wind behind it. In the second, love is absent; the sea is wide and empty. And the last quotation reminds us that even love cannot exist in the waste land.

The next passage, that in which Madame Sosostris figures, calls for futher reference to Miss Weston's book. As Miss Weston has shown, the Tarot cards were originally used to determine the event of highest importance to the people, the rising of the waters. Madame Sosostris has fallen a long way from the high function of her predecessors. She is engaged merely in vulgar fortune-telling – is merely one item in a generally vulgar civilization. But the symbols of the Tarot pack are still unchanged. The various characters are still inscribed on the cards, and she is reading in reality (though she does not know it) the fortune of the protagonist. She finds that his card is that of the drowned Phoenician Sailor, and so she warns him against death by water, not realizing any more than do the other inhabitants of the modern waste land that the way into life may be by death itself. The drowned Phoenician Sailor is a type of the fertility god whose image was thrown into the sea annually as a symbol of the death of summer. As for the other figures in the pack: Belladonna, the Lady of the Rocks, is woman in the waste land. The man with three staves, Eliot says he associates rather arbitrarily with the Fisher King. The term 'arbitrarily' indicates that we are not to attempt to find a logical connection here. (It may be interesting to point out, however, that Eliot seems to have given, in a later poem, his reason for making the association. In 'The Hollow Men' he writes, speaking as one of the Hollow Men:

> Let me also wear
> Such deliberate disguises
> Rat's coat, crowskin, crossed staves
> In a field
> Behaving as the wind behaves.

The figure is that of a scarecrow, fit symbol of the man who possesses no reality, and fit type of the Fisher King, the maimed, impotent king who ruled over the waste land of the legend. The man with three staves in the deck of cards may thus have appealed to the poet as an appropriate figure to which to assign the function of the Fisher King, although the process of identification was too difficult to expect the reader to follow and although knowledge of the process was not necessary to an understanding of the poem.)

The Hanged Man, who represents the hanged god of Frazer (including the Christ), Eliot states in a note, is associated with the hooded figure who appears in 'What the Thunder Said'. That he is hooded accounts for Madame Sosostris' inability to see him; or rather, here again the palaver of the modern fortune-teller is turned to new and important account by the poet's shifting the reference into a new and serious context. The Wheel and the one-eyed merchant will be discussed later.

After the Madame Sosostris passage, Eliot proceeds to complicate his symbols for the sterility and unreality of the modern waste land by associating it with Baudelaire's 'fourmillante cité' and with Dante's Limbo. The passages already quoted from Eliot's essay on Baudelaire will indicate one of the reasons why Baudelaire's lines are evoked here. In Baudelaire's city, dream and reality seem to mix, and it is interesting that Eliot in 'The Hollow Men' refers to this same realm of death-in-life as 'death's dream kingdom' in contradistinction to 'death's other kingdom'.

The references to Dante are most important. The line, 'I had not thought death had undone so many', is taken from the Third Canto of the *Inferno*; the line, 'Sighs, short and infrequent, were exhaled', from the Fourth Canto. Mr Matthiessen has already pointed out that the Third Canto deals with Dante's Limbo which is occupied by those who on earth had 'lived without praise or blame'. They share this abode with the angels 'who were not rebels, nor were faithful to God, but were for themselves'. They exemplify almost perfectly the secular attitude which dominates the modern world. Their grief, according to Dante, arises from the fact that they 'have no hope of death; and their blind life is so debased, that they are envious of every other lot'. But though they may not hope for death, Dante calls them 'these wretches who never were alive'. The people described in the Fourth Canto are those who lived virtuously but who died before the proclamation of the Gospel – they are the unbaptized. They form the second of the two classes of people who inhabit the modern waste land: those who are secularized and those who have no knowledge of the faith. Without a faith their life is in reality a death. To repeat the sentence from Eliot previously quoted: 'So far as we do evil or good, we are human; and it is better, in a paradoxical way, to do evil than to do nothing: at least, we exist.'

The Dante and Baudelaire references, then, come to the same thing as the allusion to the waste land of the medieval legends; and these various allusions, drawn from widely differing sources, enrich the comment on the modern city so that it becomes 'unreal' on a number of levels: as seen through 'the brown fog of a winter dawn'; as the medieval waste land and Dante's Limbo and Baudelaire's Paris are unreal.

The reference to Stetson stresses again the connection between the modern London of the poem and Dante's hell. After the statement, 'I could never have believed death had undone so many', follow the words, 'After I had distinguished some among them, I saw and knew the shade of him who made, through cowardice, the great refusal.' The protagonist, like Dante, sees among the inhabitants of the contemporary waste land one whom he recognizes. (The name 'Stetson' I take to have no ulterior significance. It is merely an ordinary name such as might be borne by the friend one might see in a crowd in a great city.) Mylae, as Mr Matthiessen has pointed out, is the name of a battle between the Romans and the Carthaginians in the Punic War. The Punic War was a trade war – might be considered a rather close parallel to our late war. At any rate, it is plain that Eliot in having the protagonist address the friend in a London street as one who was with him in the Punic War rather than as one who was with him in the World War is making the point that all the wars are one war; all experience, one experience. As Eliot put the idea in *Murder in the Cathedral*:

> We do not know very much of the future
> Except that from generation to generation
> The same things happen again and again

I am not sure that Leavis and Matthiessen are correct in inferring that the line, 'That corpse you planted last year in your garden', refers to the attempt to bury a memory. But whether or not this is true, the line certainly refers also to the buried god of the old fertility rites. It also is to be linked with the earlier passage – 'What are the roots that clutch, what branches grow', etc. This allusion to the buried god will account for the ironical, almost taunting tone of the passage. The burial of the dead is now a sterile planting – without hope. But the advice to 'keep the Dog far hence', in spite of the tone, is, I believe, well taken and serious. The passage in Webster goes as follows

> But keep the wolf far thence, that's foe to men,
> For with his nails he'll dig them up again.

Why does Eliot turn the wolf into a dog? And why does he reverse the point of importance from the animal's normal hostility to men to its friendliness? If, as some critics have suggested, he is merely interested in making a reference to Webster's darkest play, why alter the line? I am inclined to take

the Dog (the capital letter is Eliot's) as Humanitarianism* and
the related philosophies which, in their concern for man, extirpate
the supernatural – dig up the corpse of the buried god and thus
prevent the rebirth of life. For the general idea, see Eliot's essay,
'The Humanism of Irving Babbitt'.

The last line of 'The Burial of the Dead' – 'You! hypocrite
lecteur! – mon semblable, – mon frère!' the quotation from
Baudelaire, completes the universalization of Stetson begun by
the reference to Mylae. Stetson is every man including the
reader and Mr Eliot himself.

II

If 'The Burial of the Dead' gives the general abstract statement
of the situation, the second part of *The Waste Land*, 'A Game
of Chess', gives a more concrete illustration. The easiest contrast
in this section – and one which may easily blind the casual reader
to a continued emphasis on the contrast between the two kinds
of life, or the two kinds of death, already commented on – is the
contrast between life in a rich and magnificent setting, and life
in the low and vulgar setting of a London pub. But both scenes,
however antithetical they may appear superficially, are scenes
taken from the contemporary waste land. In both of them life
has lost its meaning.

I am particularly indebted to Mr Allen Tate's comment on the
first part of this section. To quote from him, 'The woman . . . is,
I believe, the symbol of man at the present time. He is surrounded
by the grandeurs of the past, but he does not participate in them;
they don't sustain him.' And to quote from another section of
his commentary: 'The rich experience of the great tradition
depicted in the room receives a violent shock in contrast with a
game that symbolizes the inhuman abstraction of the modern
mind.' Life has no meaning; history has no meaning; there is no
answer to the question: 'What shall we ever do?' The only

* The reference is perhaps more general still: it may include
Naturalism, and Science in the popular conception as the new magic
which will enable man to conquer his environment completely.

thing that has meaning is the abstract game which they are to play, a game in which the meaning is assigned and arbitrary, meaning by convention only – in short, a game of chess.

This interpretation will account in part for the pointed reference to Cleopatra in the first lines of the section. But there is, I believe, a further reason for the poet's having compared the lady to Cleopatra. The queen in Shakespeare's drama – 'Age cannot wither her, nor custom stale Her infinite variety' – is perhaps the extreme exponent of love for love's sake, the feminine member of the pair of lovers who threw away an empire for love. But the infinite variety of the life of the woman in 'A Game of Chess' *has* been staled. There is indeed no variety at all, and love simply does not exist. The function of the sudden change in the description of the carvings and paintings in the room from the heroic and magnificent to 'and other withered stumps of time' is obvious. But the reference to Philomela is particularly important, for Philomela it seems to me, is one of the major symbols of the poem.

Miss Weston points out (in *The Quest of the Holy Grail*) that a section of one of the Grail manuscripts, which is apparently intended to be a gloss on the Grail story, tells how the court of the rich Fisher King was withdrawn from the knowledge of men when certain of the maidens who frequented the shrine were raped and had their golden cups taken from them. The curse on the land follows from this act. Miss Weston conjectures that this may be a statement, in the form of a parable, of the violation of the older mysteries which were probably once celebrated openly, but were later forced underground. Whether or not Mr Eliot noticed this passage or intends a reference, the violation of a woman makes a very good symbol of the process of secularization. John Crowe Ransom makes the point very neatly for us in *God Without Thunder*. Love is the aesthetic of sex; lust is the science. Love implies a deferring of the satisfaction of the desire; it implies a certain asceticism and a ritual. Lust drives forward urgently and scientifically to the immediate extirpation of the desire. Our contemporary waste land is in large part the result of our scientific attitude – of our complete secularization. Needless to say, lust defeats its own ends. The portrayal of 'the change of Philomel, by the barbarous king' is a fitting commentary on the scene which it ornaments. The waste land of the legend came in this way; the modern waste land has come in this way.

This view is corroborated by the change of tense to which Edmund Wilson has called attention: 'And still she *cried*, and still the world *pursues* [italics mine].' Apparently the 'world' partakes in the barbarous king's action, and still partakes in that action.

To 'dirty ears' the nightingale's song is not that which filled all the desert with inviolable voice – it is 'jug, jug'. Edmund Wilson has pointed out that the rendition of the bird's song here represents not merely the Elizabethans' neutral notation of the bird's song, but carries associations of the ugly and coarse. The passage is one, therefore, of many instances of Eliot's device of using something which in one context is innocent but in another context becomes loaded with a special meaning.

The Philomela passage has another importance, however. If it is a commentary on how the waste land became waste, it also repeats the theme of the death which is the door to life, the theme of the dying god. The raped woman becomes transformed through suffering into the nightingale; through the violation comes the 'inviolable voice'. The thesis that suffering is action, and that out of suffering comes poetry is a favorite one of Eliot's. For example, 'Shakespeare, too, was occupied with the struggle – which alone constitutes life for a poet – to transmute his personal and private agonies into something rich and strange, something universal and impersonal.' Consider also his statement with reference to Baudelaire: 'Indeed, in his way of suffering is already a kind of presence of the supernatural and of the superhuman. He rejects always the purely natural and the purely human; in other words, he is neither "naturalist" nor "humanist".' The theme of the life which is death is stated specifically in the conversation between the man and the woman. She asks the question, 'Are you alive, or not?' Compare the Dante references in 'The Burial of the Dead'. (She also asks,

'Is there nothing in your head?' He is one of the Hollow Men – 'Headpiece filled with straw'.) These people, as people living in the waste land, know nothing, see nothing, do not even live.

But the protagonist, after this reflection that in the waste land of modern life even death is sterile – 'I think we are in rats' alley/Where the dead men lost their bones' – remembers a death that was transformed into something rich and strange, the death described in the song from *The Tempest* – 'Those are pearls that were his eyes.'

The reference to this section of *The Tempest* is, like the Philomela reference, one of Eliot's major symbols. A general comment on it is therefore appropriate here, for we are to meet with it twice more in later sections of the poem. The song, one remembers, was sung by Ariel in luring Ferdinand, Prince of Naples, on to meet Miranda, and thus to find love, and through this love, to effect the regeneration and deliverance of all the people on the island. Ferdinand, hearing the song, says:

> The ditty does remember my drowned father.
> This is no mortal business, nor no sound
> That the earth owes . . .

The allusion is an extremely interesting example of the device of Eliot's already commented upon, that of taking an item from one context and shifting it into another in which it assumes a new and powerful meaning. The description of a death which is a portal into a realm of the rich and strange – a death which becomes a sort of birth – assumes in the mind of the protagonist an association with that of the drowned god whose effigy was thrown into the water as a symbol of the death of the fruitful powers of nature but which was taken out of the water as a symbol of the revivified god. (See *From Ritual to Romance.*) The passage therefore represents the perfect antithesis to the passage in 'The Burial of the Dead': 'That corpse you planted last year in your garden', etc. It also, as we have already pointed out, finds its antithesis in the sterile and unfruitful death 'in rats' alley' just commented upon. (We shall find that this contrast between the death in rats' alley and the death in *The Tempest* is made again in 'The Fire Sermon'.)

We have yet to treat the relation of the title of the second section, 'A Game of Chess', to Middleton's play, *Women Beware Women*, from which the game of chess is taken. In the play, the game is used as a device to keep the widow occupied while her daughter-in-law is being seduced. The seduction amounts almost to a rape, and in a *double entendre* the rape is actually described in terms of the game. We have one more connection with the Philomela symbol, therefore. The abstract game is being used in the contemporary waste land, as in the play, to cover up a rape and is a description of the rape itself.

In the latter part of 'A Game of Chess' we are given a picture of spiritual emptiness, but this time, at the other end of the social scale, as reflected in the talk between two cockney women in a London pub. (It is perhaps unnecessary to comment on the relation of their talk about abortion to the theme of sterility and the waste land.)

The account here is straightforward enough, and the only matter which calls for comment is the line spoken by Ophelia in *Hamlet*, which ends the passage. Ophelia, too, was very much concerned about love, the theme of conversation between the women in the pub. As a matter of fact, she was in very much the same position as that of the woman who has been the topic of conversation between the two ladies whom we have just heard. And her poetry, like Philomela's, had come out of suffering. We are probably to look for the relevance of the allusion to her here rather than in an easy satiric contrast between Elizabethan glories and modern sordidness. After all, Eliot's criticism of the present world is not merely the sentimental one that this happens to be the twentieth century after Christ and not the seventeenth.

III

'The Fire Sermon' makes much use of several of the symbols already developed. The fire is the sterile burning of lust, and the section is a sermon, although a sermon by example only. This section of the poem also contains some of the most easily apprehended uses of literary allusion. The poem opens on a vision of the modern river. In Spenser's 'Prothalamion' the scene described is also a river scene at London, and it is dominated by nymphs and their paramours, and the nymphs are preparing for a wedding. The contrast between Spenser's scene and its twentieth century equivalent is jarring. The paramours are now 'the loitering heirs of city directors', and, as for the nuptials of Spenser's Elizabethan maidens, in the stanzas which follow we learn a great deal about those. At the end of the section the speech of the third of the Thames-nymphs summarizes the whole matter for us.

The waters of the Thames are also associated with those of Leman – the poet in the contemporary waste land is in a sort of Babylonian Captivity.

The castle of the Fisher King was always located on the banks of a river or on the sea shore. The title 'Fisher King', Miss Weston shows, originates from the use of the fish as a fertility or life symbol. This meaning, however, was often forgotten, and so his title in many of the later Grail romances is accounted for by describing the king as fishing. Eliot uses the reference to fishing for reverse effect. The reference to fishing is part of the realistic detail of the scene – 'While I was fishing in the dull canal.' But to the reader who knows the Weston references, the reference is to that of the Fisher King of the Grail legends. The protagonist is the maimed and impotent king of the legends.

Eliot proceeds now to tie the waste-land symbol to that of *The Tempest*, by quoting one of the lines spoken by Ferdinand, Prince of Naples, which occurs just before Ariel's song, 'Full Fathom Five', is heard. But he alters *The Tempest* passage somewhat, writing not, 'Weeping again the king my father's wreck', but

> Musing upon the king my brother's wreck
> And on the king my father's death before him.

It is possible that the alteration has been made to bring the account taken from *The Tempest* into accord with the situation in the Percival stories. In Wolfram von Eschenbach's *Parzival*, for instance, Trevrezent, the hermit, is the brother of the Fisher King, Anfortas. He tells Parzival, 'His name all men know as Anfortas, and I weep for him evermore.' Their father, Frimutel, is dead.

The protagonist in the poem, then, imagines himself not only in the situation of Ferdinand in *The Tempest* but also in that of one of the characters in the Grail legend; and the wreck, to be applied literally in the first instance, applies metaphorically in the second.

After the lines from *The Tempest*, appears again the image of a sterile death from which no life comes, the bones, 'rattled by the rat's foot only, year to year'. (The collocation of this figure with the vision of the death by water in Ariel's song has already been commented on. The lines quoted from *The Tempest* come just before the song.)

The allusion to Marvell's 'To His Coy Mistress' is of course one of the easiest allusions in the poem. Instead of 'Time's winged chariot' the poet hears 'the sound of horns and motors' of contemporary London. But the passage has been further complicated. The reference has been combined with an allusion to Day's 'Parliament of Bees'. 'Time's winged chariot' of Marvell has not only been changed to the modern automobile; Day's 'sound of horns and hunting' has changed to the horns of the motors. And Actaeon will not be brought face to face with Diana, goddess of chastity; Sweeney, type of the vulgar bourgeois, is to be brought to Mrs Porter, hardly a type of chastity. The reference in the ballad to the feet 'washed in soda water' reminds the poet ironically of another sort of foot-washing, the sound of the children singing in the dome heard at the ceremony of the foot-washing which precedes the restoration of the wounded Anfortas (the Fisher King) by Parzival and the taking away of the curse from the waste land. The quotation thus completes the allusion to the Fisher King commenced in line 189 – 'While I was fishing in the dull canal.'

The pure song of the children also reminds the poet of the

song of the nightingale which we have heard in 'The Game of Chess.' The recapitulation of symbols is continued with a repetition of 'Unreal city' and with the reference to the one-eyed merchant.

Mr Eugenides, the Smyrna merchant, is the one-eyed merchant mentioned by Madame Sosostris. The fact that the merchant is one-eyed apparently means, in Madame Sosostris' speech, no more than that the merchant's face on the card is shown in profile. But Eliot applies the term to Mr Eugenides for a totally different effect. The defect corresponds somewhat to Madame Sosostris' bad cold. He is a rather battered representative of the fertility cults: the prophet, the *seer*, with only one eye.

The Syrian merchants, we learn from Miss Weston's book, were, along with slaves and soldiers, the principal carriers of the mysteries which lie at the core of the Grail legends. But in the modern world we find both the representatives of the Tarot divining and the mystery cults in decay. What he carries on his back and what the fortune-teller is forbidden to see is evidently the knowledge of the mysteries (although Mr Eugenides himself is hardly likely to be more aware of it than Madame Sosostris is aware of the importance of her function). Mr Eugenides, in terms of his former function, ought to be inviting the protagonist into the esoteric cult which holds the secret of life, but on the realistic surface of the poem in his invitation to 'a weekend at the Metropole' he is really inviting him to a homosexual debauch. The homosexuality is 'secret' and now a 'cult' but a very different cult from that which Mr Eugenides ought to represent. The end of the new cult is not life but, ironically, sterility.

In the modern waste land, however, even the relation between man and woman is also sterile. The incident between the typist and the carbuncular young man is a picture of 'love' so exclusively and practically pursued that it is not love at all. The tragic chorus to the scene is Tiresias, into whom perhaps Mr Eugenides may be said to modulate, Tiresias, the historical 'expert' on the relation between the sexes.

The fact that Tiresias is made the commentator serves a further irony. In *Oedipus Rex*, it is Tiresias who recognizes that the curse which has come upon the Theban land has been caused by the sinful sexual relationship of Oedipus and Jocasta. But Oedipus' sin has been committed in ignorance, and knowledge of it brings horror and remorse. The essential horror of the act which Tiresias witnesses in the poem is that it is not regarded as a sin at all – is perfectly casual, is merely the copulation of beasts.

The reminiscence of the lines from Goldsmith's song in the description of the young woman's actions after the departure of her lover, gives concretely and ironically the utter break-down of traditional standards.

It is the music of her gramophone which the protagonist hears 'creep by' him 'on the waters'. Far from the music which Ferdinand heard bringing him to Miranda and love, it is, one is tempted to think, the music of 'O O O O that Shakespeherian Rag'.

But the protagonist says that he can *sometimes* hear 'the pleasant whining of a mandoline'. Significantly enough, it is the music of the fishmen (the fish again as a life symbol) and it comes from beside a church (though – if this is not to rely too much on Eliot's note – the church has been marked for destruction). Life on Lower Thames Street, if not on the Strand, still has meaning as it cannot have meaning for either the typist or the rich woman of 'A Game of Chess'.

The song of the Thames-daughters brings us back to the opening section of 'The Fire Sermon' again, and once more we have to do with the river and the river-nymphs. Indeed, the typist incident is framed by the two river-nymph scenes.

The connection of the river-nymphs with the Rhine-daughters of Wagner's *Götterdämmerung* is easily made. In the passage in Wagner's opera (to which Eliot refers in his note), the opening of Act III, the Rhine-daughters bewail the loss of the beauty of the Rhine occasioned by the theft of the gold, and then beg Siegfried to give them back the Ring made from this gold, finally threatening him with death if he does not give it up. Like the Thames-daughters they too have been violated; and like the maidens mentioned in the Grail legend the violation has brought a curse on gods and men. The first of the songs depicts the modern river, soiled with oil and tar. (Compare also with the description of the river in the first part of 'The Fire Sermon'.) The second song depicts the Elizabethan river, also evoked in the first part of 'The Fire Sermon'. (Leicester and Elizabeth ride upon it in a barge of state. Incidentally, Spenser's 'Prothalamion' from which quotation is made in the first part of 'The Fire Sermon' mentions Leicester as having formerly lived in the house which forms the setting of the poem.)

In this second song there is also a definite allusion to the passage in *Antony and Cleopatra* already referred to in the opening line of 'A Game of Chess'.

> Beating oars
> The stern was formed
> A gilded shell

And if we still have any doubt of the allusion, Eliot's note on the passage with its reference to the 'barge' and 'poop' should settle the matter. We have already commented on the earlier allusion to Cleopatra as the prime example of love for love's sake. The symbol bears something of the same meaning here, and the note which Eliot supplies does something to reinforce the 'Cleopatra' aspect of Elizabeth. Elizabeth in the presence of the Spaniard De Quadra, though negotiations were going on for a Spanish marriage, 'went so far that Lord Robert at last said, as I [De Quadra was a bishop] was on the spot there was no reason why they should not be married if the queen pleased'. The passage has a sort of double function. It reinforces the general contrast between Elizabethan magnificence and modern sordidness: in the Elizabethan age love for love's sake has some meaning and therefore some magnificence. But the passage gives something of an opposed effect too: the same sterile love, emptiness of love, obtained in this period too: Elizabeth and the typist are alike as well as different. (One of the reasons for the frequent allusion to Elizabethan poetry in this and the preceding section of the poem may be the fact that with the English Renaissance the old set of supernatural sanctions had begun to break up. See Eliot's various essays on Shakespeare and the Elizabethan dramatists.)

The third Thames-daughter's song depicts another sordid 'love' affair, and unites the themes of the first two songs. It begins 'Trams and *dusty* trees'. With it we are definitely in the waste land again. Pia, whose words she echoes in saying 'Highbury bore me. Richmond and Kew/Undid me' was in Purgatory and had hope. The woman speaking here has no hope – she too is in the Inferno: 'I can connect/Nothing with nothing.' She has just completed, floating down the river in the canoe, what Eliot has described in *Murder in the Cathedral* as

> . . . the effortless journey, to the empty land
>
> .   .   .
>
> Where those who were men can no longer turn the mind
> Where the soul is no longer deceived, for there are no objects,
>   no tones,
> To distraction, delusion, escape into dream, pretence,
> No colours, no forms to distract, to divert the soul
> From seeing itself, foully united forever, nothing with
>   nothing,
> Not what we call death, but what beyond death is not death . . .

Now, 'on Margate Sands', like the Hollow Men, she stands 'on this beach of the tumid river'.

The songs of the three Thames-daughters, as a matter of fact, epitomize this whole section of the poem. With reference to the quotations from St Augustine and Buddha at the end of 'The Fire Sermon' Eliot states that 'the collocation of these two representatives of eastern and western asceticism, as the culmination of this part of the poem, is not an accident'.

It is certainly not an accident. The moral of all the incidents which we have been witnessing is that there must be an asceticism – something to check the drive of desire. The wisdom of the East and the West comes to the same thing on this point. Moreover, the imagery which both St Augustine and Buddha use for lust is fire. What we have witnessed in the various scenes of 'The Fire Sermon' is the sterile burning of lust. Modern man, freed from all restraints, in his cultivation of experience for experience's

sake burns, but not with a 'hard and gemlike flame'. One ought
not to pound the point home in this fashion, but to see that the
imagery of this section of the poem furnishes illustrations leading
up to the Fire Sermon is the necessary requirement for feeling
the force of the brief allusions here at the end to Buddha and
St Augustine.

IV

Whatever the specific meaning of the symbols, the general
function of the section, 'Death by Water', is readily apparent.
The section forms a contrast with 'The Fire Sermon' which
precedes it – a contrast between the symbolism of fire and that of
water. Also readily apparent is its force as a symbol of surrender
and relief through surrender.

Some specific connections can be made, however. The
drowned Phoenician Sailor recalls the drowned god of the
fertility cults. Miss Weston tells that each year at Alexandria an
effigy of the head of the god was thrown into the water as a
symbol of the death of the powers of nature, and that this head
was carried by the current to Byblos where it was taken out of
the water and exhibited as a symbol of the reborn god.

Moreover, the Phoenician Sailor is a merchant – 'Forgot . . .
the profit and loss.' The vision of the drowned sailor gives a
statement of the message which the Syrian merchants originally
brought to Britain and which the Smyrna merchant, unconsciously and by ironical negatives, has brought. One of Eliot's
notes states that the 'merchant . . . melts into the Phoenician
Sailor, and the latter is not wholly distinct from Ferdinand
Prince of Naples'. The death by water would seem to be equated
with the death described in Ariel's song in *The Tempest.* There
is a definite difference in the tone of the description of this death
– 'A current under sea/Picked his bones in whispers', as compared with the 'other' death – 'bones cast in a little low dry
garret,/Rattled by the rat's foot only, year to year'.

Further than this it would not be safe to go, but one may
point out that whirling (the whirlpool here, the Wheel of

Madame Sosostris' palaver) is one of Eliot's symbols frequently used in other poems (*Ash Wednesday*, 'Gerontion', *Murder in the Cathedral*, and 'Burnt Norton') to denote the temporal world. And I may point out, supplying the italics myself, the following passage from *Ash Wednesday*:

> Although I do not hope to *turn* again
>
> . . .
>
> Wavering between the *profit and the loss*
> In this brief transit where the dreams cross
> The dreamcrossed twilight *between birth and dying*.

At least, with a kind of hindsight, one may suggest that 'Death by Water' gives an instance of the conquest of death and time, the 'perpetual recurrence of determined seasons', the 'world of spring and autumn, birth and dying' through death itself.

V

The reference to the 'torchlight red on sweaty faces' and to the 'frosty silence in the gardens' obviously associates Christ in Gethsemane with the other hanged gods. The god has now died, and in referring to this the basic theme finds another strong restatement:

> He who was living is now dead
> We who were living are now dying
> With a little patience

The poet does not say 'We who *are* living'. It is 'We who *were* living'. It is the death-in-life of Dante's Limbo. Life in the full sense has been lost.

The passage on the sterility of the waste land and the lack of water provides for the introduction later of two highly important passages:

> There is not even silence in the mountains
> But dry sterile thunder without rain –

lines which look forward to the introduction later of 'what the thunder said' when the thunder, no longer sterile, but bringing rain, speaks.

The second of these passages is, 'There is not even solitude in the mountains', which looks forward to the reference to the Journey to Emmaus theme a few lines later: 'Who is the third who walks always beside you?' The god has returned, has risen, but the travelers cannot tell whether it is really he, or mere illusion induced by their delirium.

The parallelism between the 'hooded figure' who 'walks always beside you', and the 'hooded hordes' is another instance of the sort of parallelism that is really a contrast. In the first case, the figure is indistinct because spiritual; in the second, the hooded hordes are indistinct because completely *unspiritual* – they are the people of the waste land –

> Shape without form, shade without colour,
> Paralysed force, gesture without motion –

to take two lines from 'The Hollow Men', where the people of the waste land once more appear. Or to take another line from the same poem, perhaps their hoods are the 'deliberate disguises' which the Hollow Men, the people of the waste land, wear.

Eliot, as his notes tell us, has particularly connected the description here with the 'decay of eastern Europe'. The hordes represent, then, the general waste land of the modern world with a special application to the breakup of Eastern Europe, the region with which the fertility cults were especially connected and in which today the traditional values are thoroughly discredited. The cities, Jerusalem, Athens, Alexandria, Vienna, like the London of the first section of the poem are 'unreal', and for the same reason.

The passage which immediately follows develops the unreality into nightmare, but it is a nightmare vision which is something more than an extension of the passage beginning, 'What is the city over the mountains' – in it appear other figures from earlier in the poem: the lady of 'A Game of Chess', who, surrounded by the glory of history and art, sees no meaning in either and threatens to rush out into the street 'With my hair down, so', has here let down her hair and fiddles 'whisper music on those strings'. One remembers in 'A Game of Chess' that it was the woman's hair that spoke:

> ... her hair
> Spread out in fiery points
> Glowed into words, then would be savagely still.

The hair has been immemorially a symbol of fertility, and Miss Weston and Frazer mention sacrifices of hair in order to aid the fertility god.

As we have pointed out earlier, this passage is also to be connected with the twelfth chapter of Ecclesiastes. The doors 'of mudcracked houses', and the cisterns in this passage are to be found in Ecclesiastes, and the woman fiddling music from her hair is one of 'the daughters of musick' brought low. The towers and bells from the Elizabeth and Leicester passage of 'The Fire Sermon' also appear here, but the towers are upside down, and the bells, far from pealing for an actual occasion or ringing the hours, are 'reminiscent'. The civilization is breaking up.

The 'violet light' also deserves comment. In 'The Fire Sermon' it is twice mentioned as the 'violet hour', and there it has little more than a physical meaning. It is a description of the hour of twilight. Here it indicates the twilight of the civilization, but it is perhaps something more. Violet is one of the liturgical colors of the Church. It symbolizes repentance and it is the color of baptism. The visit to the Perilous Chapel, according to Miss Weston, was an initiation – that is, a baptism. In the nightmare vision, the bats wear baby faces.

The horror built up in this passage is a proper preparation for the passage on the Perilous Chapel which follows it. The journey has not been merely an agonized walk in the desert, though it is that; nor is it merely the journey after the god has died and hope has been lost; it is also the journey to the Perilous Chapel of the Grail story. In Miss Weston's account, the Chapel was part of the ritual, and was filled with horrors to test the candidate's courage. In some stories the perilous cemetery is also mentioned. Eliot has used both: 'Over the tumbled graves, about the chapel.' In many of the Grail stories the Chapel was haunted by demons.

The cock in the folk-lore of many people is regarded as the bird whose voice chases away the powers of evil. It is significant that it is after his crow that the flash of lightning comes and the 'damp gust Bringing rain'. It is just possible that the cock has a connection also with *The Tempest* symbols. The first song which Ariel sings to Ferdinand as he sits 'Weeping again the king my father's wreck' ends

> The strain of strutting chanticleer,
> Cry, cock-a-doodle-doo.

The next stanza is the 'Full Fathom Five' song which Eliot has used as a vision of life gained through death. If this relation holds, here we have an extreme instance of an allusion, in itself innocent, forced into serious meaning through transference to a new context.

As Miss Weston has shown, the fertility cults go back to a very early period and are recorded in Sanscrit legends. Eliot has been continually, in the poem, linking up the Christian doctrine with the beliefs of as many peoples as he can. Here he goes back to the very beginnings of Aryan culture, and tells the rest of the story of the rain's coming, not in terms of the setting already developed but in its earliest form. The passage is thus a perfect parallel in method to the passage in 'The Burial of the Dead':

> You who were with me in the ships *at Mylae*!
> That corpse you planted *last year* in your garden . . .

The use of Sanscrit in what the thunder says is thus accounted for. In addition, there is of course a more obvious reason for casting what the thunder said into Sanscrit here: onomatopoeia.

The comments on the three statements of the thunder imply an acceptance of them. The protagonist answers the first question, 'What have we given?' with the statement:

> The awful daring of a moment's surrender
> Which an age of prudence can never retract
> By this, and this only, we have existed.

Here the larger meaning is stated in terms which imply the sexual meaning. Man cannot be absolutely self-regarding. Even the propagation of the race – even mere 'existence' – calls for such a surrender. Living calls for – see the passage already quoted from Eliot's essay on Baudelaire – belief in something more than 'life'.

The comment on *dayadhvam* (sympathize) is obviously connected with the foregoing passage. The surrender to something outside the self is an attempt (whether on the sexual level or some other) to transcend one's essential isolation. The passage gathers up the symbols previously developed in the poem just as the foregoing passage reflects, though with a different implication, the numerous references to sex made earlier in the poem. For example, the woman in the first part of 'A Game of Chess' has also heard the key turn in the door, and confirms her prison by thinking of the key:

> Speak to me. Why do you never speak. Speak.
> What are you thinking of? What thinking? What?
> I never know what you are thinking. Think.

The third statement made by the thunder, *damyata* (control), follows the condition necessary for control, sympathy. The figure of the boat catches up the figure of control already given in 'Death by Water' – 'O you who turn the wheel and look to windward' – and from 'The Burial of the Dead' the figure of happy love in which the ship rushes on with a fair wind behind it: '*Frisch weht der Wind* . . .'.

I cannot accept Mr Leavis' interpretation of the passage, 'I sat upon the shore/Fishing, with the arid plain behind me', as meaning that the poem 'exhibits no progression'. The comment upon what the thunder says would indicate, if other passages did not, that the poem does 'not end where it began'. It is true that the protagonist does not witness a revival of the waste land; but there are two important relationships involved in his case: a personal one as well as a general one. If secularization has destroyed, or is likely to destroy, modern civilization, the protagonist still has a private obligation to fulfill. Even if the civilization is breaking up – 'London Bridge is falling down falling down falling down' – there remains the personal obligation: 'Shall I at least set my lands in order?' Consider in this connection the last sentences of Eliot's 'Thoughts After Lambeth': 'The World is trying the experiment of attempting to form a civilized but non-Christian mentality. The experiment will fail; but we must be very patient in awaiting its collapse; meanwhile redeeming the time: so that the Faith may be preserved alive through the dark ages before us; to renew and rebuild civilization, and save the World from suicide.'

The bundle of quotations with which the poem ends has a very definite relation to the general theme of the poem and to several of the major symbols used in the poem. Before Arnaut leaps back into the refining fire of Purgatory with joy he says: 'I am Arnaut who weep and go singing; contrite I see my past folly, and joyful I see before me the day I hope for. Now I pray you by that virtue which guides you to the summit of the stair, at times be mindful of my pain.' This theme is carried forward by the quotation from 'Pervigilium Veneris': 'When shall I be like the swallow.' The allusion is also connected with the Philomela symbol. (Eliot's note on the passage indicates this clearly.) The sister of Philomela was changed into a swallow as Philomela was changed into a nightingale. The protagonist is asking therefore when shall the spring, the time of love, return, but also when will he be reborn out of his sufferings, and – with the special meaning which the symbol takes on from the preceding Dante quotation and from the earlier contexts already discussed – he is asking what is asked at the end of one of the minor poems: 'When will Time flow away.'

The quotation from 'El Desdichado', as Edmund Wilson has pointed out, indicates that the protagonist of the poem has been disinherited, robbed of his tradition. The ruined tower is perhaps also the Perilous Chapel, 'only the wind's home', and it is also the whole tradition in decay. The protagonist resolves to claim his tradition and rehabilitate it.

The quotation from *The Spanish Tragedy* – 'Why then Ile fit you. Hieronymo's mad againe' – is perhaps the most puzzling of all these quotations. It means, I believe, this: The protagonist's acceptance of what is in reality the deepest truth will seem to the present world mere madness. (And still she cried . . . "Jug Jug" to dirty ears.') Hieronymo in the play, like Hamlet, was 'mad' for a purpose. The protagonist is conscious of the interpretation which will be placed on the words which follow – words which will seem to many apparently meaningless babble, but which contain the oldest and most permanent truth of the race:

Datta. Dayadhvam. Damyata.

Quotation of the whole context from which the line is taken confirms this interpretation. Hieronymo, asked to write a play for the court's entertainment, replies:

Why then, I'll fit you; say no more.
When I was young, I gave my mind
And plied myself to fruitless poetry;
Which though it profit the professor naught,
Yet it is passing pleasing to the world.

He sees that the play will give him the opportunity he has been seeking to avenge his son's murder. Like Hieronymo, the protagonist in the poem has found his theme; what he is about to perform is not 'fruitless'.

After this repetition of what the thunder said comes the benediction:

Shantih　　Shantih　　Shantih

The foregoing account of *The Waste Land* is, of course, not to be substituted for the poem itself. Moreover, it certainly is not to be considered as representing *the method by which the poem was composed*. Much which the prose expositor must represent as though it had been consciously contrived obviously was arrived at unconsciously and concretely.

The account given above is a statement merely of the 'prose meaning', and bears the same relation to the poem as does the 'prose meaning' of any other poem. But one need not perhaps apologize for setting forth such a statement explicitly, for *The Waste Land* has been almost consistently misinterpreted since its first publication. Even a critic so acute as Edmund Wilson has seen the poem as essentially a statement of despair and disillusionment, and his account sums up the stock interpretation of the poem. Indeed, the phrase, 'the poetry of drouth', has become a cliché of left-wing criticism. It is such a misrepresentation of *The Waste Land* as this which allows Eda Lou Walton to entitle an essay on contemporary poetry, 'Death in the Desert'; or which causes Waldo Frank to misconceive of Eliot's whole position and personality. But more than the meaning of one poem is at stake. If *The Waste Land* is not a world-weary cry of despair or a sighing after the vanished glories of the past, then not only the popular interpretation of the poem will have to be altered but also the general interpretations of post-War poetry which begin with such a misinterpretation as a premise.

Such misinterpretations involve also misconceptions of Eliot's technique. Eliot's basic method may be said to have passed relatively unnoticed. The popular view of the method used in *The Waste Land* may be described as follows: Eliot makes use of ironic contrasts between the glorious past and the sordid present – the crashing irony of

> But at my back from time to time I hear
> The sound of horns and motors, which shall bring
> Sweeney to Mrs Porter in the spring.

But this is to take the irony of the poem at the most superficial level, and to neglect the other dimensions in which it operates. And it is to neglect what are essentially more important aspects of his method. Moreover, it is to over-emphasize the difference between the method employed by Eliot in this poem and that employed by him in later poems.

The basic method used in *The Waste Land* may be described as the application of the principle of complexity. The poet works in terms of surface parallelisms which in reality make ironical contrasts, and in terms of surface contrasts which in reality constitute parallelisms. (The second group sets up effects which may be described as the obverse of irony.) The two aspects taken together give the effect of chaotic experience ordered into a new whole, though the realistic surface of experience is faithfully retained. The complexity of the experience is not violated by the apparent forcing upon it of a predetermined scheme.

The fortune-telling of 'The Burial of the Dead' will illustrate the general method very satisfactorily. On the surface of the poem the poet reproduces the patter of the charlatan, Madame Sosostris, and there is the surface irony: the contrast between the original use of the Tarot cards and the use made by Madame Sosostris. But each of the details (justified realistically in the palaver of the fortune-teller) assumes a new meaning in the general context of the poem. There is then, in addition to the surface irony, something of a Sophoclean irony too, and the 'fortune-telling', which is taken ironically by a twentieth-century audience, becomes *true* as the poem develops – true in a sense in which Madame Sosostris herself does not think it true. The surface irony is thus reversed and becomes an irony on a deeper level. The items of her speech have only one reference in terms of the context of her speech: the 'man with three staves', the 'one-eyed merchant', the 'crowds of people, walking round in a ring', etc. But transferred to other contexts they become loaded with special meanings. To sum up, all the central symbols of the poem head up here; but here, in the only section in which they are explicitly bound together, the binding is slight and accidental. The deeper lines of association only emerge in terms of the total context as the poem develops – and this is, of course, exactly the effect which the poet intends.

This transference of items from an 'innocent' context into a context in which they become charged and transformed in meaning will account for many of the literary allusions in the poem. For example, the 'change of Philomel' is merely one of the items in the decorative detail in the room in the opening of 'A Game of Chess'. But the violent change of tense – 'And still she cried, and still the world pursues' – makes it a comment upon, and a symbol of, the modern world. And further allusions to it through the course of the poem gradually equate it with the general theme of the poem. The allusions to *The Tempest* display the same method. The parallelism between Dante's Hell and the waste land of the Grail legends is fairly close; even the equation of Baudelaire's Paris to the waste land is fairly obvious. But the parallelism between the death by drowning in *The Tempest* and the death of the fertility god is, on the surface, merely accidental, and the first allusion to Ariel's song is merely an irrelevant and random association of the stream-of-consciousness:

> Is your card, the drowned Phoenician Sailor,
> (Those are pearls that were his eyes. Look!)

And on its second appearance in 'A Game of Chess' it is still only an item in the protagonist's abstracted reverie. Even the association of *The Tempest* symbol with the Grail legends in the lines

> While I was fishing in the dull canal
>
>   .   .   .
>
> Musing upon the king my brother's wreck

and in the passage which follows, is ironical merely. But the associations have been established, even though they may seem to be made in ironic mockery, and when we come to the passage, 'Death by Water', with its change of tone, they assert themselves positively. We have a sense of revelation out of material apparently accidentally thrown together. I have called the effect the obverse of irony, for the method, like that of irony, is indirect, though the effect is positive rather than negative.

The melting of the characters into each other is, of course, an aspect of this general process. Elizabeth and the girl born at Highbury both ride on the Thames, one in the barge of state, the other supine in a narrow canoe, and they are both Thames-nymphs, who are violated and thus are like the Rhine-nymphs who have also been violated, etc. With the characters as with the other symbols, the surface relationships may be accidental and apparently trivial and they may be made either ironically or through random association or in hallucination, but in the total context of the poem the deeper relationships are revealed. The effect is a sense of the oneness of experience, and of the unity of all periods, and with this a sense that the general theme of the poem is true. But the theme has not been imposed – it has been revealed.

This complication of parallelisms and contrasts makes, of course, for ambiguity, but the ambiguity, in part, resides in the poet's fidelity to the complexity of experience. The symbols resist complete equation with a simple meaning. To take an example, 'rock' throughout the poem seems to be one of the 'desert' symbols. For example, the 'dry stone' gives 'no sound of water'; woman in the waste land is 'the Lady of the Rocks', and most pointed of all, there is the long delirium passage in 'What the Thunder Said': 'Here is no water but only rock', etc. So much for its general meaning, but in 'The Burial of the Dead' occur the lines

> Only
> There is shadow under this red rock,
> (Come in under the shadow of this red rock).

Rock here is a place of refuge. (Moreover, there may also be a reference to the Grail symbolism. In *Parzival*, the Grail is a stone: 'And this stone all men call the grail. . . . As children the Grail doth call them, 'neath its shadow they wax and grow.') The paradox, life through death, penetrates the symbol itself.

To take an even clearer case of this paradoxical use of symbols, consider the lines which occur in the hyacinth girl passage. The vision gives obviously a sense of the richness and beauty of life. It is a moment of ecstasy (the basic imagery is obviously sexual); but the moment in its intensity is like death. The protagonist looks in that moment into the 'heart of light, the silence', and so looks into – not richness – but blankness: he is neither 'living nor dead'. The symbol of life stands also for a kind of death. This duality of function may, of course, extend to a whole passage. For example, consider:

Where fishmen lounge at noon: where the walls
Of Magnus Martyr hold
Inexplicable splendour of Ionian white and gold.

The function of the passage is to indicate the poverty into
which religion has fallen: the splendid church now surrounded
by the poorer districts. But the passage has an opposed effect
also: the fishmen in the 'public bar in Lower Thames Street'
next to the church have a meaningful life which has been largely
lost to the secularized upper and middle classes.

The poem would undoubtedly be 'clearer' if every symbol
had a single, unequivocal meaning; but the poem would be
thinner, and less honest. For the poet has not been content to
develop a didactic allegory in which the symbols are two-
dimensional items adding up directly to the sum of the general
scheme. They represent dramatized instances of the theme,
embodying in their own nature the fundamental paradox of the
theme.

We shall better understand why the form of the poem is right
and inevitable if we compare Eliot's theme to Dante's and to
Spenser's. Eliot's theme is not the statement of a faith held and
agreed upon (Dante's *Divine Comedy*) nor is it the projection
of a 'new' system of beliefs (Spenser's *Faerie Queene*). Eliot's
theme is the rehabilitation of a system of beliefs, known but now
discredited. Dante did not have to 'prove' his statement; he
could assume it and move within it about a poet's business. Eliot
does not care, like Spenser, to force the didacticism. He prefers
to stick to the poet's business. But, unlike Dante, he cannot
assume acceptance of the statement. A direct approach is calculated to elicit powerful 'stock responses' which will prevent the
poem's being *read* at all. Consequently, the only method is to
work by indirection. The Christian material is at the center, but
the poet never deals with it directly. The theme of resurrection is
made on the surface in terms of the fertility rites; the words
which the thunder speaks are Sanscrit words.

We have been speaking as if the poet were a strategist trying
to win acceptance from a hostile audience. But of course this is

true only in a sense. The poet himself is audience as well as speaker; we state the problem more exactly if we state it in terms of the poet's integrity rather than in terms of his strategy. He is so much a man of his own age that he can indicate his attitude toward the Christian tradition without falsity only in terms of the difficulties of a rehabilitation; and he is so much a poet and so little a propagandist that he can be sincere only as he presents his theme concretely and dramatically.

To put the matter in still other terms: the Christian terminology is for the poet a mass of clichés. However 'true' he may feel the terms to be, he is still sensitive to the fact that they operate superficially as clichés, and his method of necessity must be a process of bringing them to life again. The method adopted in *The Waste Land* is thus violent and radical, but thoroughly necessary. For the renewing and vitalizing of symbols which have been crusted over with a distorting familiarity demands the type of organization which we have already commented on in discussing particular passages: the statement of surface similarities which are ironically revealed to be dissimilarities, and the association of apparently obvious dissimilarities which culminates in a later realization that the dissimilarities are only superficial – that the chains of likeness are in reality fundamental. In this way the statement of beliefs emerges *through* confusion and cynicism – not in spite of them.

George Williamson

THE WASTE LAND AND 'DANS LE RESTAURANT' (1953)

SOME consideration of 'Dans le Restaurant' is relevant, if not imperative, to a discussion of *The Waste Land*, not merely because its conclusion provides the fourth part of the larger poem. Rather because, as I venture to think, it is a conclusion in that poem also, the dramatic conclusion to its negative movement. This conjecture and the fact that it was translated so as to form a distinct part of the new poem suggest that there is a similarity in the sequence of both poems. The nature of this sequence first becomes clear in 'Dans le Restaurant', but it is the negative development of the 'La Figlia' experience, which in that poem remains equivocal.

A brief recapitulation of the development of 'Dans le Restaurant' must suffice. A dirty, debilitated, old waiter becomes confidential with a diner, and tells the story of his earliest sex experience. Incidentally, the reader will do well to compare this poem with Eliot's explanation of Dante's experience as reflected in his work. The *garçon* begins by saying. 'In my country it is the rainy season, with wind, fine sunshine, and rain; it is what we call the wash-day of the beggars.' He describes the soaked and budding willows where one takes refuge in a shower. He was seven, and she younger. He tickled her to make her laugh; and he adds, 'J'éprouvais un instant de puissance et de délire.'

'But then, old lecher,' interrupts the diner, 'at that age!' The waiter continues that events are cruel. A big dog came to romp with them; he was frightened and had to stop midway. 'It is a pity.' 'Mais alors,' responds the diner, 'you have your lust.' Then the diner, who has shown disgust throughout, orders him to clean himself up, exclaiming, 'By what right do you pay for experiences like mine?' He concludes by giving the waiter ten *sous* for the bathroom.

The last section of this poem, reproduced with slight changes as Part IV of *The Waste Land*, supplies the old foreign waiter with his ultimate cleansing. Phlebas, still the trading Phoenician, is drowned, deprived of his lust and greed. It was a painful fate, yet he 'was once handsome and tall as you'. But *The Waste Land* omits the cargo of tin, is not explicit about the painful fate, and less specific about passing the stages of his prior life. It adds details like 'picked his bones in whispers' – a rather grim cleansing image – and specifies the audience as those 'who turn the wheel and look to windward' – a homogeneous image of those who resemble Phlebas the sailor.

Now let us review the sequence of this experience in its elements. In the rainy season, when nature is renewed, Phlebas experienced the stirring of sex, and was giving it expression when he was frightened and frustrated. Later, in another country, he is debilitated, dirty, in need of 'the wash-day of the beggars'; but he has this memory and his greed. Finally he is drowned, subjected to a painful cleansing, and we are reminded that he was once a fine figure of a man. This conclusion is reinforced by the action of his confidant, who gives him money for a bath because, despite his disgust, he has had similar experience. Hence we may infer that the experience is not regarded as unique, nor must its issue always be the same. Another issue is discussed in Eliot's essay on Dante. And the ironic '*dédoublement* of the personality' reaches its most complex form in *The Waste Land*, but as defined in his essay on Blake (II).

The way of Phlebas and the way of Dante are the two opposite issues for the experience that first centers in 'La Figlia Che Piange'. We shall do well not to forget them when we are puzzled by the sex symbolism in Eliot. Of course we cannot interpret *The Waste Land* by 'Dans le Restaurant'; but neither can we ignore a poem which supplies a distinct part of another poem, including an important character, and otherwise resembles the later and more complicated poem. It may not be going too far to regard 'Dans le Restaurant' (1918) as an earlier exploration of the vein of thought and feeling that is plumbed in *The Waste Land*. The translation of part of it bears some testimony to its anticipation of the later verse, especially in its basic symbolism, to which 'Gerontion' also contributed.

In *The Waste Land* (1922) the experience of the old waiter becomes relevant to a whole land, at once the Fisher King myth and the modern reality. One may assume that the French poem was already behind the poet – four years separate their publication – when it suddenly fell into the larger scheme suggested by Jessie L. Weston's book on the Grail legend, *From Ritual to Romance*.

George L. K. Morris

'MARIE, MARIE, HOLD ON TIGHT' (1954)

As a rented house in Provence provided somewhat sparse reading matter, I took up a volume with the unpromising title *My Past*, by a Countess Marie Larisch. To my surprise, it proved thoroughly engrossing. Perhaps it was a book which everybody read when it was first published (1916). T. S. Eliot was certainly one who read it, and before he wrote *The Waste Land*.

For a variety of reasons, the book should have created a sensation. To begin with, Countess Larisch was a niece and confidante of the Austrian Empress Elizabeth, who was famous in her time for a glamorous combination of good looks and neurasthenia; secondly, the author had been the unwilling go-between for the Archduke Rudolph and Maria Vetsera, and was blamed by almost everyone for the tragedy at Mayerling; and thirdly, she was endowed with a surprising gift for vivid characterizations.

Anyone familiar with Eliot's poem does not read very far before coming upon a similarity of names and places that can hardly be fortuitous. We have seen that the Countess' name was Marie.* Moreover her home was on the Starnberger-See (*Waste Land*, l. 8). Marie's family, the Wittelsbachs – which included the Empress and their cousin, the 'mad king' Ludwig – occupied various castles around the Bavarian lake. 'The archduke my cousin' (ll. 13–14 of the poem): Marie had several archduke cousins, but Rudolph was her first cousin; although they always disliked each other cordially, they had been forced to associate since childhood – and each unknowingly brought about the other's downfall. Marie went 'south in winter' (l. 18) – Menton, to be specific; and – to clinch matters – she frequently observed

* It might be noted that *Marie* is a most unusual name in central Europe; the German form is customarily *Maria*.

that only in the mountains she felt free (l. 17); when the Mayerling catastrophe caused her to leave Vienna, it was to the mountains that she retired for good. Richard Wagner had a humorous rendezvous with Marie when she was a girl; in the poem he intrudes only through a stanza of *Tristan.*

The *Waste Land* décor, moreover, bears kinship to certain passages in Countess Larisch's book. The opening lines of Part II echo an account of the Empress' dressing room, with its notable combination of magnificence and *ennui.* And the 'Chapel Perilous' of Part V curiously resembles the tumbledown chapter-house at Heiligenkreuz, to which the uncles of Maria Vetsera carried her mangled remains, through the windy night with a pale moon; the police allowed only a moment for the burial, and no time at all to say a prayer.

On another level we can find more subtle points of contact between the book and poem. I know few autobiographies that encompass so many violent deaths – notably death by drowning and death by fire. And, as we might expect, there was considerable superstition and fortune-telling in the Hapsburg wasteland. The most noteworthy 'death-by-drowning' episode concerns the suicide of the Bavarian king in the Starnberger-See. Of all her relatives, it was to Ludwig that the imaginative Empress always felt most closely drawn. A striking chapter gives Elizabeth's account of his reappearance several nights after his death, and the apparition she always insisted was not at all in a dream. She was awakened by the drip-drip of water in her room, and saw Ludwig standing by her bed, his hair and clothes drenched and hung with sea-weed. He foretold that her sister (who had been his fiancée) would join him before long, and already he saw her surrounded by flames and smoke. She was later burnt to death at the Bazar de la Charité fire in Paris. And he added that she herself would follow, after a death that would be 'short and painless'. The Empress was assassinated the following year, while boarding a steamer on Lac Leman ('by the waters of Leman I sat down and wept').*

* Eliot commentators have ascribed the curious Lac Leman reference variously, from the League of Nations to a medieval word for 'lover'.

As I seem to have intruded into these pages in the guise of detective, I have no business to be reviewing a forty-year-old book. But I find it difficult to close without paying homage to some of the more preposterous characters who accompany the narrative. My favorite was an Archduchess who thought she'd swallowed a sofa which had become permanently lodged in her head, and she refused to leave her room for fear that the ends would stick in the door-jambs. A quick-witted attendant performed a miraculous cure by gaining admission to one of Her Highness' frequent bilious attacks and slipping a doll's sofa into the basin. And in more serious vein, there was the noble Archduke John of Tuscany, whom Marie links with Rudolph in a plot to overthrow Franz-Joseph and to build a democratic Hungary. She hints that its failure was the real motive behind Rudolph's suicide. John of Tuscany was drowned in a shipwreck off Cape Horn.

It will be understood, I hope, that there has been no intent here to detract from the formidable merits of Eliot's work. On the contrary, I find an added interest if one of the monuments of modern literature should be connected with a source so unexpected. And some day, perhaps, the copious *Waste Land* notes – always diligent in their tributes to Dante, Shakespeare, and Miss Jessie Weston – will also put in a word for Marie Larisch.

Hugh Kenner

THE INVISIBLE POET (1959)

> This dust will not settle in our time.
> — Samuel Beckett

I

The Waste Land was drafted during a rest cure at Margate ('I can connect Nothing with nothing') and Lausanne ('In this decayed hole among the mountains') during the autumn of 1921 by a convalescent preoccupied partly with the ruin of post-war Europe, partly with his own health and the conditions of his servitude to a bank in London, partly with a hardly exorable apprehension that two thousand years of European continuity had for the first time run dry. It had for epigraph a phrase from Conrad's *Heart of Darkness* ('The horror! The horror!'); embedded in the text were a glimpse, borrowed from Conrad's opening page, of the red sails of barges drifting in the Thames Estuary, and a contrasting reference to 'the heart of light'. 'Nothing is easier', Conrad had written, '. . . than to evoke the great spirit of the past upon the lower reaches of the Thames.'

In Paris that winter, Ezra Pound has recalled, '*The Waste Land* was placed before me as a series of poems. I advised him what to leave out.' Eliot, from about the same distance of time, recalls showing Pound 'a sprawling chaotic poem . . . which left his hands, reduced to about half its size, in the form in which it appears in print'. Since 'the form in which it appears in print', with its many sudden transitions and its implication, inhering in tone and cross-references and reinforced by notes, of a centre of gravity nowhere explicitly located, remained for many years the most sensational aspect of *The Waste Land*, this transaction requires looking into. The manuscript with the Conrad epigraph and Pound's blue-pencilling has been lost sight of; John Quinn appears to have made a private bestowal of it before his collection was dispersed in 1924. From surviving clues – chiefly three letters that passed between Pound and Eliot in the winter of 1921–2 – one may hazard guesses concerning the nature of the original series.

The letters, though they were exchanged after the major operation on the poem had been performed, disclose Eliot still in the act of agonizing not only about residual verbal details but about the desirability of adding or suppressing whole sections. 'There were long passages in different metres, with short lyrics sandwiched in between,' he has since recalled. The long passages included 'a rather poor pastiche of Pope', which was presumably the occasion of Pound's dictum, elsewhere recorded, that pastiche is only justified if it is better than the original; 'another passage about a fashionable lady having breakfast in bed, and another long passage about a shipwreck, which was obviously inspired by the Ulysses episode in the *Inferno*'. This would have led up to the 'death by water' of the 'drowned Phoenician sailor'; Victor Bérard's speculations concerning the possible origin of the *Odyssey* in Phoenician *periploi* had been in print for twenty years and had occupied the attention of James Joyce. The deletion of these passages was apparently accepted without protest. The lyrics, on the other hand, contained elements Eliot struggled to preserve. After they have been removed from the body of *The Waste Land* he proposes putting them at the end, and is again dissuaded: 'The thing now runs from "April..." to "shantih" without a break. That is 19 pages, and let us say the longest poem in the Englisch langwidge. Don't try to bust all records by prolonging it three pages further.' One of the lyrics contained a 'sweats with tears' passage which Eliot, after deletion from its original context, proposed working into the 'nerves monologue: only place where it can go'. Pound vetoed it again: 'I dare say the sweats with tears will wait.' It didn't wait long; we find it in a poem contributed pseudonymously to Wyndham Lewis' *Tyro* a little before the publication of *The Waste Land*, and later revised for publication in a triad of *Dream Songs*, all three of which may have descended from the *ur-Waste Land*.*

* Two of them, 'The wind sprang up' and 'Eyes that last I saw in tears', are preserved in the collected volume as 'Minor Poems'. The

Pound also dissuaded Eliot from installing 'Gerontion' as a prelude to the sequence, forebade him to delete 'Phlebas the Phoenician', and nagged about the Conrad epigraph until a better one was discovered in Petronius.

These events are worth reconstructing because they clarify a number of things about the scope and intention of the poem. It was conceived as a somewhat loose medley, as the relief of more diffuse impulses than those to which its present compacted form corresponds. The separate preservation of the *Dream Songs* and the incorporation of some of their motifs, after much trial and error, into what is now 'The Hollow Men', testifies to Eliot's stubborn conviction that there was virtue in some of the omitted elements, whether or not their presence could be justified within the wholeness, not at first foreseen by the author, which the greater part of *The Waste Land* at length assumed. That wholeness, since it never did incorporate everything the author wanted it to, was to some extent a compromise, got by permuting with another's assistance materials he no longer had it in him to rethink; and finally, after Pound, by simply eliminating everything not of the first intensity, had revealed an unexpected corporate substantiality in what survived, Eliot's impulse was to 'explain' the poem as 'thoughts of a dry brain in a dry season' by prefixing 'Gerontion'.

That is to say, the first quality of *The Waste Land* to catch a newcomer's attention, its self-sufficient juxtaposition without copulae of themes and passages in a dense mosaic, had at first a novelty which troubled even the author. It was a quality arrived at by Pound's cutting; it didn't trouble Pound, who had already begun work on *The Cantos*. But Eliot, preoccupied as always with the seventeenth-century drama and no doubt tacitly encouraged by the example of Browning, naturally conceived a long poem as somebody's spoken or unspoken monologue, its

---

third is now pt. iii of 'The Hollow Men'. The poem in the *Tyro* is called 'Song to the Opherian' and signed 'Gus Krutzsch', a portmanteau-name of which Kurtz seems to be one of the components. There are many small signs that 'The Hollow Men' grew from rejected pieces of *The Waste Land.*

shifts of direction and transition from theme to theme psychologically justified by the workings of the speakers' brain. 'Prufrock' and 'Gerontion' elucidate not only a phase of civilization but a perceiving – for the purpose of the poem, a presiding – consciousness. For anyone who has undergone immersion in the delicate phenomenology of Francis Herbert Bradley, in fact, it is meaningless to conceive of a presentation that cannot be resolved into an experienced content and a 'finite centre' which experiences. The perceiver is describable only as the zone of consciousness where that which he perceives can coexist; but the perceived, conversely, can't be accorded independent status; it is, precisely, all that can coexist in this particular zone of consciousness. In a loose sequence of poems these considerations need give no trouble; the pervading zone of consciousness is that of the author: as we intuit Herrick in *Hesperides*, or Herbert in *The Temple*. But a five-parted work of 433 lines entitled *The Waste Land*, with sudden wrenching juxtapositions, thematic links between section and section, fragments quoted from several languages with no one present to whose mind they can occur: this dense textural unity, as queer as *Le Sacre du Printemps*, must have seemed to Eliot a little factitious until he had got used to the poem in its final form; which, as everyone who has encountered it knows, must take some time. So we discover him endeavouring to square the artistic fact with his pervasive intuition of fitness by the note on Tiresias, which offers to supply the poem with a nameable point of view:

Tiresias, although a mere spectator and not indeed a 'character', is yet the most important personage in the poem, uniting all the rest. Just as the one-eyed merchant, seller of currants, melts into the Phoenician Sailor, and the latter is not wholly distinct from Ferdinand Prince of Naples, so all the women are one woman, and the two sexes meet in Tiresias. What Tiresias *sees*, in fact, is the substance of the poem.

If we take this note as an afterthought, a token placation, say, of the ghost of Bradley, rather than as elucidative of the assumption under which the writing was originally done, our approach to *The Waste Land* will be facilitated. In fact we shall do well to discard the notes as much as possible; they have bedevilled discussion for decades.

The writing of the notes was a last complication in the fractious history of the poem's composition; it is doubtful whether any other acknowledged masterpiece has been so heavily marked, with the author's consent, by forces outside his control. The notes got added to *The Waste Land* as a consequence of the technological fact that books are printed in multiples of thirty-two pages.

The poem, which had appeared without any annotation whatever in the *Criterion* and in the *Dial* (October and November, 1922, respectively), was in book form too long for thirty-two pages of decent-sized print and a good deal too short for sixty-four. So Eliot (at length disinclined, fortunately, to insert 'Gerontion' as a preface or to append the cancelled lyrics) set to work to expand a few notes in which he had identified the quotations, 'with a view to spiking the guns of critics of my earlier poems who had accused me of plagiarism'.* He dilated on the Tarot Pack, copied out nineteen lines from Ovid and thirty-three words from Chapman's *Handbook of Birds of Eastern North America*, recorded his evaluation of the interior of the Church of St Magnus Martyr, saluted the late Henry Clarke Warren as one of the great pioneers of Buddhist studies in the Occident, directed the reader's attention to a hallucination recorded on one of the Antarctic expeditions ('I forget which, but I think one of Shackleton's'), and eventually, with the aid of quotations from Froude, Bradley, and Hermann Hesse's *Blick ins Chaos*, succeeded in padding the thing out to a suitable length. The keying of these items to specific passages by the academic device of numbering lines – hence Eliot's pleasantry, twenty-four years later, about 'bogus scholarship' – may be surmised to have been done in haste: early in *What the Thunder Said* a line was missed in the counting. 'I have sometimes thought', Eliot

---

* This incredibly illiterate literary society seems to have been wholly unaware of the methods of Pope, or else to have supposed that a period allegedly devoted to 'profuse strains of unpremeditated art' had rendered such methods obsolete.

has said, 'of getting rid of these notes; but now they can never be unstuck. They have had almost greater popularity than the poem itself. . . . It was just, no doubt, that I should pay my tribute to the work of Miss Jessie Weston; but I regret having sent so many enquirers off on a wild goose chase after Tarot cards and the Holy Grail.' We have license therefore to ignore them, and instead 'endeavour to grasp what the poetry is aiming to be . . . to grasp its entelechy'.

That the entelechy is graspable without source-hunting, and without even appeal to any but the most elementary knowledge of one or two myths and a few Shakespearean tags, is a statement requiring temerity to sustain in the face of all the scholarship that has been expended during a third of a century on these 433 lines. It inheres, however, in Dr Leavis' admirably tactful account of the poem in *New Bearings*, and in Pound's still earlier testimony. In 1924 Pound rebutted a piece of reviewers' acrimony with the flat statement that the poem's obscurities were reducible to four Sanskrit words, three of which are

so implied in the surrounding text that one can pass them by . . . without losing the general tone or the main emotion of the passage. They are so obviously the words of some ritual or other.

[One does need to be told that 'shantih' means 'peace'.]

For the rest, I saw the poem in typescript, and I did not see the notes till 6 or 8 months afterward; and they have not increased my enjoyment of the poem one atom. The poem seems to me an emotional unit. . . .

I have not read Miss Weston's *Ritual to Romance*, and do not at present intend to. As to the citations, I do not think it matters a damn which is from Day, which from Milton, Middleton, Webster, or Augustine. I mean so far as the functioning of the poem is concerned. One's incult pleasure in reading *The Waste Land* would be the same if Webster had written 'Women Before Woman' and Marvell the *Metamorphoses*.

His parting shot deserves preservation:

This demand for clarity in every particular of a work, whether essential or not, reminds me of the Pre-Raphaelite painter who was doing a twilight scene but rowed across the river in day time to see the shape of the leaves on the further bank, which he then drew in with full detail.

II

A Game of Chess is a convenient place to start our investigations. Chess is played with Queens and Pawns: the set of pieces mimics a social hierarchy, running from 'The Chair she sat in, like a burnished throne', to 'Goonight Bill. Goonight Lou. Goonight May. Goonight.' It is a silent unnerving warfare

> ('Speak to me. Why do you never speak. Speak.
>   'What are you thinking of? What thinking? What?
> 'I never know what you are thinking. Think.')

in which everything hinges on the welfare of the King, the weakest piece on the board, and in this section of the poem invisible (though a 'barbarous king' once forced Philomel). Our attention is focused on the Queen.

> The Chair she sat in, like a burnished throne,
> Glowed on the marble, where the glass
> Held up by standards wrought with fruited vines
> From which a golden Cupidon peeped out
> (Another hid his eyes behind his wing)
> Doubled the flames of sevenbranched candelabra
> Reflecting light upon the table as
> The glitter of her jewels rose to meet it,
> From satin cases poured in rich profusion. . . .

This isn't a Miltonic sentence, brilliantly contorted; it lacks nerve, forgetting after ten words its confident opening ('The Chair she sat in') to dissipate itself among glowing and smouldering sensations, like a progression of Wagner's. Cleopatra 'o'erpicturing that Venus where we see/The fancy outwork nature') sat outdoors; this Venusberg interior partakes of 'an atmosphere of Juliet's tomb', and the human inhabitant appears once, in a perfunctory subordinate clause. Pope's Belinda conducted 'the sacred rites of pride' —

> This casket India's glowing gems unlocks,
> And all Arabia breathes from yonder box.

The woman at the dressing-table in *The Waste Land*, implied but never named or attended to, is not like Belinda the moral centre of an innocent dislocation of values, but simply the implied sensibility in which these multifarious effects dissolve and find congruence. All things deny nature; the fruited vines are carved, the Cupidons golden, the light not of the sun, the perfumes synthetic, the candelabra (seven-branched, as for an altar) devoted to no rite, the very colour of the fire-light perverted by sodium and copper salts. The dolphin is carved, and swims in a 'sad light', not, like Antony's delights, 'showing his back above the element he lives in'.

No will to exploit new sensations is present; the will has long ago died; this opulent ambience is neither chosen nor questioned. The 'sylvan scene' is not Eden nor a window but a painting, and a painting of an unnatural event:

> The change of Philomel, by the barbarous king
> So rudely forced; yet there the nightingale
> Filled all the desert with inviolable voice
> And still she cried, and still the world pursues,
> 'Jug Jug' to dirty ears.

Her voice alone, like the voice that modulates the thick fluid of this sentence, is 'inviolable'; like Tiresias in Thebes, she is prevented from identifying the criminal whom only she can name. John Lyly wrote down her song more than two centuries before Keats (who wasn't interested in what she was saying):

> What bird so sings yet so dos wayle?
> O 'Tis the ravishd Nightingale.
> Jug, Jug, Jug, tereu, shee cryes,
> And still her woes at Midnight rise.
> Brave prick song! . . .

Lyly, not being committed to the idea that the bird was pouring forth its soul abroad, noted that it stuck to its script ('prick song') and himself attempted a transcription. Lyly of course is perfectly aware of what she is trying to say: 'tereu' comes very close to 'Tereus'. It remained for the nineteenth century to dissolve her plight into a symbol of diffuse *Angst*, indeed to impute 'ecstasy' amid human desolation, 'here, where men sit and hear each other groan'; and for the twentieth century to hang up a painting of the event on a dressing-room wall, as pungent sauce to appetites jaded with the narrative clarity of mythologies, but responsive to the visceral thrill and the pressures of 'significant form'. The picture, a 'withered stump of time', hangs there, one item in a collection that manages to be not edifying but sinister:

> staring forms
> Leaned out, leaning, hushing the room enclosed.

Then the visitor, as always in Eliot, mounts a stairway –

> Footsteps shuffled on the stair.

– and we get human conversation at last:

> 'What is that noise?'
> The wind under the door.
> 'What is that noise now? What is the wind doing?'
> Nothing again nothing.
>   'Do
> 'You know nothing? Do you see nothing? Do you remember
> 'Nothing?'
>   I remember
> Those are pearls that were his eyes.

'My experience falls within my own circle, a circle closed on the outside; and, with all its elements alike, every sphere is opaque to the other which surrounded it.' What is there to say but 'nothing'? He remembers a quotation, faintly apposite; in this room the European past, effects and *objets d'art* gathered from many centuries, has suffered a sea-change, into something rich and strange, and stifling. Sensibility here is the very inhibition of life; and activity is reduced to the manic capering of 'that

Shakespeherian Rag', the past imposing no austerity, existing simply to be used.

> 'What shall we do tomorrow?'
> 'What shall we ever do?'
> The hot water at ten.
> And if it rains, a closed car at four.
> And we shall play a game of chess,
> Pressing lidless eyes and waiting for a knock upon the door.

If we move from the queens to the pawns, we find low life no more free or natural, equally obsessed with the denial of nature, artificial teeth, chemically procured abortions, the speaker and her interlocutor battening fascinated at second-hand on the life of Lil and her Albert, Lil and Albert interested only in spurious ideal images of one another

(He'll want to know what you done with that money he gave you
To get yourself some teeth. . . .
He said, I swear, I can't bear to look at you.)

And this point – nature everywhere denied, its ceremonies simplified to the brutal abstractions of a chess-game

(He's been in the army four years, he wants a good time,
And if you don't give it him, there's others will, I said.
Oh is there, she said. Something o' that, I said.
Then I'll know who to thank, she said, and give me a straight look.)

– this point is made implicitly by a device carried over from 'Whispers of Immortality', the juxtaposition without comment or copula of two levels of sensibility: the world of one who reads Webster with the world of one who knows Grishkin, the world of the inquiring wind and the sense drowned in odours with the world of ivory teeth and hot gammon. In Lil and Albert's milieu there is fertility, in the milieu where golden Cupidons peep out there is not; but Lil and Albert's breeding betokens not a harmony of wills but only Albert's improvident refusal to leave Lil alone. The chemist with commercial impartiality supplies one woman with 'strange synthetic perfumes' and the other with 'them pills I took, to bring it off', aphrodisiacs and abortifacients; he is the tutelary deity, uniting the offices of Cupid and Hymen, of a world which is under a universal curse.

From this vantage-point we can survey the methods of the first section, which opens with a denial of Chaucer:

> Whan that Aprille with his shoures soote
> The droughte of March hath perced to the roote
> And bathed every veyne in swich licour
> Of which vertu engendred is the flour. . . .
> Thanne longen folk to goon on pilgrimages. . . .

In the twentieth-century version we have a prayer-book heading, 'The Burial of the Dead', with its implied ceremonial of dust thrown and of souls reborn; and the poem begins,

> April is the cruellest month, breeding
> Lilacs out of the dead land, mixing
> Memory and desire, stirring
> Dull roots with spring rain.

No 'vertu' is engendered amid this apprehensive reaching forward of participles, and instead of pilgrimages we have European tours:

> we stopped in the colonnade,
> And went on in sunlight, into the Hofgarten,
> And drank coffee, and talked for an hour.

Up out of the incantation breaks a woman's voice, giving tongue to the ethnological confusions of the new Europe, the subservience of *patria* to whim of statesmen, the interplay of immutable fact and national pride:

> Bin gar keine Russin, stamm' aus Litauen, echt deutsch.

– a mixing of memory and desire. Another voice evokes the vanished Austro-Hungarian Empire, the inbred *malaise* of Mayerling, regressive thrills, objectless travels:

> And when we were children, staying at the archduke's,
> My cousin's, he took me out on a sled,
> And I was frightened. He said, Marie,

> Marie, hold on tight. And down we went.
> In the mountains, there you feel free.
> I read, much of the night, and go south in the winter.

'In the mountains, there you feel free.' We have only to delete 'there' to observe the collapse of more than a rhythm: to observe how the line's exact mimicry of a fatigue which supposes it has reached some ultimate perception can telescope spiritual bankruptcy, deracinated ardour, and an illusion of liberty which is no more than impatience with human society and relief at a temporary change. It was a restless, pointless world that collapsed during the war, agitated out of habit but tired beyond coherence, on the move to avoid itself. The memories in lines 8 to 18 seem spacious and precious now; then, the events punctuated a terrible continuum of boredom.

The plight of the Sibyl in the epigraph rhymes with that of Marie; the terrible thing is to be compelled to stay alive. 'For I with these my own eyes have seen the Cumaean Sibyl hanging in a jar; and when the boys said, "What do you want, Sibyl?" she answered, "I want to die." ' The sentence is in a macaronic Latin, posterior to the best age, pungently sauced with Greek; Cato would have contemplated with unblinking severity Petronius' readers' jazz-age craving for the cosmospolitan. The Sibyl in her better days answered questions by flinging from her cave handfuls of leaves bearing letters which the postulant was required to arrange in a suitable order; the wind commonly blew half of them away. Like Tiresias, like Philomel, like the modern poet, she divulged forbidden knowledge only in riddles, fitfully. (Tiresias wouldn't answer Oedipus at all; and he put off Odysseus with a puzzle about an oar mistaken for a winnowing-fan). *The Waste Land* is suffused with a functional obscurity, sibylline fragments so disposed as to yield the utmost in connotative power, embracing the fragmented present and reaching back to 'that vanished mind of which our mind is a continuation'. As for the Sibyl's present exhaustion, she had foolishly asked Apollo for as many years as the grains of sand in her hand; which is one layer in the multi-layered line, 'I will show you fear in a handful of dust.' She is the prophetic power, no longer consulted by heroes but tormented by curious boys, still answering because she must; she is Madame Sosostris, consulted by dear Mrs Equitone and harried by police ('One must be so careful these days'); she is the image of the late phase of Roman civilization, now vanished; she is also 'the mind of Europe', a mind more important than one's own private mind, a mind which changes but abandons nothing *en route*, not superannuating either Shakespeare, or Homer, or the rock drawing of the Magdalenian draughtsmen; but now very nearly exhausted by the effort to stay interested in its own contents.

Which brings us to the 'heap of broken images': not only desert ruins of some past from which life was withdrawn with the failure of the water supply, like the Roman cities in North Africa, or Augustine's Carthage, but also the manner in which Shakespeare, Homer, and the drawings of Michelangelo, Raphael, and the Magdalenian draughtsmen coexist in the contemporary cultivated consciousness: fragments, familiar quotations: *poluphloisboio thalasse*, to be or not to be, undo this button, one touch of nature, etc., God creating the Sun and Moon, those are pearls that were his eyes: For one man who knows *The Tempest* intimately there are a thousand who can identify the lines about the cloud-capp'd towers; painting is a miscellany of reproductions, literature a potpourri of quotations, history a chaos of theories and postures (Nelson's telescope, Washington crossing the Delaware, government of, for and by the people, the Colosseum, the guillotine). A desert wind has blown half the leaves away; disuse and vandals have broken the monuments –

> What are the roots that clutch, what branches grow
> Out of this stony rubbish? Son of man,
> You cannot say, or guess, for you know only
> A heap of broken images, where the sun beats,
> And the dead tree gives no shelter, the cricket no relief,
> And the dry stone no sound of water. . . .

Cities are built out of the ruins of previous cities, as *The Waste Land* is built out of the remains of older poems. But at this stage no building is yet in question; the 'Son of man' (a portentously generalizing phrase) is moving tirelessly eastward, when the speaker accosts him with a sinister 'Come in under the shadow of this red rock', and offers to show him not merely horror and desolation but something older and deeper: fear.

Hence the hyacinth girl, who speaks with urgent hurt simplicity, like the mad Ophelia:

> 'You gave me hyacinths first a year ago;
> They called me the hyacinth girl.'

They are childlike words, self-pitying, spoken perhaps in memory, perhaps by a ghost, perhaps by a wistful woman now out of her mind. The response exposes many contradictory layers of feeling:

> — Yet when we came back, late, from the Hyacinth garden,
> Your arms full, and your hair wet, I could not
> Speak, and my eyes failed, I was neither
> Living nor dead, and I knew nothing,
> Looking into the heart of light, the silence.

The context is erotic, the language that of mystical experience: plainly a tainted mysticism. 'The Hyacinth garden' sounds queerly like a lost cult's sacred grove, and her arms were no doubt full of flowers; what rite was there enacted or evaded we can have no means of knowing.

But another level of meaning is less ambiguous: perhaps in fantasy, the girl has been drowned. Five pages later 'A Game of Chess' ends with Ophelia's words before her death; Ophelia gathered flowers before she tumbled into the stream, then lay and chanted snatches of old tunes —

> Frisch weht der Wind
> Der Heimat zu . . .

while her clothes and hair spread out on the waters. 'The Burial of the Dead' ends with a sinister dialogue about a corpse in the garden —

> Has it begun to sprout? Will it bloom this year?
> Or has the sudden frost disturbed its bed?

— two Englishmen discussing their tulips, with a note of the
terrible intimacy with which murderers imagine themselves
being taunted. The traditional British murderer — unlike his
American counterpart, who in a vast land instinctively puts
distance between himself and the corpse — prefers to keep it
near at hand; in the garden, or behind the wainscoting, or

> bones cast in a little low dry garret,
> Rattled by the rat's foot only, year to year.

'The Fire Sermon' opens with despairing fingers clutching and
sinking into a wet bank; it closes with Thames-daughters
singing from beneath the oily waves. The drowned Phlebas in
Section IV varies this theme; and at the close of the poem the
response to the last challenge of the thunder alludes to something that happened in a boat:

> your heart would have responded
> Gaily, when invited, beating obedient
> To controlling hands

— but what in fact did happen we are not told; perhaps nothing,
or perhaps the hands assumed another sort of control.

In *The Waste Land* as in *The Family Reunion*, the guilt of
the protagonist seems coupled with his perhaps imagined
responsibility for the fate of a perhaps ideally drowned woman.

> One thinks to escape
> By violence, but one is still alone
> In an over-crowded desert, jostled by ghosts.

(Ghosts that beckon us under the shadow of some red rock)

> It was only reversing the senseless direction
> For a momentary rest on the burning wheel
> That cloudless night in the mid-Atlantic
> When I pushed her over

It must give this man an unusual turn when Madame Sosostris
spreads her pack and selects a card as close to his secret as the
Tarot symbolism can come:

> Here, said she,
> Is your card, the drowned Phoenician Sailor,
> (Those are pearls that were his eyes. Look!) –

and again:

> this card,
> Which is blank, is something he carries on his back
> Which I am forbidden to see.

(In what posture did they come back, late, from the Hyacinth Garden, her hair wet, before the planting of the corpse?) It is not clear whether he is comforted to learn that the clairvoyante does not find the Hanged Man.

Hence, then, his inability to speak, his failed eyes, his stunned movement, neither living nor dead and knowing nothing: as Sweeney later puts it,

> He didn't know if he was alive
>   and the girl was dead
> He didn't know if the girl was alive
>   and he was dead
> He didn't know if they both were alive
>   or both were dead. . . .

The heart of light, the silence, seems to be identified with a waste and empty sea, 'Oed' und leer das Meer'; so Harry, Lord Monchensey gazed, or thought he remembered gazing, over the rail of the liner:

> You would never imagine anyone could sink so quickly. . . .
> That night I slept heavily, alone. . . .
> I lay two days in contented drowsiness;
> Then I recovered.

He recovered into an awareness of the Eumenides.

At the end of 'The Burial of the Dead' it is the speaker's acquaintance Stetson who has planted a corpse in his garden and awaits its fantastic blooming 'out of the dead land': whether a hyacinth bulb or a dead mistress there is, in this phantasmagoric cosmos, no knowing. Any man, as Sweeney is to put it,

has to, needs to, wants to
Once in a lifetime, do a girl in.

Baudelaire agrees:

> Si le viol, le poison, le poignard, l'incendie,
> N'ont pas encore brodé de leurs plaisants dessins
> Le canevas banal de nos piteux destins,
> C'est que notre âme, hélas! n'est pas assez hardie.

This is from the poem which ends with the line Eliot has appropriated to climax the first section of *The Waste Land*:

> You! hypocrite lecteur! – mon semblable, – mon frère!

Part II, 'A Game of Chess' revolves around perverted nature, denied or murdered offspring; Part III, 'The Fire Sermon', the most explicit of the five sections, surveys with grave denunciatory candour a world of automatic lust, in which those barriers between person and person which so troubled Prufrock are dissolved by the suppression of the person and the transposition of all human needs and desires to a plane of genital gratification.

> The river's tent is broken: the last fingers of leaf
> Clutch and sink into the wet bank. The wind
> Crosses the brown land, unheard. The nymphs are departed.
> Sweet Thames, run softly, till I end my song.

The 'tent', now broken, would have been composed of the overarching trees that transformed a reach of the river into a tunnel of love; the phrase beckons to mind the broken maidenhead; and a line later the gone harmonious order, by a half-realizable metamorphosis, struggles exhausted an instant against drowning. 'The nymphs are departed' both because summer is past, and because the world of Spenser's 'Prothalamion' (when nymphs scattered flowers on the water) is gone, if it ever existed except as an ideal fancy of Spenser's.

> The river bears no empty boxes, sandwich papers,
> Silk handkerchiefs, cardboard boxes, cigarette ends
> Or other testimony of summer nights. The nymphs are departed.

From the 'brown land', amorists have fled indoors, but the river is not restored to a sixteenth-century purity because the debris of which it is now freed was not a sixteenth-century strewing of petals but a discarding of twentieth-century impedimenta. The nymphs who have this year departed are not the same nymphs who departed in autumn known to Spenser; their friends are 'the loitering heirs of city directors', who, unwilling to assume responsibility for any untoward pregnancies,

> Departed, have left no addresses.

Spring will return and bring Sweeney to Mrs Porter; Mrs Porter, introduced by the sound of horns and caressed by the moonlight while she laves her feet, is a latter-day Diana bathing; her daughter perhaps, or any of the vanished nymphs, a latter-day Philomel

> (So rudely forc'd.
> Tereu.)

Next Mr Eugenides proposes what appears to be a pederastic assignation; and next the typist expects a visitor to her flat.

The typist passage is the great *tour de force* of the poem; its gentle lyric melancholy, its repeatedly disrupted rhythms, the automatism of its cadences, in alternate lines aspiring and falling nervelessly –

> The time is now propitious, as he guesses,
> The meal is ended, she is bored and tired,
> Endeavours to engage her in caresses
> Which still are unreproved, if undesired.

– constitute Eliot's most perfect liaison between the self-sustaining gesture of the verse and the presented fact. Some twenty-five lines in flawlessly traditional iambic pentameter, alternately rhymed, sustain with their cadenced gravity a moral context in which the dreary business is played out; the texture is lyric rather than dramatic because there is neither doing nor suffering here but rather the mutual compliance of a ritual scene. The section initiates its flow with a sure and perfect line composed according to the best eighteenth-century models:

> At the violet hour, when the eyes and back

which, if the last word were, for instance, 'heart', we might
suppose to be by a precursor of Wordsworth's. But the harsh
sound and incongruous specification of 'back' shift us instead
to a plane of prosodic disintegration:

> when the eyes and back
> Turn upward from the desk, when the human engine waits
> Like a taxi throbbing waiting,

The upturned eyes and back – nothing else, no face, no torso –
recall a Picasso distortion; the 'human engine' throws pathos
down into mechanism. In the next line the speaker for the first
time in the poem identifies himself as Tiresias:

> I Tiresias, though blind, throbbing between two lives,
> Old man with wrinkled female breasts, can see . . .

There are three principal stories about Tiresias, all of them
relevant. In *Oedipus Rex*, sitting 'by Thebes below the wall' he
knew why, and as a consequence of what violent death and what
illicit amour, the pestilence had fallen on the unreal city, but
declined to tell. In the *Odyssey* he 'walked among the lowest of
the dead' and evaded predicting Odysseus' death by water; the
encounter was somehow necessary to Odysseus' homecoming,
and Odysseus was somehow satisfied with it, and did get home,
for a while. In the *Metamorphoses* he underwent a change of sex
for watching the coupling of snakes: presumably the occasion
on which he 'foresuffered' what is tonight 'enacted on this same
divan or bed'. He is often the prophet who knows but withholds
his knowledge, just as Hieronymo, who is mentioned at the close
of the poem, knew how the tree he had planted in his garden
came to bear his dead son, but was compelled to withhold that
knowledge until he could write a play which, like *The Waste
Land*, employs several languages and a framework of allusions
impenetrable to anyone but the 'hypocrite lecteur'. It is an inescapable shared guilt that makes us so intimate with the contents
of this strange deathly poem; it is also, in an age that has eaten of
the tree of the knowledge of psychology and anthropology

('After such knowledge, what forgiveness?'), an inescapable morbid sympathy with everyone else, very destructive to the coherent personality, that (like Tiresias' years as a woman) enables us to join with him in 'foresuffering all'. These sciences afford us an *illusion* of understanding other people, on which we build sympathies that in an ideal era would have gone out with a less pathological generosity, and that are as likely as not projections of our self-pity and self-absorption, vices for which Freud and Frazer afford dangerous nourishment. Tiresias is he who has lost the sense of other people as inviolably other, and who is capable neither of pity nor terror but only of a fascination spuriously related to compassion, which is merely the twentieth century's special mutation of indifference. Tiresias can see

> At the violet hour, the evening hour that strives
> Homeward, and brings the sailor home from sea,
> The typist home at teatime, clears her breakfast, lights
> Her stove, and lays out food in tins.

Syntax, like his sensibility and her routine, undergoes total collapse. A fine throbbing line intervenes:

> Out of the window perilously spread

and bathos does not wholly overtopple the completing Alexandrine:

> Her drying combinations touched by the sun's last rays.

'Combinations' sounds a little finer than the thing it denotes; so does 'divan':

> On the divan are piled (at night her bed)
> Stockings, slippers, camisoles and stays.

Some transfiguring word touches with glory line after line:

> He, the young man carbuncular, arrives,

If he existed, and if he read those words, how must he have marvelled at the alchemical power of language over his inflamed skin! As their weary ritual commences, the diction alters; it moves to a plane of Johnsonian dignity without losing touch with them; they are never 'formulated, sprawling on a pin'.

'Endeavours to engage her in caresses' is out of touch with the small house-agent's clerk's speech, but it is such a sentence as he might *write*; Eliot has noted elsewhere how 'an artisan who can talk the English language beautifully while about his work or in a public bar, may compose a letter painfully written in a dead language bearing some resemblance to a newspaper leader and decorated with words like "maelstrom" and "pandemonium" '. So it is with the diction of this passage: it reflects the words with which the participants might clothe, during recollection in tranquillity, their own notion of what they have been about, presuming them capable of such self-analysis; and it maintains simultaneously Tiresias' fastidious impersonality. The rhymes come with a weary inevitability that parodies the formal elegance of Gray; and the episode modulates at its close into a key to which Goldsmith can be transposed:

> When lovely woman stoops to folly and
> Paces about her room again, alone,
> She smoothes her hair with automatic hand,
> And puts a record on the gramophone.

With her music and her lures 'perilously spread' she is a London siren; the next line, 'This music crept by me upon the water', if it is lifted from the *Tempest*, might as well be adapted from the twelfth book of the *Odyssey*.

After the Siren, the violated Thames-daughters, borrowed from Wagner, the 'universal artist' whom the French Symbolists delighted to honour. The opulent Wagnerian pathos, with its harmonic rather than linear development and its trick of entrancing the attention with *leitmotifs*, is never unrelated to the methods of *The Waste Land*. One of the characters in 'A Dialogue on Dramatic Poetry', though he has railed at Wagner as 'pernicious', yet would not willingly resign his experience of Wagner; for Wagner had more than a bag of orchestral tricks and a corrupt taste for mythologies, he had also an indispensable sense of his own age, something that partly sustains and justifies his methods. 'A sense of his own age' – the ability to 'recognize its pattern while the pattern was yet incomplete' – was a quality Eliot in 1930 was to ascribe to Baudelaire.* One who has possessed it cannot simply be ignored, though he is exposed to the follies of his age as well as sensitive to its inventions. At the very least he comes to symbolize a phase in 'the mind of Europe' otherwise difficult to locate or name; at best, his methods, whether or not they merited his own fanaticism, are of permanent value to later artists for elucidating those phases of human sensibility to the existence of which they originally contributed. This principle is quite different from the academic or counter-academic notion that art must be deliberately adulterated because its preoccupations are.

Wagner, more than Frazer or Miss Weston, presides over the introduction into *The Waste Land* of the Grail motif. In Wagner's opera, the Sangreal quest is embedded in an opulent and depraved religiosity, as in Tennyson's *Holy Grail* the cup, 'rose-red, with beatings in it, as if alive, till all the white walls of my cell were dyed with rosy colours leaping on the wall', never succeeds in being more than the reward of a refined and sublimated erotic impulse. Again Eliot notes of Baudelaire that 'in much romantic poetry the sadness is due to the exploitation of the fact that no human relations are adequate to human desires, but also to the disbelief in any further object for human desires than that which, being human, fails to satisfy them'. The Grail was in mid-nineteenth-century art an attempt to postulate such an object; and the quest for that vision unites the poetry of baffled sadness to 'the poetry of flight', a genre which Eliot distinguishes in quoting Baudelaire's 'Quand partons-nous vers le bonheur?' and characterizes as 'a dim recognition of the direction of beatitude'.

So in Part V of *The Waste Land* the journey eastward among the red rocks and heaps of broken images is fused with the journey to Emmaus ('He who was living is now dead. We who

---

* The quoted phrases are from a book by Peter Quennell, which Eliot cites in his essay on Baudelaire.

were living are now dying') and the approach to the Chapel
Perilous.

The quester arrived at the Chapel Perilous had only to ask the
meaning of the things that were shown him. Until he has asked
their meaning, they have none; after he has asked, the king's
wound is healed and the waters commence again to flow. So in a
civilization reduced to 'a heap of broken images' all that is
requisite is sufficient curiosity; the man who asks what one or
another of these fragments means – seeking, for instance, 'a first-
hand opinion about Shakespeare' – may be the agent of regeneration. The past exists in fragments precisely because nobody cares
what it meant; it will unite itself and come alive in the mind of
anyone who succeeds in caring, who is unwilling that Shakespeare
shall remain the name attached only to a few tags everyone half-
remembers, in a world where 'we know too much, and are
convinced of too little'.

Eliot develops the nightmare journey with consummate skill,
and then manœuvres the reader into the position of the quester,
presented with a terminal heap of fragments which it is his
business to inquire about. The protagonist in the poem perhaps
does not inquire; they are fragments he has shored against his
ruins. Or perhaps he does inquire; he has at least begun to put
them to use, and the 'arid plain' is at length behind him.

The journey is prepared for by two images of asceticism: the
brand plucked from the burning, and the annihilation of Phlebas
the Phoenician. 'The Fire Sermon', which opens by Thames
water, closes with a burning, a burning that images the restless
lusts of the nymphs, the heirs of city directors, Mr Eugenides, the
typist and the young man carbuncular, the Thames-daughters.
They are unaware that they burn. 'I made no comment. What
should I resent?' They burn nevertheless, as the protagonist
cannot help noticing when he shifts his attention from commercial London to commercial Carthage (which stood on the
North African shore, and is now utterly destroyed). There
human sacrifies were dropped into the furnaces of Moloch, in a
frantic gesture of appeasement. There Augustine burned with
sensual fires: 'a cauldron of unholy loves sang all about mine

ears'; and he cried, 'O Lord, Thou pluckest me out.' The Buddhist ascetic on the other hand does not ask to be plucked out; he simply turns away from the senses because (as the Buddhist Fire Sermon states) they are each of them on fire. As for Phlebas the Phoenician, a trader sailing perhaps to Britain, his asceticism is enforced: 'A current under sea picked his bones in whispers', he forgets the benisons of sense, 'the cry of gulls and the deep sea swell' as well as 'the profit and loss', and he spirals down, like Dante's Ulysses, through circling memories of his age and youth, 'as Another chose'. (An account of a ship-wreck, imitated from the Ulysses episode in Dante, was one of the long sections deleted from the original *Waste Land*.) Ulysses in hell was encased in a tongue of flame, death by water having in one instance secured not the baptismal renunciation of the Old Adam, but an eternity of fire. Were there some simple negative formula for dealing with the senses, suicide would be the sure way to regeneration.

Part V opens, then, in Gethsemane, carries us rapidly to Golgotha, and then leaves us to pursue a nightmare journey in a world now apparently deprived of meaning.

> Here is no water but only rock
> Rock and no water and the sandy road
> The road winding above among the mountains
> Which are mountains of rock without water
> If there were water we should stop and drink. . . .

The whirling, obsessive reduplication of single words carries the travellers through a desert, through the phases of hallucination in which they number phantom companions, and closes with a synoptic vision of the destruction of Jerusalem ('Murmur of maternal lamentation' obviously recalling 'daughters of Jerusalem, weep not for me, but for yourselves and your children') which becomes *sub specie aeternitatis* the destruction by fire of civilization after civilization

> Jerusalem Athens Alexandria
> Vienna London
> Unreal

The woman at the dressing-table recurs:

> A woman drew her long black hair out tight
> And fiddled whisper music on those strings;

her 'golden Cupidons' are transmogrified:

> And bats with baby faces in the violet light
> Whistled, and beat their wings
> And crawled head downward down a blackened wall

and where towers hang 'upside down in air' stability is imaged by a deserted chapel among the mountains, another place from which the life has gone but in which the meaning is latent, awaiting only a pilgrim's advent. The cock crows as it did when Peter wept tears of penitence; as in *Hamlet*, it disperses the night-spirits.

> Then a damp gust
> Bringing rain.

There the activity of the protagonist ends. Some forty remaining lines in the past tense recapitulate the poem in terms of the oldest wisdom accessible to the West. The thunder's DA is one of those primordial Indo-European roots that recur in the *Oxford Dictionary*, a random leaf of the Sibyl's to which a thousand derivative words, now automatic currency, were in their origins so many explicit glosses. If the race's most permanent wisdom is its oldest, then DA, the voice of the thunder and of the Hindu sages, is the cosmic voice not yet dissociated into echoes. It underlies the Latin infinitive 'dare', and all its Romance derivatives; by a sound-change, the Germanic 'geben', the English 'give'. It is the root of 'datta', 'dayadhvam', 'damyata': give, sympathize, control: three sorts of giving. To sympathize is to give oneself; to control is to give governance.

> Then spoke the thunder
> DA
> *Datta*: what have we given?
> My friend, blood shaking my heart
> The awful daring of a moment's surrender
> Which an age of prudence can never retract
> By this, and this only, we have existed.

The first surrender was our parents' sexual consent; and when we are born again it is by a new surrender, inconceivable to the essentially satiric sensibility with which a Gerontion contemplates

> ... De Bailhache, Fresca, Mrs Cammel, whirled
> Beyond the circuit of the shuddering Bear,

and requiring a radical modification of even a Tiresias' negative compassion.

> The awful daring of a moment's surrender ...
> Which is not to be found in our obituaries
> Or in memories draped by the beneficent spider
> Or under seals broken by the lean solicitor
> In our empty rooms.

The lean solicitor, like the inquiring worm, breaks seals that in lifetime were held prissily inviolate; the will he is about to read registers not things given but things abandoned. The thunder is telling us what Tiresias did not dare tell Oedipus, the reason for the universal curse: 'What have we given?' As for 'Dayadhvam', 'sympathize':

> DA
> *Dayadhvam*: I have heard the key
> Turn in the door once and turn once only
> We think of the key, each in his prison
> Thinking of the key, each confirms a prison

– a prison of inviolate honour, self-sufficiency, like that in which Coriolanus locked himself away. Coriolanus' city was also under a curse, in which he participated. His energies sufficed in wartime (Eliot's poem was written three years after the close of the Great War), but in peacetime it becomes clear that 'he did it to please his mother, and to be partly proud'. He is advised to go through the forms of giving and sympathy, but

> [Not] by the matter which your heart prompts you,
> But with such words that are but rooted in
> Your tongue ...

After his banishment he goes out 'like to a lonely dragon', and plots the destruction of Rome. His final threat is to stand

> As if a man were author of himself
> And knew no other kin.

He is an energetic and purposeful Prufrock, concerned with the figure he cuts and readily humiliated; Prufrock's radical fault is not his lack of energy and purpose. Coriolanus is finally shattered like a statue; and if

> Only at nightfall, aethereal rumours
> Revive for a moment a broken Coriolanus,

it may be only as the Hollow Men in Death's dream kingdom hear voices 'in the wind's singing', and discern sunlight on a broken column. Do the rumours at nightfall restore him to momentary life, or restore his memory to the minds of other self-sufficient unsympathizing men?

> DA
> *Damyata*: The boat responded
> Gaily, to the hand expert with sail and oar
> The sea was calm, your heart would have responded
> Gaily, when invited, beating obedient
> To controlling hands

Unlike the rider, who may dominate his horse, the sailor survives and moves by co-operation with a nature that cannot be forced; and this directing, sensitive hand, feeling on the sheet the pulsation of the wind and on the rudder the momentary thrust of waves, becomes the imagined instrument of a comparably sensitive human relationship. If dominance compels response, control invites it; and the response comes 'gaily'. But — 'would have': the right relationship was never attempted.

> I sat upon the shore
> Fishing, with the arid plain behind me

The journey eastward across the desert is finished; though the king's lands are waste, he has arrived at the sea.

> Shall I at least set my lands in order?

Isaiah bade King Hezekiah set his lands in order because he was destined not to live; but Candide resolved to cultivate his own garden as a way of living. We cannot set the whole world in order; we can rectify ourselves. And we are destined to die, but such order as lies in our power is nevertheless desirable.

> London Bridge is falling down falling down falling down
> *Poi s'ascose nel foco che gli affina*
> *Quando fiam uti chelidon* – O swallow swallow
> *Le Prince d'Aquitaine à la tour abolie*
> These fragments I have shored against my ruins

An English nursery rhyme, a line of Dante's, a scrap of the late Latin 'Pervigilium Veneris', a phrase of Tennyson's ('O swallow, swallow, if I could follow') linked to the fate of Philomel, an image from a pioneer nineteenth-century French visionary who hanged himself on a freezing January morning: 'a heap of broken images', and a fragmentary conspectus of the mind of Europe. Like the Knight in the Chapel Perilous, we are to ask what these relics mean; and the answers will lead us into far recesses of tradition.

The history of London Bridge (which was disintegrating in the eighteenth century, and which had symbolized, with its impractical houses, a communal life now sacrificed to abstract transportation –

> A crowd flowed over London Bridge, so many,
> I had not thought death had undone so many.)

is linked by the nursery rhyme with feudal rituals ('gold and silver, my fair lady') and festivals older still. Dante's line focuses the tradition of Christian asceticism, in which 'burning' is voluntarily undergone. Dante's speaker was a poet:

> Ieu sui Arnaut, que plor e vau cantan;
> Consiros vei la passada folor,
> E vei jausen lo jorn, que'esper, denan. . . .

'Consiros vei la passada folor': compare 'With the arid plain

behind me'. 'Vau cantan': he goes singing in the fire, like the
children in the Babylonian furnace, not quite like Philomel
whose song is pressed out of her by the memory of pain. The
'Pervigilium Veneris' is another rite, popular, post-pagan, pre-
Christian, welcoming in the spring and inciting to love: 'Cras
amet qui numquam amavit'; he who has never loved, let him
love tomorrow; secular love, but its trajectory leads via the
swallow, aloft. Tennyson's swallow nearly two thousand years
later ('if I could follow') flies away from an earthbound poet,
grounded in an iron time, and meditating 'la poésie des départs'.
That poem is a solo, not a folk ritual. As for the Prince of
Aquitaine with the ruined tower, he is one of the numerous
personae Gérard Nerval assumes in 'El Desdichado': 'Suis-je
Amour ou Phébus, Lusignan ou Biron?' as the speaker of *The
Waste Land* is Tiresias, the Phoenician Sailor, and Ferdinand
Prince of Naples. He has lingered in the chambers of the sea

> J'ai rêvé dans la grotte où nage la sirene . . .

and like Orpheus he has called up his love from the shades:

> Et j'ai deux fois vainqueur traversé l'Achéron
> Modulant tour à tour sur la lyre d'Orphée
> Les soupirs de la sainte et les cris de la fée.

So *The Waste Land* contains Augustine's cries and the song of
the Thames-daughters; but de Nerval, the pioneer Symbolist,
is enclosed in a mood, in a poetic state, surrounded by his own
symbols ('Je suis le ténébreux, – le veuf, – l'inconsolé'), offering
to a remembered order, where the vine and the rose were one,
only the supplication of a dead man's hand, 'Dans la nuit du
tombeau', where 'ma seule étoile est morte': under the twinkle
of a fading star. It is some such state as his, these images suggest,
that is to be explored in *The Hollow Men*; he inhabits death's
dream kingdom. The mind of Europe, some time in the nineteenth century, entered an uneasy phase of sheer dream.

> These fragments I have shored against my·ruins
> Why then Ile fit you. Hieronymo's mad againe.

Here Eliot provides us with a final image for all that he has done: his poem is like Hieronymo's revenge-play. Hieronymo's enemies — the public for the poet in our time — commission an entertainment:

> It pleased you,
> At the entertainment of the ambassador,
> To grace the king so much as with a show.
> Now, were your study so well furnished,
> As for the passing of the first night's sport
> To entertain my father with the like
> Or any such-like pleasing motion,
> Assure yourself, it would content them well.
> *Hier:* Is this all?
> *Bal:*   Ay, this is all.
> *Hier:* Why then, I'll fit you. Say no more.
> When I was young, I gave my mind
> And plied myself to fruitless poetry;
> Which though it profit the professor naught,
> Yet is it passing pleasing to the world.

It profits the professor naught, like Philomel's gift of songs and pleases those who have no notion of what it has cost, of what it will ultimately cost them. Hieronymo goes on to specify:

> Each one of us
> Must act his part in unknown languages,
> That it may breed the more variety:
> As you, my lord, in Latin, I in Greek,
> You in Italian, and for because I know
> That Bellimperia hath practised the French,
> In courtly French shall all her phrases be.

Each of these languages occurs in *The Waste Land*; all but Greek, in the list of shored fragments. Balthasar responds, like a critic in the *New Statesman*,

> But this will be a mere confusion,
> And hardly shall we all be understood.

Hieronymo, however, is master of his method:

It must be so: for the conclusion
Shall prove the invention and all was good.

Hieronymo's madness, in the context provided by Eliot, is that of the Platonic bard. If we are to take the last two lines of *The Waste Land* as the substance of what the bard in his sibylline trance has to say, then the old man's macaronic tragedy appears transmuted into the thunder's three injunctions, Give, Sympathize, Control, and a triple 'Peace', 'repeated as here', says the note, 'a formal ending to an Upanishad'.

III

Within a few months Eliot found himself responsible for a somewhat bemusing success. The poem won the 1922 *Dial* award; the first impression of one thousand copies was rapidly succeeded by a second; it was rumoured that the author had perpetrated a hoax; the line 'Twit twit twit' was not liked; the 'parodies' were pronounced 'inferior' by Mr F. L. Lucas; Arnold Bennett inquired of the author whether the notes were 'a lark or serious', and was careful to specify that the question was not insulting. The author said that 'they were serious, and not more of a skit than some things in the poem itself'. Mr Bennett said that he couldn't see the point of the poem. The *Times Literary Supplement* reviewer felt that Mr Eliot was sometimes walking very near the limits of coherency, but that when he had recovered control we should expect his poetry to have gained in variety and strength from this ambitious experiment.

He had written a poem which expressed for many readers their sense of not knowing what to do with themselves; as he later put it, with Bradleyan subtlety, 'their illusion of being disillusioned'. He was credited with having created a new mode of poetic organization, as he had, though specific instances of the cinematic effect were as likely as not attributable to Pound's cutting. Also he was singled out as the man who had written an unintelligible poem, and *with notes*. The author and annotator of this 'piece that passeth understanding' was not insensitive to

the resulting climate of jest. Six years later he capped a comparison between Crashaw and Shelley by calling for elucidation of
the 'Keen as are the arrows' stanza of 'To a Skylark': 'There may
be some clue for persons more learned than I; but Shelley should
have provided notes.'

David Craig

THE DEFEATISM OF
THE WASTE LAND (1960)

T. S. ELIOT's *The Waste Land* is one of the outstanding cases in
modern times of a work which projects an almost defeatist
personal depression in the guise of a full, impersonal picture of
society. Lawrence's *Women in Love* is a much more substantial
case of the same thing, but the response it demands is much less
easy. Both, however, in my experience, encourage in readers,
especially young students, a sort of superior cynicism which
flatters the educated man by letting him feel that he is left as the
sole bearer of a fine culture which the new mass-barbarians have
spurned and spoiled. Eliot has characteristically slid out of
responsibility in the matter by means of his remark that *The
Waste Land* pleased people because of 'their own illusion of
being disillusioned'.[1] But, I suggest, the essential (and very
original) method of his poem and the peculiar sense of life
which it mediates are such that they invite that very response –
and get it from the most considerable critics as well as from
young cynics.

Before considering *The Waste Land* itself, it will be as well to
quote a case of that view of the modern 'plight' which the poem
has licensed, or seemed sufficient grounds for. Summing up the
social state of affairs which he sees as the basis for the poem's
'rich disorganisation', F. R. Leavis writes: 'The traditions and
cultures have mingled, and the historical imagination makes the
past contemporary; no one tradition can digest so great a variety
of materials, and the result is a break-down of forms and the
irrevocable loss of that sense of absoluteness which seems
necessary to a robust culture.'[2] This is suggestive, and 'that
sense of absoluteness' implies a more felt idea of what modern
rapid change has done to us than is usual in admirers of

'the organic community'. But consider what it leads on to:

In the modern Waste Land

> April is the cruellest month, breeding
> Lilacs out of the dead land,

but bringing no quickening to the human spirit. Sex here is sterile, breeding not life and fulfilment but disgust, accidia, and unanswerable questions. It is not easy today to accept the perpetuation and multiplication of life as ultimate ends.[3]

The logic of this is by no means consecutive: the critic is moving with shifts which seem not quite conscious, between life itself and the poem treated as a report on life. When he writes, 'Sex here is sterile', although the immediate reference of 'here' seems to be the world of the poem, the quick shift to 'today', which must refer directly to real life here and now, suggests that Dr Leavis considers the experience in *The Waste Land* a self-evident, perfectly acceptable version of the world we and the poet live in. That is the kind of assumption, and the pessimistic thought behind it, which I wish to challenge.

The technique of *The Waste Land* is very various; it gives the impression (compared with, say, Pound's *Cantos*) of rich, or intensely-felt, resources both of literature and of life direct. But one method stands out: that way of running on, with no marked break and therefore with a deadpan ironical effect, from one area of experience, one place or time or speech or social class, to another. Section II, 'A Game of Chess', throws shifting lights on the woman protagonist by changes of style. At first Cleopatra is present, but a Cleopatra who lives in an indoor, lifelessly ornate setting:

> The Chair she sat in, like a burnished throne,
> Glowed on the marble, where the glass
> Held up by standards wrought with fruited vines
> From which a golden Cupidon peeped out
> (Another hid his eyes behind his wing)
> Doubled the flame of sevenbranched candelabra
> Reflecting light upon the table as
> The glitter of her jewels rose to meet it . . .

By this point she has become Belinda from *The Rape of the Lock*, living in a world of 'things', make-up, dress, *bijouterie* – in Veblen's phrase, conspicuous consumption. But the modern poet does not have a mocking relish for the woman, as did Pope:

> This casket India's glowing gems unlocks,
> And all Arabia breathes from yonder box.
> The tortoise here and elephant unite,
> Transform'd to combs, the speckled and the white.
> Here files of pins extend their shining rows,
> Puffs, powders, patches, Bibles, billet-doux.

By the end of the equivalent passage in *The Waste Land*, the woman is not even Belinda, moving with assurance in her idle, expensive world. She is a neurotic who cannot stand being alone with her own thoughts – a type psychologically and socially akin to Eveline Hutchins who kills herself at the end of John Dos Passos's trilogy *U.S.A.* The change is given in the shift from a quite richly 'literary' diction –

> Under the firelight, under the brush, her hair
> Spread out in fiery points
> Glowed into words, then would be savagely still –

to a bitty, comparatively unshaped, modern spoken English (though the repetitiveness is cunningly stylised):

> 'My nerves are bad to-night. Yes, bad. Stay with me.
> 'Speak to me. Why do you never speak. Speak.
> 'What are you thinking of? What thinking? What?
> 'I never know what you are thinking. Think.'

The effect is of landing up with final disenchantment face to face with the unpleasant reality of life today.

There is then, in mid-section, a change of social class, from wealthy life ('The hot water at ten./And if it rains, a closed car at four') to ordinary ('When Lil's husband got demobbed, I said . . .'). But life is fruitless here too, and the poet's aloof revulsion is conveyed by similar means. The working-class women in the pub talk about false teeth, abortions, promiscuous sexual rivalry between the wives of Great War soldiers, in a lingo which sprawls over any kind of formal elegance of metre or rhyme; and the poet does not intrude on the common speech until the closing line:

> Goonight Bill. Goonight Lou. Goonight May. Goonight
> Ta ta. Goonight. Goonight.
> Good night, ladies, good night, sweet ladies, good night,
> good night.

'Sweet ladies' – the irony is, to say the least, obvious. As well as the effect of 'sweet' there is the reminiscence of the innocently hearty student song (this seems more relevant than Ophelia's mad snatch in *Hamlet*). The effect is identical with what he does by incorporating Goldsmith's ditty from *The Vicar of Wakefield* at the end of the typist's dreary seduction in 'The Fire Sermon':

> 'Well now that's done: and I'm glad it's over.'
> When lovely woman stoops to folly and
> Paces about her room again, alone ...

This technique, which is typical of the transitions of tone and of the collocation of two cultures which occur throughout the poem, seems to me unsatisfactory in two ways. The irony is no finer than ordinary sarcasm – the simple juxtaposing of messy reality and flattering description (as in a common phrase like 'You're a pretty sight'). The pub women and the typist have been made so utterly sour and unlovely that the poet's innuendo, being unnecessary, does no more than hint at his own superior qualities. Secondly, using earlier literature to embody the better way of life which is the poet's ideal depends on a view of the past which is not made good in the poem (it hardly could be) and which the reader may well not share – unless he is pessimistic. Consider some further instances. The Thames as it is now is given thus at the beginning of 'The Fire Sermon':

> Sweet Thames, run softly till I end my song.
> The river bears no empty bottles, sandwich papers,
> Silk handkerchiefs, cardboard boxes, cigarette ends
> Or other testimony of summer nights ...

The life evoked here is unpleasant – but so is the poet's attitude, notably the pointed but prudishly or suggestively tacit hint at contraceptives. At the same time, for us to respond as the poet means, we have to accept his glamourising view of Spenser's London, Elizabethan England with its pure rivers and stately ways. The same suggestion occurs in the lyrical passage which is meant to parallel the Rhinemaidens' song from *Götterdämmerung*. Modern:

> The river sweats
> Oil and tar
> The barges drift
> With the turning tide ...
> The barges wash
> Drifting logs
> Down Greenwich reach
> Past the Isle of Dogs.

Renaissance:

> Elizabeth and Leicester
> Beating oars
> The stern was formed
> A gilded shell
> Red and gold
> The brisk swell
> Rippled both shores ...

The poet's meaning is clear: modern civilisation does nothing but spoil what was once gracious, lovely, ceremonious, and natural.

Here it must be said that the poet's comparative view of old and modern culture is not quite one-sided. As Hugh Kenner suggests, it may not be implied that Spenser's nymph-world 'ever existed except as an ideal fancy of Spenser's',[4] and as Cleanth Brooks suggests, the Elizabeth passage has 'a sort of double function': historically, Elizabeth flirted so wantonly with Leicester, in the presence of the Spanish bishop de Quadra, that Cecil at last suggested that as there was a bishop on the spot they might as well be married there and then (Froude's *Elizabeth*, quoted in Eliot's note). As Brooks says, the passage 'reinforces the general contrast between Elizabethan magnificence and modern sordidness: in the Elizabethan age love for love's sake has some meaning and therefore some magnificence. But the passage gives something of an opposed effect too: the same sterile love, emptiness of love, obtained in this period too: Elizabeth and the typist are alike as well as different.' 5 In the whole poem, however, it is certainly old magnificence which is given the advantage, and it is as well to say straight out that this is an absurdly partial outlook on culture – groundlessly idealising about the old and warped in its revulsion from the modern. If magnificence is desired, modern life can supply it well enough, whether the show of Royalty or big-business ostentation. And if one thinks of the filth, poverty, superstition, and brutal knock-about life invariable in town or country four centuries ago, one realises how fatuous it is to make flat contrasts between then and now. History, reality, are being manipulated to fit an escapist kind of prejudice, however detached the writer may feel himself to be.

As one would expect, the cultural warp has as strong an equivalent in the poet's way of presenting personal experience. Consider the attitudes implied in the seduction of the typist. In this most cunningly-managed episode, one is induced to feel, by means of the fastidiously detached diction and movement, that a scene part commonplace, part debased, is altogether unpleasant. The experience is a more intimate meeting between people than Eliot deals with directly anywhere else in his work, but here is the style he finds for it:

> He, the young man carbuncular, arrives,
> A small house agent's clerk, with one bold stare,
> One of the low on whom assurance sits
> As a silk hat on a Bradford millionaire.
> The time is now propitious, as he guesses,
> The meal is ended, she is bored and tired,
> Endeavours to engage her in caresses
> Which still are unreproved, if undesired.
> Flushed and decided, he assaults at once;
> Exploring hands encounter no defence;
> His vanity requires no response,
> And makes a welcome of indifference.

The unfeeling grossness of the experience is held off at the finger-
tips by the analytic, unphysical diction – 'Endeavours to engage
her in caresses' – and by the movement, whose even run is not
interrupted by the violence of what is 'going on'. The neat
assimilation of such life to a formal verse paragraph recalls
Augustan modes. But if one thinks of the sexual passage concerning the 'Imperial Whore' in Dryden's translation of Juvenal's
sixth Satire, or even the one concerning the unfeeling Chloe in
Pope's *Moral Essay* 'Of the Characters of Women',[6] one realises
that the Augustans did not stand off from the physical with anything like Eliot's distaste. Eliot's style is carefully impersonal; it
enumerates with fastidious care the sordid details:

> On the divan are piled (at night her bed)
> Stocking, slippers, camisoles, and stays.

But here one has doubts. This is given as a typically comfortless
modern apartment, suggesting a life which lacks the right pace,
the right sociableness, the right instinctive decency for it to merit
the name of civilisation. (Were Elizabethan houses and habits any
better?) But the touch in the second line feels uncertain: is the
heavily careful art with which the line is built up not too contrived for the rather ordinary modern habit it is meant to satirise?
When we come to 'carbuncular' – an adjective which, placed after
the noun and resounding in its slow movement and almost orna-
mental air, is deliberately out of key with the commonplace life
around it – I think we begin to feel that Eliot's conscious
literariness is working, whatever his intention, more to hold at
arm's length something which he personally shudders at than to
convey a poised criticism of behaviour.[7] There is a shudder in
'carbuncular'; it is disdainful, but the dislike is disproportionately
strong for its object; queasy emotions of the writer's seem to be
at work.[8] The snobbery is of a piece with this. 'He is a nobody –
a mere clerk, and clerk to a *small* house agent at that. What right
has *he* to look assured?' That is the suggestion; and we are also
left wondering what warrant the poet has for uniting himself
with some class finer, it seems, than the provincial bourgeoisie.

And the passage ends with the snatch of Goldsmith, 'When lovely woman stoops to folly':

> She smoothes her hair with automatic hand,
> And puts a record on the gramophone.

Here the nerveless movement and the ordinariness of the detail are deftly managed. And the human poverty of the scene has never been in doubt. But the writer's means of conveying *his valuation* of it are surely objectionable. One may agree or not that modern civilisation has its own kind of health; one may agree or not that the petty bourgeoisie are a decent class. But one must surely take exception to a method which seeks its effects through an irony which is no more than smart sarcasm. It is amazing that Dr Leavis should speak of 'delicate collocations',[9] when the contrasts are regularly so facile in their selection of old grandeur and modern squalor.

To put the matter in terms which refer directly to life: if, as Brooks says, 'the same sterile love, emptiness of love, obtained in this period too', then why does the criticism work so consistently against contemporary civilisation? And when Dr Leavis says, 'Sex here is sterile', does he really mean that love between men and women has deteriorated as a whole? (One remembers similar extraordinary suggestions about intercourse now and formerly in *Lady Chatterley's Lover*.) The historian tells us that in Renaissance England,

> Wife-beating was a recognised right of man, and was practised without shame by high as well as low. Similarly, the daughter who refused to marry the gentleman of her parents' choice was liable to be locked up, beaten, and flung about the room, without any shock being inflicted on public opinion. Marriage was not an affair of personal affection but of family avarice, particularly in the 'chivalrous' upper classes.[10]

I think we may take it that the comparison of cultures to the advantage· of the older is either impossible, pointless, or else feasible only by specific fields and not overall.[11] The question remains why critics have surrendered so gratefully to an almost nastily despairing view of the civilisation we live in. This occurs in Leavis's *New Bearings* and Edmund Wilson's *Axel's Castle*.[12] It is seen at its most irresponsible in Hugh Kenner's glib explication of the pub scene: 'If we move from the queens to the pawns, we find low life no more free or natural, equally obsessed with the denial of nature, artificial teeth, chemically procured abortions, the speaker and her interlocutor battening fascinated at second-hand on the life of Lil and her Albert, Lil and Albert interested only in spurious ideal images of one another.'[13] 'Battening fascinated at second-hand' means no more than 'listening with interest to the tale of someone else's experiences': Mr Kenner's condemnation comes from the general atmosphere of moral depression which the poem generates rather than from anything established by the dramatic speech of that scene – here the critic's sourness outdoes the poet's. And the reference to false teeth, lumped with abortions, as though false teeth were not simply an admirable achievement of medical science in giving comfort where nature has broken down, is a glaring case of that blind dislike of science which nowadays has become an intellectual's disease. It is primitivist; and it thoughtlessly ignores the experience involved.

Dr Leavis's adherence to the old culture is much more scrupulously worked out, and must be considered by itself. A key term in that part of *New Bearings* (as in his early *Scrutiny* editorials) is 'continuity':

In considering our present plight we have also to take account of the incessant rapid change that characterises the Machine Age. The result is breach of continuity and the uprooting of life. This last metaphor has a peculiar aptness, for what we are witnessing today is the final uprooting of the immemorial ways of life, of life rooted in the soil. . . . There are ways in which it is possible to be too conscious; and to be so is, as a result of the break-up of forms and the loss of axioms noted above, one of the troubles of the present age. . . .[14]

Now, it would be foolish to burke the truth that the rapid disruption started by the Industrial Revolution undermined, and actually demoralised, the masses who were uprooted from the country and flung into the towns. But there are ways and ways of viewing this change – defeatist ways and constructive ways. The description of the old village culture which opens Engels's *Condition of the Working Class in England in 1844*[15] is remarkably similar to the main 'line' of *Scrutiny*; it belongs to the same humane tradition of protest at the harrow of industrialism. But realisation of such sufferings and social deterioration may lead on to a practical will to reconstruct, using the new social instruments, or it may lead on to a really helpless fixation on the past which comes from a distaste for the raw difficulties and uncomelinesses of the life around us. An outlook which assumes the fineness of the older culture belongs to the defeatist class. Dr Leavis of course cannot back up his assumptions in a book mainly on modern poetry. But if we are to keep our thought grounded, we must notice that the obverse could be stated to every one of the advantages he sees in the 'organic' culture. Marx and Engels no doubt went too far the other way when they referred summarily to 'the idiocy of rural life'.[16] But when we speak of immemorial ways of life, we must remember how cramped a range of vocations they offered: consider the release of wider human talents made possible by the growth of technology and of organisation (both treated as evils by the *Scrutiny* critics). The village life was socially healthy in various ways, but it also ground down people cruelly: consider the lives of Burns and Gorky. When 'axioms' are mentioned, we must remember that they reflected fixed habits which held human possibilities in rigid bounds. I have suggested that it is futile to draw up an overall comparison between the old and contemporary types of culture. This is partly because we are now as we are; we have the means we now have; it is these alone that we can use. Therefore the only positive course is to co-operate with the hopeful present trends. No one saw more piercingly into the anti-human effects of industrial labour as it once was than Marx; but he knew that that was the very means by which we must win through to the *new* good life. He gives this balance of possibilities in passages such as these from *Capital*, vol. I:

Modern Industry, on the other hand, through its catastrophes imposes the necessity of recognising, as a fundamental law of production, variation of work, consequently fitness of the labourer for varied work, consequently the greatest possible development of his varied aptitudes. . . . Modern Industry, indeed, compels society, under penalty of death, to replace the detail-worker of today, crippled by lifelong repetition of one and the same trivial operation, and thus reduced to the mere fragment of a man, by the fully developed individual, fit for a variety of labours, ready to face any change of production, and to whom the different social functions he performs are but so many modes of giving free scope to his own natural and acquired powers.

(As a step towards this he then cites the setting up of agricultural and technical schools.) And again:

However terrible and disgusting the dissolution, under the capitalist system, of the old family ties may appear, nevertheless, modern industry, by assigning as it does an important part in the process of production, outside the domestic sphere, to women, to young persons, and to children of both sexes, creates a new economical foundation for a higher form of the family and of the relations between the sexes . . . the fact of the collective working group being composed of individuals of both sexes and all ages, must necessarily, under suitable conditions, become a source of humane development.[17] . . .

The Waste Land, then, seems to me to work essentially against life, for the range of opinions it mobilises, that come welling up in response to it, are all negative. In the final section Eliot uses the philosophy of F. H. Bradley. The lines

> I have heard the key
> Turn in the door once and turn once only
> We think of the key, each in his prison
> Thinking of the key, each confirms a prison . . .

he himself glosses from Bradley's *Appearance and Reality*:

My external sensations are no less private to myself than are my thought or my feelings. In either case my experience falls within my own circle, a circle closed on the outside; and, with all its elements alike, every sphere is opaque to the others which surround it . . . In brief, regarded as an existence which appears in a soul, the whole world for each is peculiar and private to that soul.[18]

This thought of Bradley's has led on to that barren line of philosophy which includes John Wisdom's *Other Minds*. To say what must suffice here: if our sensations, thoughts, and feelings are perfectly private and the sphere of each person's life 'opaque', how is it that speech and literature themselves are intelligible — and intelligible so fully and intimately that to reach understanding with a person or appreciate a piece of writing can seem to take us inside another existence? That the question of whether one mind can get through to another should even have arisen seems to me a perversion of thought. (Historically, it is perhaps a cast from the anti-co-operative state of existence brought about by entrepreneur capitalism. It seems similar to the helplessly solipsistic 'denial of objective truth' which Lenin refutes in *Materialism and Empirio-Criticism*. In each case the individual ego relies less and less on anything outside itself.)

The obscurity of *The Waste Land* is significant likewise, for though the trained reader no longer jibs at it, it is certainly impossible that it should ever become popular reading as did earlier important literature (Burns, Byron, George Eliot, D. H. Lawrence). Dr Leavis writes on the issue of 'minority culture' which this raises: 'that the public for it is limited is one of the symptoms of the state of culture which produced the poem. Works expressing the finest consciousness of the age in which the word "high-brow" has become current are almost inevitably such as to appeal only to a tiny minority.' [19] The argument that follows is dubious at a number of points. In the first place, Lawrence expressed many sides of the 'finest consciousness of the age' and he has been read in cheap editions by the million (as has Gorky in the Soviet Union and James T. Farrell in the United States). The usual obstinately pessimistic reply is that 'They only read Lawrence for the sex, or the love story'. But this is only reaching for another stick to beat the times, for is it not good that a major writer should have devoted himself to the universal subject of love and sex? Dr Leavis goes on to say that the idea that the poem's obscurity is symptomatic of our cultural condition 'amounts to an admission that there must be something limited about the kind of artistic achievement possible in our time'. But if this were so, how account for the work of Lawrence and of the many other considerable novelists of our time? Finally his question 'how large in any age has the minority been that has really comprehended the masterpieces?' contains an equivocation – 'really'. If one sets the highest standard, of course 'real' (that is, full) comprehension is attained by few; but if the numbers of even the *total* public reached are small, as has happened with *The Waste Land*, then there is indeed a significant difference between its meaningfulness and appeal for readers and that which the major novelists have regularly achieved (George Eliot, Hardy, Lawrence, Tolstoy, Gorky, Farrell). *The Waste Land*, in short, is *not* the representative work of the present age, and to make it so implies that pessimistic view of the present age which I have already challenged.

What has been made of *The Waste Land* illustrates two more issues important in our times. It is significant that Dr Leavis should meet the charge that the poem is a 'dead end', literarily and morally. When he says, 'So complete and vigorous a statement of the Waste Land could hardly . . . forecast an exhausted and hopeless sojourn there',[20] he implies a proper distinction between Eliot's quality of art and that of Pound's *Cantos* or Joyce's *Ulysses* – both recognisably from the same line of art distorted by the break-up of cultural forms. *The Waste Land*, it is true, does not cut life into bits and juggle them into patterns interesting only for their intricacy, or meaningful only to their manipulator. At the same time there turns out to be little that Dr Leavis can plead convincingly when he has to say what way beyond the Waste Land Eliot found. He quotes some bracing sermons from the *Criterion*: 'a tendency – discernible even in art – towards a higher and clearer conception of Reason, and a more severe and serene control of the emotions by Reason', and 'the generation which is beginning to turn its attention to an athleticism, a *training*, of the soul as severe and ascetic as the training of the body of a runner'.[21] The vague 'dedication' of this recalls the loftiness with no definite direction which characterised the more serious of the *fin de siècle* writers, notably Yeats, when they were being Hellenic or religiose. Its abstractness, its lack of reference to any social facts, suggests Eliot's inveterate drift away from anything progressive in society with which he might have co-operated in a practical way.[22]

The wider affiliations of such defeatism come out in the agreement Eliot and Leavis reach on 'eastern Europe'. Eliot's note introducing the final section of the poem says: 'In the first part of Part V three themes are employed: the journey to Emmaus, the approach to the Chapel Perilous (see Miss Weston's book) and the present decay of eastern Europe.'[23] This is very bland. The final phrase has that characteristic air of stating the unanswerable – he would explain further if he wished but he does not condescend to. Actually it must have behind it the most reactionary politics. How did Bela Kun's Communist régime in Hungary, for example, represent decay? or is Eliot sympathising with the Russian Tsars?[24] Dr Leavis's interpretation is still more unacceptable: 'These "hooded hordes", "ringed by the flat horizon only", are not merely Russians, suggestively related to the barbarian invaders of civilisation.[25] . . .' Eliot's poem, we need only recall, was being written when the civilised armies of Britain, America, France, and Japan were invading Russia on twenty-three fronts.[26] But there is nothing with which the pessimistic liberal *can* associate himself – neither the new civilisation which is being founded in the East nor the ordinary life of the West which he is so ready to write off.[27]

NOTES

1. T. S. Eliot, 'Thoughts after Lambeth', in *Selected Essays* (1951 ed.) p. 368.
2. *New Bearings in English Poetry* (1950 ed.) pp. 90–1.
3. Ibid. p. 93.
4. *The Invisible Poet: T. S. Eliot* (New York, 1959) p. 165.

5. Cleanth Brooks, Jr, '*The Waste Land*: An Analysis', in *Southern Review* (Louisiana State University, Summer 1937) vol. III, no. 1, p. 123.

6. Dryden, 'The Sixth Satyr' of Juvenal, 11. 161–89; Pope, 'Of the Characters of Women', 11. 157–70.

7. Compare Lawrence's analysis of Thomas Mann: 'Thomas Mann, like Flaubert, feels vaguely that he has in him something finer than ever physical life revealed. Physical life is a disordered corruption against which he can fight with only one weapon, his fine aesthetic sense, his feeling for beauty, for perfection, for a certain fitness which soothes him, and gives him an inner pleasure, however corrupt the stuff of life may be.... And so, with real suicidal intention, like Flaubert's, he sits, a last too-sick disciple, reducing himself grain by grain to the statement of his own disgust, patiently, self-destructively, so that his statement at least may be perfect in a world of corruption.' (See *Phoenix*, ed. Edward D. Macdonald, 1936, p. 312.)

8. Compare 'The young are red and pustular' (from 'Mr Eliot's Sunday Morning Service', in *Collected Poems*, 1909–1935, 1946 ed., p. 53).

9. *New Bearings*, p. 112.

10. G. M. Trevelyan, *A Shortened History of England* (Pelican ed., 1959) p. 196.

11. An interesting suggestion has been made by the Communist Party Historians' Group that, as it is desirable that history should be taught as 'a matter of cause and effect, and, too, of human progress; as opposed to the view that history has nothing to teach, no meaning nor pattern', it should be taught through the history of technique 'because progress in this field is clear ... there is never total retrogression'. ('The Teaching of History', in *Marxism Today*, Jan 1959, p. 30).

12. (New York, 1936) p. 106.

13. *The Invisible Poet*, p. 156.

14. *New Bearings*, pp. 91, 93–4.

15. See Marx and Engels, *On Britain* (Moscow, 1953) pp. 35–8.

16. *The Manifesto of the Communist Party* (Moscow, 1957) p. 55.

17. Trans. Moore and Aveling (New York, Modern Library) pp. 534, 536.

18. Note to 1. 411, in *Collected Poems*, p. 84.

19. *New Bearings*, p. 104.

20. Ibid. pp. 113–14.

21. Ibid. p. 114.

22. Compare Edmund Wilson's sensible criticism of Eliot's set of reactionary slogans, Royalist, classicist, and Anglo-Catholic: see

'T. S. Eliot and the Church of England', in *The Shores of Light* (1952) pp. 437–41.

23. *Collected Poems*, p. 82.

24. Various touches suggest that he moves naturally amongst upper-class émigrés, e.g.:

> Bin gar keine Russin, stamm' aus Litauen, echt deutsch.
> And when we were children, staying at the arch-duke's . . .
> (Section I: *Collected Poems*, p. 61)

25. *New Bearings*, p. 101.

26. This episode is summarised and placed by R. Palme Dutt in his *World Politics, 1918–1936* (1936) pp. 45–6.

27. Compare L. C. Knights, who argues straight from the debased mass media to the mentality of the people themselves: 'Those Elizabethans who never got beyond Deloney, even those who remembered nothing of *King Lear* beyond the action and a couple of bawdy jokes, were not doomed to pass their lives in the emotional and intellectual muddledom of the readers of the *Daily Mail*.' ('Elizabethan Prose': see *Drama and Society in the Age of Jonson*, 1951 ed., pp. 313–14.)

C. K. Stead

THE POEM AND ITS SUBSTITUTES
(1964)

THE comparison which perhaps more than any other has confused discussions of Eliot's poetry, is the comparison with Donne and the Metaphysicals. When F. O. Matthiessen, for example, writes that 'the condensation of form that was demanded both by Donne and the Symbolists *logically* builds its effects upon sharp contrasts',[1] the word 'logically', if it means anything, is being used in two quite different senses at once. The conscious, directing intellect, the sinewy logic, the drive towards a particular point, all present in Donne, are absent in Symbolist poetry; on the other hand, there is no room, within the exacting intellectual structure of a Metaphysical poem, for the Symbolists' repetitive, dream-like music – the style which is brought to perfection in *The Waste Land*.

Three general statements made by early critics of *The Waste Land* establish a firm basis for the discussion of all Eliot's major poems before *Four Quartets*. The first of these is by I. A. Richards. It may be that Richards's accuracy in describing *The Waste Land* resulted in part from the perfect correspondence of that poem with the generalization Richards was at that time attempting to make about *all* poetry. Nevertheless, the following remarks, published only two years after the appearance of *The Waste Land*, remain an accurate description of the poem and a serviceable warning to its critics:

Mr Eliot's poetry has occasioned an unusual amount of irritated or enthusiastic bewilderment. The bewilderment has several sources. The most formidable is the unobtrusiveness, in some cases the absence, of any coherent intellectual thread upon which the items of the poem are strung. A reader of 'Gerontion', of 'Preludes', or of *The Waste Land* may, if he will, after repeated readings, introduce such a thread. Another reader after much effort may fail to contrive one. But in either case energy will have been misapplied. For the items are united by the accord, contrast, and interaction of their emotional effects, not by an intellectual scheme that analysis must work out. The value lies in the unified response which this interaction creates in the right reader. The only intellectual activity required takes place in the realization of the separate items. We can, of course, make a 'rationalization' of the whole experience, as we can of any experience. If we do, we are adding something which does not belong to the poem.[2]

The second general statement comes from R. P. Blackmur, who wrote in 1928:

The Waste Land is neither allegory, nor metaphysics in verse, *nor anything else but poetry.*[3]

In the same article Blackmur spoke of the 'astonishing purity' of the poem, and added:

The reason Mr Eliot leaves aside English poetry since the Restoration is that its inspiration is impure . . . its emotions not founded on the facts of feeling exclusively.

And third, F. R. Leavis writing in 1932:

. . . the unity of *The Waste Land* is no more 'metaphysical' than it is narrative or dramatic, and to try to elucidate it metaphysically reveals complete misunderstanding. The unity the poem aims at is that of an inclusive consciousness: the organization it achieves as a work of art is . . . an organization that may, by analogy, be called musical. It exhibits no progression.[4]

These critics, in the passages I have quoted, looked at the poem and described it accurately in general terms. But an adequate critical procedure was lacking. As more and more information about the *material* of the poem has been made available, these early critical observations have been set aside. The raw material has been re-used by critics to construct a formula, a 'statement of beliefs', which is then said to be *in* the poem itself. That Eliot went to the trouble of transmuting this material into non-discursive form is ignored. Mr George Williamson in his 'poem by poem analysis'[5] specifically disagrees with Leavis's description (quoted above) and proceeds to unfold what he calls 'the basic scheme' of the poem – a task which he finds himself able to accomplish *almost entirely without quotation*. Cleanth Brooks declares of *The Waste Land*:

> The moral of all the incidents which we have been witnessing is that there must be an asceticism – something to check the drive of desire.[6]

– a statement which, again, fails to bring us closer to the poetry.

I shall discuss a short passage from *The Waste Land*, together with some of the critical commentaries which deal with it, in order to distinguish more exactly between what I am declaring valid and invalid procedures.

In 'The Fire Sermon' Tiresias observes, and experiences, the seduction of the typist by the house agent's clerk. Alone after the event, the 'lovely woman' who has 'stooped to folly'

> smoothes her hair with automatic hand,
> And puts a record on the gramophone.

Then follows one of the most beautiful lyric passages in the poem:

> 'This music crept by me upon the waters'
> And along the Strand, up Queen Victoria Street.
> O City city, I can sometimes hear
> Beside a public bar in Lower Thames Street,
> The pleasant whining of a mandoline
> And a clatter and a chatter from within
> Where fishmen lounge at noon: where the walls
> Of Magnus Martyr hold
> Inexplicable splendour of Ionian white and gold.

Three commentaries on these lines will illustrate certain points I have been attempting to make about the deficiencies of most criticism of the poem.

Cleanth Brooks[7] considers that the music which 'crept by' the protagonist 'upon the waters' is probably 'O O O O that Shakespeherian Rag', but notes that the latter can also hear, sometimes, the music of the fishmen. This other music – and the location of the fishmen near a church – is 'significant', because the fish is a 'life-symbol'. On the basis of these observations Brooks draws out the statement he believes implicit in the lines:

Life on Lower Thames Street, if not on the Strand, still has meaning as it cannot have meaning for either the typist or the rich woman of 'A Game of Chess'.

D. E. S. Maxwell[8] follows Brooks's observations:

The music leads the poem's action to one of the few manifestations of virility in the waste land, in Lower Thames Street, abode of the fishmen, those who continue to give allegiance to the source of life. They live by the river, and by the church.

George Williamson[9] is at once more abstract and more confident:

The music which creeps by Ferdinand upon the waters of Leman develops the lust or death theme, reveals its moral significance, and suggests its moral need. Since his fate has been connected with water, water has assumed a fateful attraction for the protagonist, who both fears and craves it. In terms of the fortune the course of these waters is highly significant.

Later Williamson repeats Brooks's main point.

It will be noticed that these critics are looking for details which are 'significant' – and that 'significance' for each of them resides in the ease with which the chosen details can be accommodated in an abstract system of ideas. But if we return to the lines themselves I think it will be found that none of the remarks quoted above has brought us nearer to their essential quality:

> 'This music crept by me upon the waters'
> And along the Strand, up Queen Victoria Street.
> O City city, I can sometimes hear
> Beside a public bar in Lower Thames Street,
> The pleasant whining of a mandoline

And a clatter and a chatter from within
Where fishmen lounge at noon: where the walls
Of Magnus Martyr hold
Inexplicable splendour of Ionian white and gold.

This passage projects, creates an image of, a particular state of mind. This image or projection is composed out of the indissoluble union of, on the one hand, a particular poetic music, and on the other an edited recreation of the experience – auditory and visual – of a specific time and place. The state is one of melancholy and loneliness in a city, the mind aware of itself alone, quiet and passive, yet on the fringes of human society, noise and action. It is a state of tranquil self-pity and tranquil pleasure. The consciousness of the poem focuses first on the music, which passes it by 'upon the waters'; then on the noises of the pub which it leaves behind; and comes to rest finally on the 'inexplicable splendour' of the silent, solid, visible object.

This is the effect of the lines as they exist alone. Their place in the poem, however, must condition our reading.

Lines 215 to 256, which precede the passage under discussion, enact a sordid event, in verse whose heroic flavour is capable of both mocking and intensifying the sordidness:

Out of the window perilously spread
Her drying combinations, touched by the sun's last rays ...

But the quality achieved in these lines is not precisely that of satire. There is objectivity, 'impersonality' ...; but not the detachment of the satirist who stands apart from the events he describes. There is, perhaps, disgust. But there is also in the lines a caressing quality which lingers upon the events, like Prufrock's smoke over the pools that stand in drains. Tiresias, the poem's 'inclusive consciousness', is sensitive to human degradation. But there is no hint of an implicit moral imperative – no suggestion that such things ought not to happen. This is, in fact, what *happens*, and what must go on happening: it is an image of human life consistent with the state of feeling which governs the poem. The passage is not a detached account of an event, but an *enactment*. The poet's mind is the mind of Tiresias, the 'inclusive consciousness' that has 'foresuffered all'. By its intimate participation in the event, that mind is released of a common burden; and in this process of enactment and release, Eliot's unique music achieves perfect ease of movement. At the climax of the event, the consciousness of the poem is forced into an indissoluble union with the participants:

> And I, Tiresias, have foresuffered all
> Enacted on this same divan or bed;
> I who have sat by Thebes below the wall
> And walked among the lowest of the dead.

There is in this moment the physical climax of the 'lovers', and the literary climax which forces 'Tiresias' into a humble understanding of himself and of all human kind. What follows can only be peace and sadness, in which the 'lovers', Tiresias, the poet, and his readers (*Vous, hypocrite lecteur!*) concur as one mind.

> Well, now that's done: and I'm glad it's over.

However sordid and mechanical the event has been, the typist's 'half-formed thought' proceeds out of a feeling which is not despair. This is her post-coital sadness, the 'music' of which comes inevitably to the protagonist and creates the equivalent melancholy of the nine lines under specific discussion. So, in these lines, the mind ranges about among impressions, but comes to rest at last on the walls of St Magnus Martyr. The 'inexplicable splendour' is not wholly separated from, nor even a judgement on, the action through which the poem has passed. It is a conclusion generated in the enactment.

In these remarks I have attempted to write some commentary on a direct experience of a passage of the poem. This whole section of 'The Fire Sermon' is, I should think, poetry of the kind described by Eliot in his remarks about 'the first voice' of poetry: it has broken forth from the depths of the mind, after what seems a long gestation, taking its form first as a particular rhythm, gradually solidifying into words, taking into itself a series of visual impressions which in turn attain narrative and symbolic semblance. It is a product of the 'unified sensibility', the imagination heightened, the will kept down to its humble task of arrangement. A critic who is to write adequately of such a passage of poetry cannot, therefore, approach it as if it contained an 'intellectual scheme', slightly obscured, but deliberately planted to be found. If the apparatus of criticism, the notes and the sources, were necessary before the poem could be fully experienced, then *The Waste Land* would have to be dismissed as inferior poetry. But Eliot clearly meant what he said when he wrote: 'I myself should like an audience which could neither read nor write',[10] and when he argued that poetry could communicate even *before* it was understood. In this he was acknowledging that the experience of his poetry is foremost an aural, emotional experience, one which approximates in many ways to the experience of listening to music; and that an 'intellectual' apparatus can easily impede a full and unified experience of the poetry. One would not, of course, deny all validity to a discussion which draws attention to the anthropological and literary symbolism that has found its way into *The Waste Land*. But there is clearly a danger that such discussions will offer us Jessie Weston and an assortment of Elizabethan dramatists as a substitute for the poem which ought to be the object of our attention.

NOTES

1. *The Achievement of T. S. Eliot* (1958) p. 15 (italics mine).

2. *Principles of Literary Criticism*, pp. 289–90. On p. 130 of *The Use of Poetry* Eliot expresses disapproval of Richards' statement (in *Science and Poetry*) that *The Waste Land* effects a 'severance between poetry and *all* beliefs'. Eliot's failure to understand what Richards means here seems deliberate obtuseness, especially since we find him writing on p. 151 of the same book that 'meaning' is only something to keep the reader's mind diverted and quiet while the poem does its work on him. Eliot also seems to have forgotten his own dictum (in 'Shakespeare and the Stoicism of Seneca') that the poet *qua* poet does not believe or disbelieve anything.

3. *The Hound and the Horn*, vol. i, no. 3 (1928) p. 195 (italics mine).

4. *New Bearings in English Poetry* (1932) p. 103.
5. *A Reader's Guide to T. S. Eliot* (1955) pp. 121 and 126.
6. *Modern Poetry and the Tradition* (Chapel Hill, 1939) p. 156.
7. Ibid. p. 154.
8. *The Poetry of T. S. Eliot* (1952) p. 110.
9. *A Reader's Guide to T. S. Eliot*, p. 128.
10. *The Use of Poetry and the Use of Criticism* (1933) p. 152.

Frank Kermode

A BABYLONISH DIALECT (1967)[1]

In the middle thirties, emerging from my remote provincial background (but we wrote poems and asked whether Browning didn't sometimes go beyond bounds), I at last discovered Yeats and Eliot; and in that bewilderment one truth seemed worth steering by, which was that these men were *remaking* poetry. Although this recognition had very little to do with knowledge, and one waited years before being granted any real notion of the character of such poetry, it was nevertheless, as I still believe, a genuine insight. As one came to know the other great works of the wonderful years, one also came with increasing certainty to see that the imperative of modernism was 'make it new': a difficult but in the end satisfactory formula.

These were the years of Auden, of a poetry oscillating between an inaccessible private mythology and public exhortation, an in-group apocalypse and a call for commitment to 'the struggle'. It was going to be our war; we were committed whether or not we wanted to be; and there were many poems of Auden especially which have by now disappeared from the canon, but not from the memories of men in their forties. Meanwhile, as the war approached, the indisputably great, the men of the wonderful years, were still at work. What were they doing? Their commitment they consigned, mostly, to the cooler element of prose; but we could hardly suppose they were with any part of their minds on our side. 'Making it new' seemed to be a process which had disagreeable consequences in the political sphere. I forget how we explained this to ourselves, but somehow we preserved the certainty that the older poets who behaved so strangely, seemed so harshly to absent themselves from our world – to hold opinions in the age of the Bristol Bomber which were appropriate to the penny-farthing – were nevertheless the men on whom all depended.

The death of Yeats in January 1939 therefore seemed to us an event of catastrophic importance. The news of Eliot's death immediately brought to mind, in surprising detail, the events and feelings of that dark, cold day nearly twenty-six years earlier. These were the men who had counted most, yet had seemed to have so little in common with us. Yet on the face of it the two events seemed to have little similarity beyond what is obvious. In the months preceding Yeats's death there had been an extraordinary outpouring of poetry – how impatiently one awaited the next issue of the *London Mercury*, and, later, the publication in the spring of 1940 of *Last Poems and Plays*! And that wasn't all: there was the poet himself, masked as a wild old man or a dangerous sage; there was the samurai posturing, the learned, more than half-fascist, shouting about eugenics and war, and this at a moment when we were beginning to understand that the enemy would soon be imposing both these disciplines on Europe. But one didn't hate the poet for what he thought he knew, remembering that he had always held strange opinions without damaging his verse. 'Man can embody truth but he cannot know it,' he said in his last letter; and years before, in a line which gives modern poetry its motto, 'In dreams begin responsibilities.' He made no order, but showed that our real lives begin when we have been shown that order ends: it is for the dreams, the intuitions of irregularity and chaos, of the tragic rag-and-bone shop, that we value him, and not for his 'system' or his 'thought'. The time of his death seemed appropriate to the dream; in a few months the towns lay beaten flat.

History did not collaborate in the same way to remind us of the responsibilities begun in Eliot's dream. His farewell to poetry was taken only a couple of years after Yeats's. It was no deathbed 'Cuchulain Comforted'; it was 'Little Gidding'. Perhaps the Dantesque section of that poem grew in part from Yeats's strange poem; certainly Yeats predominates over the others who make up the 'familiar compound ghost'. The famous lines tell us what we ought to make of our great poetry and of our great poets:

> ... I am not eager to rehearse
>   My thoughts and theory which you have forgotten.
>   These things have served their purpose: let them be.
> So with your own. ...

So much for the using up of a poet's thought. As a man he continues to suffer and without reward:

> Let me disclose the gifts reserved for age
>   To set a crown upon your lifetime's effort.
>   First, the cold friction of expiring sense. ...
> Second, the conscious impotence of rage
>   At human folly. ...
> And last, the rending pain of re-enactment
>   Of all that you have done, and been. ...

So the ghost speaks of a Yeatsian guilt, remorse, and purgation. The man who suffers is now truly distinct from the mind that creates poems that have to be, as Picasso said of paintings, 'hordes of destructions'.

It is customary now to speak of a 'tradition of the new' in American painting, and it may even be possible to do the same of American poetry. There is no such tradition in English poetry. That our contemporaries on the whole avoid Eliot's influence is probably not important; perhaps it is the case, as Auden said in his obituary notice, that Eliot cannot be imitated, only parodied. But it *is* important, I think, that his insistence on making it new, on treating every attempt as a wholly new start, is now discounted. It may be true, as is sometimes said, that this wholly exhausting doctrine is on cultural grounds more likely to be successful in the United States than in England; certainly much of the evidence points that way. But that does not entitle us to ignore the doctrine. After such knowledge, what forgiveness? The lesson was that the craft of poetry can no longer be a matter of perpetuating dialects and imitating what was well made; it lies in an act of radical analysis, a return to the brute elements, to the matter which may have a potentiality of form; but last year's words will not find it. In consequence, the writing of major poetry seems more than ever before a ruinous and exhausting undertaking, and no poet deserves blame for modestly refusing to take it on, or even for coming to think of Eliot and his peers as Chinese walls across their literature.

This, of course, is to apply to Eliot the damaging epigram he devised for Milton. Sir Herbert Read tells me that the English poet for whom Eliot felt a conscious affinity, and upon whom he perhaps in some degree modelled himself, was Johnson. All the same it seems to me that the more we see of the hidden side of Eliot the more he seems to resemble Milton, though he thought of Milton as a polar opposite. As we look at all the contraries reconciled in Eliot – his schismatic traditionalism, his romantic classicism, his highly personal impersonality – we are prepared for the surprise (which Eliot himself seems in some measure to have experienced) of finding in the dissenting Whig regicide a hazy mirror-image of the Anglo-Catholic royalist. Each, having prepared himself carefully for poetry, saw that he must also, living in such times, explore prose, the cooler element. From a consciously archaic standpoint each must characterize the activities of the sons of Belial. Each saw that fidelity to tradition is ensured by revolutionary action. (Eliot would hardly have dissented from the proposition that 'a man may be a heretic in the truth'.) Each knew the difficulty of finding 'answerable style' in an age too late. With the Commonwealth an evident failure, Milton wrote one last book to restore it, and as the élites crumbled and reformed Eliot wrote his *Notes*. If Milton killed a king, Eliot attacked vulgar democracy and shared with the 'men of 1914' and with Yeats some extreme authoritarian opinions.

Milton had his apocalyptic delusions, but settled down in aristocratic patience to wait for the failure of the anti-Christian experiment, 'meanwhile', as Eliot said in the conclusion of 'Thoughts after Lambeth', 'redeeming the time: so that the Faith may be preserved alive through the dark ages before us'. In the end, they thought, the elect, however shorn of power, all bring down the Philistine temple; and the self-begotten bird will return. As poets, they wrote with voluptuousness of youth, and with unmatched force of the lacerations of age. And each of them lived on into a time when it seemed there was little for them to say to their compatriots, God's Englishmen. Eliot can scarcely have failed to see this left-handed image of himself in a poet who made a new language for his poetry and who transformed what he took from a venerable tradition:

Our effort is not only to explore the frontiers of the spirit, but as much to regain, under very different conditions, what was known to men writing at remote times and in alien languages.

This is truly Miltonic; but Eliot at first moved away and pretended to find his reflection in the strong and lucid Dryden, deceiving many into supposing that he resembled that poet more than the lonely, fiercer maker of the new, of whom he said that it was 'something of a problem' to decide in what his greatness consisted.

However, a great poet need not always understand another; there may be good reasons why he should not. And Eliot certainly has the marks of a modern kind of greatness, those beneficial intuitions of irregularity and chaos, the truth of the foul rag-and-bone shop. Yet we remember him as celebrating order. Over the years he explored the implications of his attitudes to order, and it is doubtful whether many people capable of understanding him now have much sympathy with his views. His greatness will rest on the fruitful recognition of disorder, though the theories will have their interest as theories held by a great man.

Many of the doctrines are the product of a seductive thesis and its stern antithesis. The objective correlative, a term probably developed from the 'object correlative' of Santayana,[2] is an attempt to depersonalize what remains essentially the image of romantic poetry, and to purge it of any taint of simple expressiveness or rational communication. Its propriety is limited to Eliot's own earlier verse, which is deeply personal but made inexplicably so by the arbitrariness of its logical relations, its elaborate remoteness from the personal, and its position within a context which provides a sort of model of an impersonal 'tradition' – the fragments shored against our ruin. It is neither a matter of 'the logic of concepts' nor something that welled up from an a-logical unconscious; in so far as it has 'meaning', it has it in order to keep the intellect happy while the poem does its work, and in so far as it has not, it has not in order to distinguish it from poems that 'make you conscious of having been written by somebody'.[3] The 'dissociation of sensibility' is an historical theory to explain the dearth of objective correlatives in a time when the artist, alienated from his environment, *l'immonde cité*, is working at the beginning of a dark age 'under conditions that seem unpropitious', in an ever-worsening climate of imagination.

Such theories, we now see, are highly personal versions of stock themes in the history of ideas of the period. They have been subtly developed and are now increasingly subject to criticism. The most persistent and influential of them, no doubt, is the theory of tradition. In a sense it is Cubist historiography, unlearning the trick of perspective and ordering history as a system of perpetually varying spatial alignments. Tradition is always unexpected, hard to find, easily confused with worthless custom; and it is emblematic that a father of modernism should call himself Anglican, for the early Anglicans upset the whole idea of tradition in much this way.

He also called himself royalist, and this is an aspect of a larger and even more surprising traditionalism; for Eliot, in a weirdly pure sense, was an imperialist. This may seem at odds with certain aspects of his thought – his nostalgia for closed societies, his support for American agrarianism; but in the end, although he suppressed *After Strange Gods*, they grow from the same root. The essay on Dante, which is one of the true masterpieces of modern criticism, has been called a projection on to the medieval poet of Eliot's own theories of diction and imagery; but it has an undercurrent of imperialism, and can usefully be read with the studies of Virgil and Kipling.

This imperialist Eliot is the poet of the *urbs aeterna*, of the transmitted but corrupted dignity of Rome. Hence his veneration not only for Baudelaire (where his Symbolist predecessors would have agreed) but for Virgil (where they would not). The other side of this city is the Babylon of *Apocalypse*, and when the *imperium* is threadbare and the end approaches of that which

Virgil called endless, this is the city we see. It is the *Blick ins Chaos*.

The merchants of the earth are waxed rich through the abundance of her delicacies. . . . And the kings of the earth, who have committed fornication and live deliciously with her, shall bewail her, and lament for her, when they shall see the smoke of her burning. . . . And the merchants of the earth shall weep and mourn over her . . . saying, Alas, alas that great city, that was clothed in fine linen, and purple, and scarlet, and decked with gold, and precious stones, and pearls! For in one hour so great riches is come to naught. And every shipmaster, and the company in ships, and sailors, and as many as trade by sea, stood afar off, and cried when they saw the smoke of her burning, saying What city is like unto this great city!

Here is the imagery of sea and imperial city, the city which is the whore and the mother of harlots, with Mystery on her forehead: Mme Sosostris and the bejewelled lady of the game of chess – diminished as the sailors and merchants have dwindled to Phlebas, the sea swallowing his concern for profit and loss, and to Mr Eugenides, his pocket full of currants (base Levantine trade) and his heart set on metropolitan whoring. This is the London of *The Waste Land*, the City by the sea with its remaining flashes of inexplicable imperial splendor: the Unreal City, the *urbs aeterna* declined into *l'immonde cité*.

In another mood, complementary to this of Babylon, Eliot still imagined the Empire as without end, and Virgil, its prophet, became the central classic, *l'altissimo poeta*, as Dante called him. In him originated the imperial tradition. To ignore the 'consciousness of Rome' as Virgil crystallized it is simply to be provincial. It is to be out of the historical current which bears the imperial dignity. In this way Eliot deepened for himself the Arnoldian meanings of the word *provincial*. The European destiny, as prophesied by Virgil, was imperial; the Empire became the secular body of the Church. The fact that it split is reflected in *The Waste Land*, where the hooded Eastern hordes swarm over their plains, and the towers of the city fall. And as the dignity of empire was split among the nations, the task of

the chosen, which is to defeat the proud and be merciful to the
subject, was increasingly identified with Babylonian motives of
profit – a situation in which Kipling's relevance is obvious. Eliot
speaks of his 'imperial imagination'; and, given a view of history
as having a kind of perspectiveless unity, Virgil, Dante, Baudelaire, and Kipling can exist within the same plane, like Babylon
and the *urbs aeterna*, or like the inter-related motifs of *The
Waste Land*. Thus does the poet-historian redeem the time. His
is a period of waiting such as occurs before the apocalypse of
collapsing cities. But behind the temporal disaster of Babylon he
knows that the timeless pattern of the eternal city must survive.

Some such imagery of disaster and continuity – 'that the wheel
may turn and still/Be forever still' – lies under *The Waste Land*
and is reflected also in Eliot's cults of continuity and renovation
'under conditions/That seem unpropitious'. Yet when we think
of the great poem, we think of it as an image of imperial catastrophe, of the disaster and not of the pattern. For that pattern
suggests a commitment, a religion; and the poet retreats to it.
But the poem is a great poem because it will not force us to
follow him. It makes us wiser without committing us. Here I
play on the title of William Bartley's recent book, *Retreat to
Commitment*; but one remembers that Eliot himself is aware of
these distinctions. Art may lead one to a point where something
else must take over, as Virgil led Dante; it 'may be affirmed to
serve ends beyond itself', as Eliot himself remarked; but it 'is
not required to be aware of these ends' – an objective correlative
has enough to do existing out there without joining a church.
It joins the mix of our own minds, but it does not tell us what
to believe. Whereas Mr Bartley's theologians sometimes feel
uneasily that they should defend the rationality of what they are
saying, the poets in their rival fictions do not. One of the really
distinctive features of the literature of the modernist *anni mirabiles* was that variously and subtly committed writers blocked the
retreat to commitment in their poems. Eliot ridiculed the critics
who found in *The Waste Land* an image of the age's despair, but
he might equally have rejected the more recent Christian
interpretations. The poem resists an imposed order; it is a part

of its greatness, and the greatness of its epoch, that it can do so. 'To find, Not to impose,' as Wallace Stevens said with a desperate wisdom, 'It is possible, possible, possible.' We must hope so.

No one has better stated the chief characteristics of that epoch than the late R. P. Blackmur in a little book of lectures, *Anni Mirabiles 1921–1925*; though it contains some of the best of his later work, it seems to be not much read. We live, wrote Blackmur, in the first age that has been 'fully self-conscious of its fictions' – in a way, Nietzsche has sunk in at last; and in these conditions we are more than ever dependent on what he calls, perhaps not quite satisfactorily, 'bourgeois humanism' – 'the residue of reason in relation to the madness of the senses'. Without it we cannot have 'creation in honesty', only 'assertion in desperation'. But in its operation this residual humanism can only deny the validity of our frames of reference and make 'an irregular metaphysic for the control of man's irrational powers'. So this kind of art is a new kind of creation, harsh, medicinal, remaking reality 'in rivalry with our own wishes', denying us the consolations of predictable form but showing us the forces of our world, which we may have to control by other means. And the great works in this new and necessary manner were the product of the 'wonderful years' – in English, two notable examples are *Ulysses* and *The Waste Land*.

The function of such a work, one has to see, is what Simone Weil called *decreation*; Stevens, whose profound contribution to the subject nobody seems to have noticed, picked the word out of *La Pesanteur et la Grâce*. Simone Weil explains the difference from destruction: decreation is not a change from the created to nothingness, but from the created to the uncreated. 'Modern reality,' commented Stevens, 'is a reality of decreation, in which our revelations are not the revelations of belief'; though he adds that he can say this 'without in any way asserting that they are the sole sources'.

This seems to me a useful instrument for the discrimination of modernisms. The form in which Simone Weil expresses it is rather obscure, though she is quite clear that 'destruction' is 'a blameworthy substitute for decreation'. The latter depends upon an act of renunciation, considered as a creative act like that of God. 'God could create only by hiding himself. Otherwise there would be nothing but himself.' She means that decreation, for men, implies the deliberate repudiation (not simply the destruction) of the naturally human and so naturally false 'set' of the world: 'we participate in the creation of the world by decreating ourselves.' Now the poets of the *anni mirabiles* also desired to create a world by decreating the self in suffering; to purge what, in being merely natural and human, was also false. It is a point often made, though in different language, by Eliot. This is what Stevens called clearing the world of 'its stiff and stubborn, man-locked set'. In another way it is what attracted Hulme and Eliot to Worringer, who related societies purged of the messily human to a radical abstract art.

Decreation, as practised by poets, has its disadvantages. In this very article I myself have, without much consideration for the hazards, provided a man-locked set for *The Waste Land*. But we can see that when Eliot pushed his objective correlative out into the neutral air – 'seeming a beast disgorged, unlike,/ Warmed by a desperate milk' – he expected it, liberated from his own fictions, to be caught up in the fictions of others, those explanations we find for all the creations. In the world Blackmur is writing about, the elements of a true poem are precisely such nuclei, disgorged, unlike, purged of the suffering self; they become that around which a possible new world may accrete.

It would be too much to say that no one now practises this poetry of decreation; but much English poetry of these days is neither decreative nor destructive, expressing a modest selfishness which escapes both the purgative effort and the blame. America has, I think, its destructive poetry, which tends to be a poetry of manifesto; and in Lowell it seems to have a decreative poet. One way to tell them is by a certain ambiguity in your own response. *The Waste Land*, and also *Hugh Selwyn Mauberley*, can strike you in certain moments as emperors without clothes; discrete poems cobbled into a sequence which is always inviting the censure of pretentiousness. It is with your own proper fictive covering that you hide their nakedness and make them wise.

Perhaps there is in *Life Studies* an ambivalence of the same sort. Certainly to have Eliot's great poem in one's life involves an irrevocable but repeated act of love. This is not called for by merely schismatic poetry, the poetry of destruction.

This is why our most lively sense of what it means to be alive in poetry continues to stem from the 'modern' of forty years ago. Deeply conditioned by the original experience of decreation, we may find it hard to understand that without it poetry had no future we can now seriously conceive of. It is true that the exhortations which accompanied Eliot's nuclear achievement are of only secondary interest. What survives is a habit of mind that looks for analysis, analysis by controlled unreason. This habit can be vulgarized: analysis of the most severe kind degenerates into chatter about breakdown and dissociation. *The Waste Land* has been used thus, as a myth of decadence, a facile evasion. Eliot is in his capacity as thinker partly to blame for this. Arnold complained that Carlyle 'led us out into the wilderness and left us there'. So did Eliot, despite his conviction that he knew the way; even before the 'conversion' he had a vision of a future dominated by Bradley, Frazer, and Henry James. We need not complain, so long as the response to the wilderness is authentic; but often it is a comfortable unfelt acceptance of tragedy. Not the least heartening aspect of Mr Bellow's recent book was his attack on this contemptible myth. *The Waste Land* is in one light an imperial epic; but such comforts as it can offer are not compatible with any illusions, past, present, or future.

This is not the way the poem is usually read nowadays; but most people who know about poetry will still admit that it is a very difficult poem, though it invites glib or simplified interpretation. As I said, one can think of it as a mere arbitrary sequence upon which we have been persuaded to impose an order. But the true order, I think, is there to be found, unique, unrepeated, resistant to synthesis. The *Four Quartets* seem by comparison isolated in their eminence, tragic, often crystalline in the presentation of the temporal agony, but personal; and closer sometimes to commentary than to the thing itself. When the *Quartets* speak of a pattern of timeless moments, of the point of intersection, they speak *about* that pattern and that point; the true image of them is *The Waste Land*. There the dreams cross, the dreams in which begin responsibilities.

NOTES

1. A short version of this essay appeared in the *New Statesman*, London, in 1965.

2. In a letter to Mr Nimai Chatterji in 1955, Eliot says he thought he 'coined' the expression, but discovered that it had been used by Washington Allston. Eliot adds characteristically that he is not 'quite sure of what I meant 35 years ago'. (Letter in *New Statesman*, 5 Mar 1965, p. 361.)

3. This is from an early essay on Pound (*Athenaeum*, 24 Oct 1919) quoted by C. K. Stead in his interesting book *The New Poetic* (1964) p. 132.

QUESTIONS

1. Is there any change of attitude to *The Waste Land* as we move from 'The Burial of the Dead' to 'What the Thunder Said'?

2. Do you think that Tiresias *does* act as the central consciousness in the poem?

3. Various critics talk of the musical structure of the poem. Do you find this comparison helpful?

4. What is the function of the allusions in the poem? Is the device successful?

5. Do you think the notes are unnecessary?

6. What is the poetic effect of the first seven lines of the poem?

7. What is the value of the references to the Tarot pack in 'The Burial of the Dead'.

8. Do you think Eliot's picture of people in a pub shows a contempt for ordinary humanity?

9. Why does Eliot break off the sentences at the end of 'The Fire Sermon' and end with the single word 'burning'?

10. 'Death by Water' has been described as a lyrical interlude, a poem of serenity and a negative acceptance of death. What is your view?

11. Discuss the religious imagery in the poem.

12. What effect have the words of the thunder in the final section?

13. The poem ends with a heap of broken images: how successful is this?

14. What do you deduce from the poem of Eliot's attitude to the past?

15. Critics in the 1920s and 1930s felt that the poem was important because it reflected the decayed condition of their civilization. Do you think they were right? Has this point of view any relevance in a discussion of the poem's artistic merits?

16. Many critics talk of the dream-like quality of the poem, or, in the words of F. R. Leavis, its 'hallucinatory quality'. Do you agree? And what is the importance of such a quality?

17. Do you agree with David Craig that the poem reflects a genteel, prudish view of life?

18. Graham Hough thinks that the poem lacks unity of tone. Do you agree?

19. Is the incorporation of Indian religion successful? What does such an inclusion do to the poem?

20. Is it still possible to maintain seriously, as Amy Lowell did, that the poem is 'a piece of tripe'?

SELECT BIBLIOGRAPHY

THE literature about T. S. Eliot is endless. A newcomer to his work could do no better than begin with M. C. Bradbrook's British Council pamphlet (Writers and Their Work, no. 8, revised 1965) which has an excellent descriptive Bibliography, or T. S. Pearce's *T. S. Eliot* (Literature in Perspective Series; Evans Bros., 1967). Good introductions to his total work can be found in Northrop Frye's *T. S. Eliot* (Oliver & Boyd, 1963) and Twentieth-century Views, *T. S. Eliot*, ed. Hugh Kenner (Prentice-Hall, 1962). Helen Gardner's *The Art of T. S. Eliot* (Cresset Press, 1949; Dutton, 1949) is particularly concerned with his later work and provides a perceptive account of *Four Quartets*. The two main works omitted from our selection are F. R. Leavis's *New Bearings in English Poetry* (Chatto & Windus, 1932) and Grover Smith's *T. S. Eliot's Poetry and Plays* (University of Chicago Press, 1956). The reasons for these omissions are given in our introduction. Another useful compilation is Leonard Unger's *T. S. Eliot: A Selected Critique* (Rinehart & Winston, 1948) which contains a selection of criticism of the 1930s and 1940s and an extensive check-list of books and articles in English about Eliot's work up to 1948. Herbert Howarth's *Notes on Some Figures Behind T. S. Eliot* (Chatto & Windus, 1965) includes much useful biographical material and an excellent section on *The Waste Land* (pp. 232–46). Other interesting comments on the poem can be found in A. Alvarez's *The Shaping Spirit* (Chatto & Windus, 1958) – Alvarez is typical of the younger generation's criticism of Eliot – Elizabeth Drew's Jungian interpretation in *T. S. Eliot: The Design of his Poetry* (Charles Scribner, 1949; Eyre & Spottiswoode, 1950), D. E. S. Maxwell's *The Poetry of T. S. Eliot* (Routledge & Kegan Paul,

1952; Hillary House, 1959), G. S. Fraser's *Vision and Rhetoric* (Faber & Faber, 1959), Kristian Smidt's *Poetry and Belief in the Work of T. S. Eliot* (Bailey Bros & Swinfen, 1949) and George Wright's *The Poet in the Poem* (University of California Press, 1960; C.U.P., 1960). *Storm over 'The Waste Land'*, ed. Robert E. Knoll (University of Nebraska Press, 1964) collects together opposing views of the poem. The curious reader of *The Waste Land* may care to follow Eliot's whimsical advice and read Jessie L. Weston's *From Ritual to Romance* (Anchor Books, 1957) and Sir James Frazer's *The Golden Bough*, now published in an abridged version by Macmillan & Co. in paperback.

NOTES ON CONTRIBUTORS

CONRAD AIKEN: American critic, novelist and poet, and early friend of T. S. Eliot.

CLEANTH BROOKS: American literary critic and Professor of English at Yale. Famous as one of the founding fathers of the New Criticism. His books include *The Well-Wrought Urn* and *Modern Poetry and the Tradition*.

DAVID CRAIG: Senior Lecturer in English at the University of Lancaster, author of *Scottish Literature and the Scottish People 1680–1830*.

WILLIAM EMPSON: British poet and literary critic. Professor of English Literature at Sheffield. His first book, *Seven Types of Ambiguity*, had a seminal influence on modern criticism.

GRAHAM HOUGH: British literary critic. Professor of English at Cambridge. His books include *The Last Romantics*, *The Dark Sun*, and *An Essay on Criticism*.

HUGH KENNER: American literary critic. Professor of English at University of California, Santa Barbara. His book on Eliot *The Invisible Poet* has become very well known.

FRANK KERMODE: British literary critic. Lord Northcliffe Professor of English at University College, London. His books include *Romantic Image* and *The Sense of An Ending*.

C. DAY LEWIS: British poet, particularly well known for his left-wing writings in the 1930s. Appointed Poet Laureate in 1968.

F. O. MATTHIESSEN: American scholar and expert on Henry

James and T. S. Eliot. *The Achievement of T. S. Eliot* is a classic of modern criticism.

GEORGE L. K. MORRIS is an abstract artist, painter and sculptor living in New York. From 1937 to 1943 he was Art Editor of *Partisan Review*.

I. A. RICHARDS: Famous for establishing 'practical criticism' in the 1920s. Professor of English at Harvard. His *Practical Criticism* and *Principles of Literary Criticism* remain standard works.

KARL SHAPIRO: American poet and critic. Professor of English at University of Nebraska.

STEPHEN SPENDER: British poet well-known from the 1930s. Editor of *Encounter* for many years. His recent book, *The Struggle of the Modern*, is widely discussed.

C. K. STEAD teaches at the University of Auckland, New Zealand. He has written a study of modern poetry, *The New Poetic*, and edited a collection of New Zealand short stories. He is editing the Casebook *Shakespeare: Measure for Measure*.

GEORGE WATSON is Fellow of St John's College and lecturer in English, University of Cambridge. His publications include *The Literary Critics* and *Coleridge the Poet*.

GEORGE WILLIAMSON was professor of English at the University of Chicago 1940–59, and has been Martin A. Ryerson distinguished service professor since 1959. His publications include *The Senecan Ramble* and *A Reader's Guide to T. S. Eliot*.

EDMUND WILSON: American literary critic, novelist, essayist. His best-known books are *Axel's Castle* and *The Wound and The Bow*.

YVOR WINTERS: American literary critic and poet, was Professor of English at Stanford, California. A highly individual, but influential, critic.

DANIEL H. WOODWARD teaches at Mary Washington College, University of Virginia.

INDEX

References to *The Waste Land* and its author are naturally too numerous to be recorded here. References to characters in the poem are not included unless they are the subject of lengthy comment.

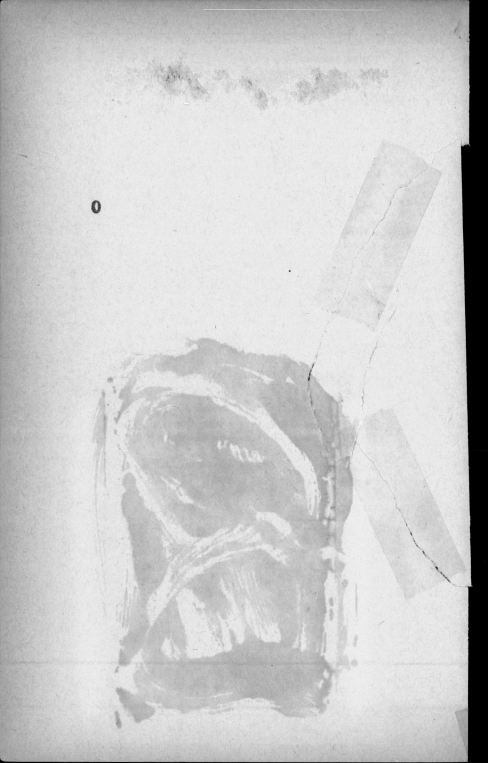